Necessary Mischief

Exploring the Shakespeare Authorship Question

Bonner Miller Cutting

Minos Publishing Company
2018

Bibliographical Information

Editing and Interior Design: Chris Pannell
Cover and Exterior Design: Caitlin Pannell-Evans
Typeset in Baskerville
Printed by CreateSpace, An Amazon.com Company

Minos Publishing Company
430 First Street,
Jennings, Louisiana
70546

Library of Congress Cataloguing Information:

Cutting, Bonner Miller, 1948, author
Necessary Mischief:
        Exploring the Shakespeare Authorship Question

ISBN 9-780692-158593

Library of Congress Control Number
2018953392

For my parents

Acknowledgements

I have an inexpressible gratitude towards the many Oxfordian Shakespeare scholars who have mentored me over many years, giving me good counsel and advice as this book was researched, written, and revised. Those who have worked to find answers to the "Shakespeare Authorship Question" know that we are, after all, a minority opinion. What we publish in articles and books must rest on bedrock facts, clearly presented and meticulously investigated.

I am deeply indebted to Roger Stritmatter, Gary Goldstein, Michael Delahoyde, Chris Pannell, Michael Egan, and Alex McNeil, editors of the journals and newsletters in which earlier versions of these chapters were published. Specifically, Roger has given me direction for research parameters throughout the years that these essays were taking shape. Chris reviewed the manuscript and provided editorial advice for this book. I am among the many Oxfordians who have benefitted from Alex's copy-editing of the *Shakespeare Fellowship Newsletter* and *Brief Chronicles*. Parts of this book previously appeared in *The Oxfordian* (vol. 13, 18, 19), *Brief Chronicles* (vol. 1, 3, 4), *Shakespeare Matters* (Summer 2006), and the book *Shakespeare Beyond Doubt?* (2013, edited by John Shahan and Alexander Waugh).

Present-day Oxfordians are indebted to those who have preceded us and brought their expertise to the quest for historical truth and cultural justice. We should take note of the work of John Thomas Looney, Bernard Ward, Eva Turner Clark, Charles Barrell, the Ogburns, and more recently Richard Paul Roe – to name just a few. For my own part, I've directed my research to areas that I thought needed to be looked at more closely.

"Knowing how vain a thing it is
to linger a necessary mischief…
that land of mine which is in Cornwall
I have appointed to be sold
for mine expenses in this travel."
                    – Edward de Vere,
                writing from Siena, Italy

Rosalind: A traveler! By my faith, you
              have great reason to be sad.
              I fear you have sold your own lands
              to see other men's; then to have seen
              much, and to have nothing, is to have
              rich eyes and poor hands.

Jaques: Yes, I have gain'd my experience.
                                    As You Like It

Table of Contents

Introduction

Let me show you, sir, how I keep finding these little
problems I shouldn't even be looking for.
— *Lieutenant Columbo*

The Shakespeare Authorship Question has been a controversial subject for many generations. The debate has been
fueled by the lack of evidence to support the idea that a
glover's son from Stratford-upon-Avon wrote the literary works
known as the Shakespeare canon. At this point, I should note that
in these pages, the man from Stratford-upon-Avon will be called
"Shakspere," as this is the most frequent spelling of his name in
the records of the town where he was born in 1564 and buried in
1616. It is the facts of his life between these dates that are debated.

The majority of English literature professors accept a story
about this individual that is built on imagination, speculation and
conjecture – and riddled with factual inconsistencies. We will examine the discrepancies, much like the intrepid Lieutenant Columbo
did in each episode of his television series *Columbo*. Although what
follows was initially written for an audience well-versed with the
problems of Shakespearean authorship, I hope those who are new
to the this question – the Shakespeare Authorship Question – will
find many points of interest and insights about the origins of Shakespeare's works.

One of the best resources on the subject is the website of the
Shakespeare Authorship Coalition (SAC) at:

https://doubtaboutwill.org

A video entitled *Why Was I Never Told This?* by Keir Cutler, PhD,
introduces the Declaration of Reasonable Doubt, a document
that has over 4,000 signatories and may be signed by any visitor to
the SAC website. Additionally, the SAC's book, *Shakespeare Beyond
Doubt? Exposing an Industry in Denial*, presents the many reasons why

we should question whether the man from Stratford actually wrote those plays and poems.

I agree with the SAC that a major purpose of the Shakespeare Industry is to promote the public reverence for the official narrative. Newspapers readily snap up stories promising a "new" discovery about Shakespeare. Each year, thousands of articles on Shakespeare pour out of academic journals, and academicians themselves are remunerated with awards, grants, and endowments. On the other hand, those who doubt the approved story have a steep hill to climb. Until the recent advent of a Research Grant Program by the Shakespeare Oxford Fellowship, there has been practically nothing for the intrepid soul who wants to research this subject. Those who do find the universities, libraries, museums, and archives unreceptive territory.

One of the best-known defenders of the Stratfordian story of Shakespeare is James Shapiro, a Professor of English and Comparative Literature at Columbia University. *Contested Will*, published in 2010, puts Shapiro's gloss on the history of the authorship question, explaining why doubts have remained through many generations. My first chapter, A Contest of Wills rebuts Shapiro's arguments and evaluates the enthusiastic reviews for *Contested Will*.

At authorship conferences, I was inspired to study Shakspere's Last Will and Testament. When fellow attendees compared notes about why they doubted the Stratfordian authorship story, many people said "I read his will and that did it for me." Shakspere's supporters have a litany of explanations for the deficiencies in his will, so a closer look was warranted. In the summer of 2008, I spent long hours in Rice University's Fondren Library looking for collections of wills from Shakspere's time, and read through about three thousand wills of the era to find out what his contemporaries had to say in their wills. I also checked out every book they had on wills, probate, death and dying in early modern England. That fall, I presented the results of this effort at the SOS/SF authorship conference in White Plains, New York. My essay appeared in 2009, in the authorship journal *Brief Chronicles*. Here it forms the basis of chapter two, Shakespeare's Will: Considered Too Curiously.

My work on Shakspere's will was noticed by the Folger Shakespeare Library when – in 2016, in conjunction with the National

Introduction

Archives – they put up a website called *Shakespeare Documented*. Twentieth century Shakespeare authorities have stood by Sir Edmund K. Chambers' proposal that the three pages of Shakspere's will were first composed in January of 1616 and revised two months later in March. Chambers and others relate a scene in which Shakspere's will was hastily prepared as the great man lay dying, and this explains why a literary genius left such a poorly composed, slovenly looking document. In a recent posting to the *Shakespeare Documented* website, the timeline has been readjusted to reflect information I put forth at that 2008 conference, where I showed how pages two and three of his will were written prior to January, 1616. In the months before Shakspere died, those pages were updated and cobbled together with the newer page one. In short, the will was composed over several years, rather than several months. This upends the traditional story of the will's composition, taking away the Stratfordian "dying man" excuse for the dismal, un-Shakespearean document.

Since a corrected transcript of Shakspere's will was made public at the end of the eighteenth century, Shakspere's bequest of his second best bed to his wife has been a thorny issue. It looks like Mr. Shakspere was disparaging Mrs. Shakspere. In chapter three, Alas Poor Anne, I explore the historical methods used by Stratfordians to make this "notorious bequest" seem more appealing. But the problem becomes more profound when the laws that governed women's rights to property in early modern England are understood. The laws of coverture dictated that a married woman owned nothing during her marriage – not even her clothes. Because of this, it was incumbent on a husband to provide for the maintenance of his surviving spouse in his will. A comparative study of spousal bequests in contemporaneous wills shows that most will-makers specified the housing, income and personal property a woman would need during her widowhood. That Shakspere fails in this duty is a serious deficiency in his story. He seems oblivious to the behavior expected from a member of the gentry class even though the word "gent" appears after his name in his will – an indication that he thought of himself as a gentleman.

Many biographers of Shakspere have taken pains to foster the impression of a congenial, well-known figure, walking the streets of London in the late sixteenth and early seventeenth centuries. In *Will in the World*, Harvard University Professor Stephen Greenblatt describes a "Shakespeare" who was "by all accounts, pleasant company, affable and witty; and his writing, even at that very early point [the early 1590s], doubtless showed that he had real talent." Greenblatt explains that his "Shakespeare" went unnoticed by Spenser, Donne, Bacon, or Raleigh because "the living writers who meant the most to him were those he encountered in the seedy inns near the theater soon after he arrived in London." How "Shakespeare" learned the customs and manners of aristocratic court circles from unknown persons in seedy inns is unexplained. Greenblatt goes on to say, "There are, in any case, enough signs of serious attention to Shakespeare's early work to suggest that the group of writers may at first have actively wanted to cultivate his acquaintance."

What is this serious attention and who are these writers Greenblatt has in mind? In *Shakespeare's Unorthodox Biography*, Diana Price disassembled Stratfordian claims such as these, and constructed a chart with ten categories for twenty-four writers of the time, plus Stratford's Shakspere. Among the categories of evidence of a writing career are ownership of books, evidence of education, records of correspondence, extant manuscripts, diaries and other miscellaneous supporting documentation, relationship to a patron, payment for writing plays, and notice of the writer's death. Stratford's Shakspere is the only individual with no hard evidence in any of the ten categories, in spite of the many biographies that put him in London from approximately 1592 until 1612.

The subject of censorship could be another category added to Price's chart. My chapter four, Let the Punishment Fit the Crime, shows that Elizabethan authorities imposed harsh punishments on writers whose work was thought to be seditious, and "Shakespeare," whoever he was, dealt with subjects that were off limits to other writers. For example, in *Richard II*, Shakespeare deals with not one but three dangerous topics: the deposition of a monarch, the succession crisis, and the royal prerogative. Yet "Shakespeare" was never noticed by the Privy Council or its enforcement arm, the Royal Commission. Unlike Marlowe, Nashe, Chapman, Marston, Hayward, Jonson, and others, "Shakespeare" was never once called to justify his writing on potentially treasonous topics for the public stage. His work was even ignored in the Bishops' Ban of 1599 when the entire output of many leading writers was burned at the command of the Archbishop of Canterbury and the Bishop of London.

But if the problems with Stratford's Shakspere are insuperable, are there historical circumstances to support a case for "someone else" as a pseudonymous Shakespeare? There existed in early modern England a social system known as wardship. Fortunately, feudal wardship, as it was practiced in the sixteenth century, has long been abandoned by a more enlightened society. But many families in sixteenth century England suffered from this abhorrent system in which the state took custody of children after a father's death and leased the heirs' lands to the highest bidder. Most pernicious of all, a guardian had the right to arrange the ward's marriage. More details are in chapter five: Evermore in Subjection.

Edward de Vere (hereafter called "Oxford" for his title as the 17th Earl of Oxford) was swept into wardship upon the death of his father when he was twelve, and an extraordinary life trajectory was set in motion. During the young Earl's wardship, he was provided with an exceptional education by England's best teachers. Prior to his father's death, Oxford's education was directed by the distinguished scholar Sir Thomas Smith; at the age of eight, Oxford attended Cambridge University. But the years in wardship left Oxford impoverished and he would become destitute after marrying the daughter of his guardian, Lord Burghley's. Marriage to a guardian's daughter is the backdrop for Shakespeare's *All's Well That Ends Well*, making this one of many parallels between the life experiences of Oxford and the works of Shakespeare.

In the sixth chapter, What's Past is Prologue: Consequences of Wardship, I propose that the losses Oxford incurred during his years in wardship unleashed in him a fury that motivated him to write the Shakespeare canon. The production of plays gave him unlimited opportunities for revenge. Those in Queen Elizabeth's court who he felt had wronged him or people he thought to be generally corrupt were models for the villainous characters in his plays.

But wait! If the 17th Earl of Oxford was mocking her courtiers, then why did the miserly Queen pay him a £1,000 annual annuity – the equivalent to a million dollars a year in today's money? After sorting through every aspect of Oxford's £1,000 annuity – in chapter seven, A Sufficient Warrant – the foremost question is: what motivated Queen Elizabeth to pay Oxford such a large sum? Oxford has been called a "feckless nobleman" by modern historians, which makes the Queen's motivation for this expenditure more mysterious. Also striking is the timeframe: the payments to Oxford began in 1586 as the expenses of war were bankrupting the Queen's Exchequer. But the annuity continued for the rest of Elizabeth's reign and was reissued by King James upon his accession to the English throne in 1603.

An explanation for the £1,000 payments may be found in the history plays of "Shakespeare." United States Supreme Court Justice John Paul Stevens has commented that Shakespeare's chronicle plays were partly propaganda to support the legitimacy of Elizabeth's rule and stir patriotism in the English people. To this end, "Shakespeare" helped the insecure Queen at a time when Spain, the most powerful country on earth, was determined to conquer England. Besides, "Shakespeare" supplied the royal court with top-notch entertainment. Although those who were taken to task were surely not pleased, a pseudonym would mask the author's identity, and the mischievous entertainments in the royal court would not be common knowledge.

Perhaps some members of the court thought that the works would lose their appeal in subsequent years, and it would not matter who wrote them. Perhaps it was thought that the author's identity would eventually seep out, but enough time would elapse that the injured parties would be gone too – and future generations would not care. If so, it has been a miscalculation on both counts. In *Born to Rule*, Ellis Wasson points out how many families of the upper strata of English society in the sixteenth century still held political power in the twentieth century. The descendants of Shakespeare's characters have been leading figures in English government through the centuries, as well as members of institutional boards, historical societies, university trustees, and grandees of high society.

The complete erasure of Oxford's identity as Shakespeare did not happen overnight. It occurred in stages and took the better part of two centuries to accomplish. A step by step tracing of the disappearing author is beyond the scope of these essays, but two articles explore the phenomenon as it was taking hold. Chapter eight – The Missing *First Folio* – deals with the absence of Shakespeare's *First Folio* from the most remarkable pictorial display of books in early modern English portraiture. Another bizarre situation is the eradication of Oxford's daughter, Susan Vere, from the Pembroke family chronicles and the false identification of Pembroke's second wife instead of Susan Vere in the magnificent Van Dyck portrait of Pembroke's family at Wilton House. We explore these problems in chapter nine, A Countess Transformed: How Susan Vere Became Anne Clifford. The vexing question is why her own descendants have sought to erase her identity in Van Dyck's painting. It is also puzzling that, with one exception, art historians have been willing to acquiesce to an erroneous identification.

My final chapter, She Will Not Be A Mother, was prompted by the 2011 film *Anonymous*. In Portland, Oregon I saw an early screening and thought it was a powerful film in many ways. However, it was a surprise to see it advocate that the 17th Earl of Oxford was secretly the son of Queen Elizabeth. It seemed an unnecessary digression. But the film also spurred me into some research. The resulting essay received tense commentary during its peer review prior to publication in *Brief Chronicles*. I have continued to investigate the issues and I hold to the conclusions of chapter ten.

I invite readers to email me with their feedback at:
jandbcutting@comcast.net

I greatly appreciate your comments on any aspect of this book, as well as the time you spend delving into the following pages.

Chapter 1

A Contest of Wills
A Response to Shapiro's *Contested Will*

In his Prologue to *Contested Will,* James Shapiro mentions a visit he made to a local elementary school where he was asked if Shakespeare wrote *Romeo and Juliet.* "I hadn't expected that doubts about Shakespeare's authorship had filtered down to the fourth grade" (5).

In *Contested Will,* Shapiro seeks to understand why the traditional story of a glover's son from Stratford-upon-Avon who became the author of the plays and poems of William Shakespeare is widely questioned. He opens with a crucial acknowledgment: the Shakespeare Authorship Question is a subject that academia strictly avoids. Those who have studied this controversial issue are well aware of the taboo, but it is a stunning admission coming from an academic of Shapiro's standing – and worth considering.

The academic taboo serves a number of useful functions: first, it deprives teachers and students of a venue for discussion; second, it keeps a substantial body of information about Shakespeare and the historical circumstances surrounding the canon off the table; and third, new research is systematically discouraged if it has the potential to conflict with the established point of view. With these advantages, it is easy for academics to maintain their ascendancy, and facts that contradict their position are not taken into consideration.

But forbidding discussion, research, or publication about authorship issues has not made the authorship question go away. Shapiro notes, "If anything, people are more drawn to it than ever" (5).

How did this problem take hold in the first place? Shapiro traces the history of the controversy, positing that for about two hundred years, nobody doubted the Stratford story. In his view, the idea of early acceptance buttresses the orthodox position.

There is a major problem with Shapiro's theory: it is not true. From the 1590s, there were rumblings of doubt. No contemporaneous reference to Shakespeare gives biographical details for a living person. In *Shakespeare's Unorthodox Biography*, Diana Price demonstrates that every single reference is only a literary allusion, containing nothing of a personal nature or anything to show that any contemporary writer had even met Shakespeare (133-144). Still, Shapiro's position as a Professor of English and Comparative Literature at Columbia University gives him a platform to influence mainstream opinion. Upon the publication of *Contested Will* in 2010, many news outlets reviewed it, some of them printing more than one review by well-known writers. But very few of them took notice of the book's mistakes, misleading statements and unsupported myths. Lloyd Rose wrote in *The Washington Post* that "the book is rich with insight and analysis." On the website *Salon*, Laura Miller gushed over his "penetrating new consideration of the debate." In *The Guardian*, Hilary Mantel congratulated Shapiro on his "glinting, steely facts."

Worse still, many reviewers injected their own nonsense and were not as crafty as Shapiro in the use of qualifiers to give plausible deniability. For example, Boyd Tonkin's review for *The Independent* imagined William to be "one of the most familiar faces in town and at court." Lauding Shakespeare as "the dramatist, executive and impresario" of the acting company, Tonkin must not know – and would not have learned from *Contested Will* – that the Stratford man was absent from important events in which the acting company was involved. Shakespeare is missing from the record of the trial and proceedings of the Essex Rebellion in 1601 and from the company's attendance at the Spanish Ambassador's visit in 1604. He is nowhere to be seen at the installation of the Prince of Wales in 1610 and not mentioned in the references to the burning of the Globe Theater in 1613. For an actor who was supposedly a familiar face, the records in London and Stratford make no mention of him as an actor. No theater-goer noted a part he played. The influential nineteenth century authority James Halliwell-Phillips searched through municipal archives from cities and towns throughout England where Shakespeare's acting company performed, and found no mention of his name (Schoenbaum 303). In the early twentieth century, Hulda and Charles Wallace rummaged through millions of documents in England's Public Record Office (Schoenbaum 464-469). Their labors produced the Stratford man's deposition with the sixth and last of his scrawled signatures – but they found nothing to indicate that this individual was a writer of any kind. These are some of the real "steely facts."

Granted, it was approximately two hundred years before doubts were openly expressed in writing and in public venues; this is where Shapiro's two hundred year notion comes from. Doubts did not surface openly and immediately because the facts of the mundane life of William Shakspere of Stratford-upon-Avon had not yet been unearthed. As early as 1728, Voltaire commented that "Shakespeare is rarely called anything but divine in England" (30). But as Shapiro knows, the "belated efforts of eighteenth-century scholars and collectors" did not turn up biographical documentation to support Shakespeare's career as a writer. Yet Shapiro does not dwell on what this absence means, so we will have to fill in the gaps.

By the mid-1700s, the search was underway for literary documents that, if found, would confirm the Stratford man's literary activity. When all that was coming up were records of the life of a country businessman interested in purchasing land, money lending, and litigating for petty sums, by the mid- nineteenth century, doubts about the Stratford story were making their way into books and articles.

Shapiro believes that cultural forces in the nineteenth century stimulated a skeptical attitude toward many subjects, and this spilled over to the Shakespeare authorship question (69-79). Be that as it may, it is not so much the cultural factors but the recognition of the weakness of the documentary evidence for the Stratford man that led to the emergence of doubts after approximately two hundred years had gone by. By this time, the appealing story of the Stratford mythos had been established, and though created out of whole cloth, it was firmly entrenched in the hearts of the general public. Shakespeare was a national hero, the focus of the national pride of the English people. Thus the commitment to the story remained.

Shapiro is troubled that "doubters" of high repute have joined the fray. The list of distinguished people who have questioned the traditional story is growing in spite of the opprobrium that will surely come their way. Just to name a few: Mark Twain, Sigmund Freud, Sir John Gielgud, Sir Derek Jacobi, Sir Mark Rylance, five United States Supreme Court Justices – after a while it starts to add up. People doubting the so-called traditional story have faced powerful opposition from the Shakespeare Industrial-Educational Complex (an appropriate term coined by Ron Rosenbaum in *The Shakespeare Wars*).

To dampen enthusiasm for the authorship question, the reviewers of *Contested Will* fill their pages with ad hominem attacks. Peter Conrad wrote for *The Guardian* that "the doubters Shapiro unearths are cranks," and Oxfordians are "a reprehensibly reactionary lot." Hilary Mantel found it "a tale of snobbery and ignorance, of unhistorical assumptions, of myths about the writing life . . ." Reviewing *Contested Will* in *The Wall Street Journal*, Terry Teachout praised Shapiro's "no-nonsense study of zanies whose theory-mongering has blighted the world of legitimate Shakespeare studies." Teachout goes on to say that there are "mountains of incontrovertible evidence proving that the not-so-mysterious man from Stratford did in fact write the greatest plays ever written."[1] Skeptics would like Teachout to tell them where these mountains of evidence are located. On this point, Oxford University history professor Hugh Trevor-Roper registered his concerns:

> Of all the immortal geniuses of literature, none is personally so elusive as William Shakespeare... particularly in the last century, he has been subjected to the greatest battery of organized research that has ever been directed upon a single person. Armies of scholars, formidably equipped, have examined all the documents which could possibly contain at least a mention of Shakespeare's name... and yet this greatest of all Englishmen, after this tremendous inquisition, remains so close to a mystery that even his identity can

still be doubted. (Ogburn 69-70).

In an effort to discredit the notable doubters, Shapiro censures Mark Twain, Helen Keller, Henry James and Sigmund Freud. Then he turns his artillery on John Thomas Looney, a schoolteacher in England who is not a household name. In describing Looney as unassuming and modest, the Dean of St. Paul's went on to call him "one of the clearest thinkers and the most effective exponent of the true art of teaching" he had ever known. Looney was intrigued, as others before him had been, by the problems and contradictions in the biography of the Stratford man as the author of the works of Shakespeare. He researched the authorship question in the early decades of the 20th century, but could not publish his book, *Shakespeare Identified*, until 1920 after the end of World War I. It is this book that brought Edward de Vere to the attention of the world as the real author hidden behind the nom de plume William Shakespeare.

As a young man, Looney had studied the Logical Positivism of Auguste Comte, a Frenchman who combined concepts of sociology and science into a philosophy intended to improve the human condition. Comte's theories had appealed to the Victorian mindset, though by the turn of the century, interest in his philosophy had run its course. However, with some free association and a touch of time traveling, Shapiro draws a tenuous line from Comte in 1850 to Hitler in 1940. Along the way he subtly creates the impression that Looney was a Nazi sympathizer. It is a low blow. Shapiro follows Stephen Greenblatt's lead in attempting to equate authorship doubters with holocaust deniers. In an effort to turn this distorted reasoning into a new paradigm, others climb on board. Katherine Duncan-Jones comments in her review of *Contested Will* in *The Literary Times*: "It seems that Freud never fully understood the Positivist ideology to which Looney had been committed, which had strong strands within it both of fascism and anti-Semitism."

****

The discovery of Edward de Vere in *Shakespeare Identified* has stood the test of time. A major reason for this is that Looney's methodology was so straightforward and reasonable that it is hard to believe it had not been done before. Prior to Looney's book, alternative candidates had been chosen by what he called a "pick and try process" (78). To this day, candidates brought forth have been known historical figures, selected because their lives are historically interesting. Then, a scenario is woven around a candidate's life story to explain how he (or she) became "Shakespeare."

Looney thought Shakespeare's true identity was unknown. He reasoned that there were too many deficiencies in the Stratford man's biography for him to have written the Shakespeare canon, but found the challengers wanting as well. In order to search for the true author, Looney developed a Shakespearean profile. Looking to the Shakespeare canon itself for the profile of its writer, Looney came up with eighteen characteristics that he expected to find in its author: nine are general and nine specific.

In addition to the profile, Looney sought a method to search systematically for Shakespeare. He thought that one of the weaknesses in the Stratford narrative is the absence of early artistic production from the pen of "Shakespeare." Orthodox scholars presume that their Shakespeare's artistic powers were well developed upon his entry to London, which they surmise occurred sometime around 1590. Orthodoxy regards Shakespeare's *Venus and Adonis*, published in 1593, as one of his earliest works. But Looney thought *Venus and Adonis* too artistically competent to be an early composition, and that, at an earlier time in the author's life, he had written similar poetry that might have been published under his true name. He would base his search on the hope that precursor poetry (perhaps even "juvenilia") in the stanza form of *Venus and Adonis* could be found with the author's name attached.

At the outset, Looney understood that the odds were against him, and his search might be futile. Even if such poetry had once existed, it was possible that it may not have survived for three hundred years. Another concern was the possibility of obstacles in the way of discovery, especially if deliberate steps had been taken either to protect the author's anonymity or, conversely, to suppress it (73). Nevertheless, with the Shakespearean profile and a plan of action in place, Looney set out to see if he could find a match. The inquiry produced one candidate, and this candidate fulfilled all eighteen characteristics. In Edward de Vere, he found a perfect fit.

In *Contested Will*, Shapiro tries to belittle Looney any way he can, and he even takes a shot at Looney's methodology. An example of Shapiro's penchant for sly innuendo is his suggestion that Looney already had Edward de Vere in mind, and that his search was not conducted in an entirely objective manner. This accusation, made strictly to undermine Looney's remarkable discovery, has the ring of jealousy on Shapiro's part.

Contested Will contains many examples of what Looney called "artifice instead of argument" (12). One of Shapiro's techniques is to combine Edward de Vere's name with as many other challengers as possible. His routine inclusion of red herrings engenders a sense that the evidence for each candidate is roughly equal. It is a false equivalence. When the case for Edward de Vere is thoroughly examined and compared with other challengers, no other candidate comes close.[2]

Since Looney's discovery nearly a hundred years ago, new information about Edward de Vere has surfaced that was not available to him; I think Looney would be pleased to know that a large body of additional data supports his original conclusions. For one thing, he did not know about the £1,000 annuity given annually to Oxford by Queen Elizabeth (approximately one million US dollars today), and this largesse, unique in the parsimonious Queen's reign, came with a non-accountability clause. Also, Looney did not know how specifically Oxford's travels in Italy coincided with Shakespeare's Italian settings. It would be almost a century before Mark Anderson would map out Oxford's itinerary in Italy, revealing the match between the cities that Oxford visited and the settings for Shakespeare's plays (Anderson *v*, Roe 4). Details like these, coming to light after *Shakespeare Identified* in 1920, further support and validate Looney's discovery.[3]

Lacking a strong evidentiary case, Shapiro pushes back with the typical screed on Shakespeare's imagination: a spin-off of the old circular reasoning that all it took was "genius" to write the works of Shakespeare. Surely the reviewers of *Contested Will* and the English professors who support Shapiro's views are well-educated, cultivated people. One might ask what goes through their minds when they pull off the shelf any one of the eight volumes of Geoffrey Bullough's *Narrative and Dramatic Sources of Shakespeare*. Can't they see that the Shakespeare canon is, among other things, an encyclopedia of classical and Renaissance knowledge? Several reviewers grapple with the problem of Shakespeare's erudition by proposing that the Stratford man learned from books. But no books are mentioned in his Last Will and Testament, and no books that he owned have been identified.[4]

Occasionally the sun breaks through the clouds. In *The Wall Street Journal*, Saul Rosenberg points out the difficulties inherent in Shapiro's scenario of an author browsing, observing and chatting his way to creating *Hamlet*, *King Lear*, and *Othello*. Although his review of *Contested Will* is favorable for the most part, Rosenberg finds it unlikely that "Shakespeare" went about casually gathering and assimilating highly esoteric information. Writing for *The Brooklyn Rail*, William S. Niederkorn gives an in depth review of the misleading statements and outright dishonest claims that fill the pages of Shapiro's book. It is reassuring that Niederkorn's review was chosen Review of the Day by the *National Book Critics Circle*.

Nevertheless, with so much reinforcement from academia and media outlets, many readers of *Contested Will* may be convinced by Shapiro's arguments. But maybe a few will want to drill down a little deeper, sensing that something more is going on than merely the solution to an intriguing historical mystery. Shapiro would agree. In an interview in *The Los Angeles Times*, he speaks of "cultural authority" and underscores that the Shakespeare Authorship Question is part of a bigger picture.

Looney, too, understood the larger cultural question:

> He [Shakespeare] is the one Englishman of whom it can be most truly said that he belongs to the world; and in any pantheon of humanity that may one day be set up he is the one of our countrymen who is already assured of an eternal place. England's negligence to put his identity beyond question would therefore be a grave dereliction of national duty if by any means his identity could be fully established. (71)

Notes

1. See comments from Terry Teachout's WSJ review reported in "Praise for Contested Will" on James Shapiro's website at:

   http://www.jamesshapiro.net/works.htm

2. The Shakespeare industry has made a concerted effort to assign dates to the plays that are as late as possible, and this artificial dating structure is used as an argument against Oxford's authorship. Various scenarios for late dates have accomplished two additional things. First, it shortens the number of years of the Stratford man's "retirement" when nothing can even be attributed to him. Second, spreading the work over a wider span of time makes the achievement seem a bit more plausible within the confines of the Stratford man's supposed time in London. Therefore, to these ends, generations of Stratfordian scholars have worked assiduously to find rationales for late dates. Today, most academic opinion falls in line with the late dates in *The Riverside Shakespeare*. The academic consensus notwithstanding, there is no hard evidence for dating any of the plays or poetry in the Shakespeare canon, and the orthodox dating methodology has serious limitations and deficiencies. For a comprehensive study, see *Dating Shakespeare's Plays*, Kevin Gilvary, ed.

3. It should be remarked how much Looney gets right in *Shakespeare Identified*. His investigation was surprisingly far-sighted considering the rank distortions in Shakespeare commentary and the paucity of historical materials available to him in the early 20th century. For the former, he relied on Halliwell-Phillips' *Outlines*; for the latter the *Dictionary of National Biography* – a fine effort for its day but full of factual errors and biased historical accounts. Looney was off-base in his chapter on *The Tempest*, but understandably he could not see past the orthodox view of its date. What appeared to be a problem was decisively put to rest in *On the Date, Sources and Design of Shakespeare's The*

Tempest by Dr. Roger Stritmatter and Lynne Kositsky. Since the advent of this book in 2013, orthodox interest in *The Tempest* (with regards to the authorship question) has abated.

4. The absence of books in the Stratford man's will is a serious problem, and Stratfordians propose that books would be mentioned in an inventory – which has been conveniently lost.

Chapter
2

Shakespeare's Will
Considered Too Curiously

Hamlet: To what base uses we may return, Horatio . . .
Horatio: Twere to consider too curiously, to consider so.

(5.1.192,195)

The last will and testament of William Shakspere went unnoticed for more than a century after his death in Stratford-upon-Avon on April 23, 1616. To this day, it is unclear how the original will came to light. From the mid-eighteenth century through most of the twentieth century, it was believed that the Reverend Joseph Greene discovered the will in 1747 when he made two transcripts of it and wrote about it to his friend, James West.

> The Legacies and Bequests therein, are undoubtedly as he
> intended; but the manner of introducing them, appears
> to me so dull and irregular, so absolutely void of the least
> particle of the Spirit which Animated Our great Poet; that
> it must lessen his Character as a Writer, to imagine the least
> Sentence of it his production.

In *Shakespeare's Lives*, Schoenbaum admitted that posterity does not know exactly where Greene found the will, but that it was somewhere in Stratford-upon-Avon. He also believed that Greene came across a copy of the will, not the original will (92-93) and that this copy was re-discovered in the late nineteenth century.[1]

Schoenbaum credited the eighteenth century engraver and antiquarian George Vertue with the discovery of the will in 1737, preceding Greene by a decade. When Vertue made the trip to

Stratford-upon-Avon in the company of Edward Harley, the 2nd Earl of Oxford, he kept notebooks. In writing about the will, Vertue made several mistakes that he surely would not have made had he actually seen the original will or a reliable copy. Among the errors, he called Shakspere's sister "Elizabeth" when she is addressed three times in the will by her name Joan Harte, a curious inaccuracy for an experienced antiquarian.[2] Vertue also wrote that he was told that the original will was located at the Doctors' Commons in London (*Shakespeare Survey 5*, 56).[3] Upon his return to London, he presumably made his way to the Commons and, if the information about the whereabouts of the original will was correct, he found the will there.[4]

It would take another hundred years until the Prerogative Court of Canterbury acquiesced to repeated requests for the original will

A derivative of George Vertue's sketch of Edward Harley, the 2nd Earl of Oxford, at the Holy Trinity Church in Stratford-upon-Avon in 1737. Artist unknown. (Courtesy of the Estate of Ruth Loyd Miller).

to be published. They allowed James Halliwell (later Halliwell-Phillips) to release it in a form as close to the original as possible (Halliwell iii). In a limited edition of one hundred copies, Halliwell set in type the original will with its interlineations and alterations.[6] When the contents of the Stratford will are seen in their entirety, the reluctance of the Prerogative Court to make it publicly available will be easily understood.

We seek to put the will of William Shakspere of Stratford-upon-Avon in historical, legal, and social perspective. For the most part, the wills of gentlemen have been chosen for comparison with the Stratford man's will, as Shakspere's claim to gentry status came with his family coat-of-arms obtained at the College of Heralds in 1596. Occasionally, the wills of esquires, yeomen, tradesmen or people with theatrical connections will be used. The wills are primarily from collections transcribed and published by historical societies in England.[7]

The Stratford Man's Will

Shakspere's will is a three page document with room to spare at the bottom of the third page. It is fairly lengthy in comparison to many wills of his day in which testators often disposed of their property in a paragraph or two. It is written in a tidy secretary hand conjectured to have been a clerk or scrivener in the office of Francis Collins, a solicitor who represented Shakspere in legal matters. Attempts to claim it as Shakspere's own hand are contradicted by his three scrawled signatures on this document.

The Stratford will is in the format set out in the handbooks of Henry Swinburne and William West. However, when other wills are examined, the mindset and personalities of the testators are readily discernable despite the occasional use of standardized language. Wills were typically dictated and the scribe wrote down the testator's exact words as best he could. In the event that a will was challenged in court, the scribe could be called in to testify that the willmaker was in charge of the process, and he faithfully set down the words as they were spoken (Alsop 19-27). Despite the passage of time, one hears the authentic voices of testators in early English wills.

Searching Shakspere's will for "Shakespeare's voice" has been discouraged by Shakespearean authorities. In his *Study of Facts and Problems*, Sir Edmund K. Chambers tried to run interference on the prospect of perusing the Stratford will for evidence of literary activity, stating that "A will is a legal instrument for devising property and not a literary auto-biography" (178). This caveat reveals that Stratfordians understand the disconnect between the Stratford man's mundane life and the great literary works he supposedly wrote. A close inspection of his will makes the disparities all the more clear.

In an attempt to put Shakspere's will in the best possible light, James Halliwell called it "the testimonies we may cherish of his last faltering accents to the world he was leaving" (Halliwell-Phillips, *Life* 2:244). Failing such eloquence, most Shakespearean authorities simply follow Dr. Karl Elze who wrote in 1888 that the will would "ever remain an insolvable enigma."[8] A closer look shows that the Stratford man's will is not an enigma; it is a disaster for the orthodox biography that Shakspere of Stratford was a writer.

The Explanations

The rationale often used to explain the deficiencies in the will is that "Shakespeare" relied on the services of an attorney. This argument has several problems. At the outset, it begs the question why an individual with the storehouse of legal knowledge manifest in the Shakespeare canon would *need* a country solicitor to write out a simple legal document. Orthodoxy credits their "Shakespeare" with legal competency obtained from his property transactions and various legal skirmishes in Stratford-upon-Avon. If this is true, then this gave him sufficient legal background to write *The Merchant of Venice, Hamlet*, and *Measure for Measure*, among other plays that show deep legal knowledge. It should not have been difficult for him to prepare his own will.

But the problem is worsened by the fact that wills of the time were rarely written by attorneys. In his helpful book *Playhouse Wills*, E.A.J. Honigmann acknowledges that it was not unusual for testators to turn to "a literate neighbor" to pen their wills and admits that wills "probably give us the testators' words as spoken" (11, 19).

In the chapter on "Wills and Their Writers" in her book *Contrasting Communities*, Margaret Spufford shows that the scribes were predominantly ordinary citizens. They could range "from the lord or lessee of the manor to the vicar, curate, church clerk or churchwarden to the schoolmaster, a shopkeeper or anyone of the literate yeoman or even husbandmen in a village who could be called in to perform this last neighborly office for a dying man" (333).[9] Even if Shakspere had been too ill to write down his own will (and this is why he needed the services of the unknown scrivener), he still should have had the ability to speak so his family and later the probate court could be assured of his testamentary capacity (Houlbrooke, *Church Courts* 99).

That neighbors served in the capacity of an amanuensis restructures the question: The right question to ask is not why Shakspere had "someone else" write his own will, but why did he not compose wills for others in the town? It would seem that during Shakspere's later years of comfortable retirement in Stratford-upon-Avon that his family, friends and neighbors would *seek him out* for this task. But no member of his family made a will at all – not his father, mother, or siblings.

Deficiencies in the Stratford Man's Will

Both sides of the authorship debate, from fiercely protective Stratfordians to skeptical authorship doubters, understand that the life of Stratford's Shakspere is poorly documented. In *Shakespeare's Unorthodox Biography*, Diana Price underscores the profound deficiencies in the known facts of the Stratford man's life (302-306).[10] The absence of books in his will is often a point of departure for the discussion of these deficiencies, so we will begin here.[11]

It's a cold, hard fact that there is no mention of books in the Stratford man's will. But his missing library is just part of the problem. There is no mention of furniture that would have held books either. Literate people had cupboards, hampers, cases, boxes, presses or chests for their books. Francis Bacon instructed his executors "to take into their hands all of my papers whatsoever, which are either in cabinets, boxes or presses, and then to seal them up until they may at their leisure peruse them" (du Maurier 198). Shakspere does not mention a desk for writing or pen and ink with which to write. John Florio bequeathed three desks replete with inkhorns. Such items were not limited to the erudite. A clothier of Gosfield had "a chest to bestow my books in," and "one little chest which I lay my writings in" (Emmison 1980: 144-145).

Some propose that the books were included in the category of "household stuff." When the use of the term is examined in other wills – and nearly all include this standard verbiage – it is clearly a catchall phrase for miscellaneous articles too inconsequential to itemize. The "household stuff" is usually intended for kitchen equipment, textiles, bedding, plate, jewels, farm implements, farm animals and foodstuffs. Typical is a testator who left to his wife his "household stuff, plate, jewels, my milch kine, six geldings, and her own colt" (Emmison 1980:95). In the Stratford will, "all the rest of my goods chattels Leases plate Jewels and household stuff whatsoever" are left to his daughter Susanna. Nothing in the language suggests that books were included in the residual clause.

A more careful testator is John Bentley, a servant to a knight, who left his wife "all the other my household stuff not hereafter specially bequeathed." That the term "household stuff" does not include books is apparent in the impressive list of books that he wills to his son. Itemized in the body of this will are music books, dictionaries of Cowper, Barrett and Thomasin, dictionaries in Greek, Latin and "other languages whatsoever," Tully's Offices, books "pertaining to divinity," and "all other my books in English written or printed whatsoever" along with statute books, law books, a Livius and "my maps." To his "singular good master," he bequeaths "my new bible in Latin, imprinted in Venice," and to his Lady "a very pleasant book" called the "Instruction of a Christian Woman made by Ludovicus Vives" (Emmison 1980:105-106).[12] Sir Thomas Smith left his Latin and Greek books to Queens' College, Cambridge, directing that the Fellows "send carts to fetch them away within 10 to 12 days" and that they "chain them up in their library." Such was the care that he took that his books be preserved for future generations (Emmison 1978:42).

Then as now, books made excellent gifts to important people. William Camden willed most of his books to Robert Cotton. In his discussion of Cotton's books and manuscripts, known today as the

Cottonian collection in the British Library, Kevin Sharpe writes that "the Antiquaries were clearly liberal in their donations of books to Cotton, Walter Cope, and George Carew" among other notables. Viscount John Scudamore "thought the present of a book the best way to reward a scholar who despised the material wealth which most men prized" (Sharpe 58-59). John Florio left 340 books to the Earl of Pembroke. It strains credulity to think that no book would have been carefully directed to any special beneficiary in "Shakespeare's" will. Surely Shakspere had a friend who would value a book that he owned, maybe his alleged patron the Earl of Southampton?

Not only did Shakspere leave nothing to Southampton, but he left nothing to anyone he supposedly knew at court. Nor did he leave anything to any fellow writer – not even to those with whom he allegedly collaborated on some of the plays. Nor did he mention any apprentices he may have had, or even the printer Richard Field who supposedly hailed from Stratford. Field was the publisher of the two narrative poems that first made Shakespeare famous, and some Stratfordians propose that Shakspere read the books in Field's print shop. This would explain, they tell us, how Shakspere had access to books, although few books printed by Field are used as sources by "Shakespeare." Stratfordians do not mention that Shakspere left no books to Field in his will, and Field was still living in 1616.

Stanley Wells, chairman of the Shakespeare Birthplace Trust in Stratford-upon-Avon, argues that the missing books were listed in a separate inventory, now lost. Proposed by E. K. Chambers in 1930, the idea is worth considering, but it comes up short. Approximately two million wills and one million inventories survive from early modern England (Erickson 103-104).[13] Of the surviving inventories, few include books. According to the Essex County historian F. G. Emmison, "wills yield far more details than some inventories in which only valuation totals of items are given." Moreover, wills themselves often functioned as "quasi-inventories" with detailed bequests of movables, furnishings, and as we have seen, books (viii). Emmison's assessment is corroborated by the will and inventory of the Reverend John Bretchgirdle, the minister who baptized William Shakspere of Stratford. Bretchgirdle made detailed bequests of books in the body of his will, but the inventory simply stated that the books were valued at ten pounds (Fripp 23-31).[14]

The inventory excuse overlooks the fact that a primary purpose of a will was to ensure that important items be well bestowed. Then as now, testators wanted their most precious possessions to go to beneficiaries who would appreciate them (Vaisey 95-98). Inventories were made by "indifferent men" after the testator's death; the testator himself had no hand in the inventory. The lack of mention of books in the Stratford will indicates that, even if this testator owned books, they were not meaningful enough to him to merit inclusion in the body of his will.

The absence of books is amplified by the absence of manuscripts or writing of any kind. The orthodox explanation is that the acting company, the Lord Chamberlain's Men (later called the King's Men) had the rights to the plays. But would not a writer have *something* to show for nearly a million words on paper? Would not he have had rough drafts, diaries, notebooks? And what was stopping "Shakespeare" from buying a quarto of his own works? Francis Bacon owned the following Shakespeare quartos: *Richard II* (1614), *King Richard III* (1602), *King Henry IV* (1613), *King Lear* (1608), *Hamlet* (1605), *Titus Andronicus* (1611), *Romeo and Juliet* (1599), and *First and Second parts of King John*, (the apocryphal quarto of 1611). These are bound together with other plays including Marston's *The Wonder of Women* (1606) and *The Malcontent* (1604) and Ben Jonson's *Sejanus* (1605) and *Volpone* (1607) (du Maurier 293-294).

Stratfordians insist that Shakspere was a shareholder in the Globe Theater, but he makes no mention of shares or income from theatrical performances in this will. Other actors account for this valuable property. From *Playhouse Wills*, one finds that Thomas Pope bequeathed in 1603 "my right title and interest which I have of in and to all that playhouse with the appurtenances called The Curtain . . . and also all my part estate and interest . . . in and to all that playhouse with the appurtenances called The Globe" (70). In 1624, John Underwood instructed his executors not to sell his share in the playhouses called the Blackfriars, the Globe, and the Curtain (143). John Heminges also accounted for his profits from the Globe and Blackfriars playhouses and mentions that "the same have been and have yielded good yearly profit as by my books will

in that behalf appear . . ." (165-167). The actor John Shank gives
details of his theatrical holdings in his will of 1635, including "my
share in the Court moneys behind" (188). It is odd that Stratford's
Shakspere often litigated for petty sums of money but took no
notice of the income that his supposed theater shares would have
brought him and his heirs.

Music and musical instruments were valuable items and ordinary people bequeathed a fair number of lutes, viols, and virgin-
als in their wills (Arkell 94). But music was part and parcel of an
actor's vocation, and an integral part of Shakespeare's imagery. In
Shakespeare's Songbook, Ross Duffin presents over a hundred songs
that "Shakespeare seems certain to have known because he inserts
them, quotes them, or simply alludes to them in his works" (15-16).
Duffin goes on to say that Shakespeare might have collected these
songs in a scrapbook. It is curious that a playwright who used so
many musical terms and metaphors and shows much knowledge of
music –far more than other writers – would have owned no musical
instruments or regarded them as not worth mentioning. By contrast, Augustine Phillips left his apprentice a bass viol, a citterne, a
bandore and a lute (Honigmann 73).

Not incidentally, Shakspere makes no mention of an apprentice, and no actor to whom he might have been apprenticed early
in his career or someone he might have mentored once he was an
established actor (as his biographers tell us he was) has made any
note of it. Surprisingly, too, no item in the will suggests Shakspere's
life as an actor other than a bequest of money for three fellow
actors to buy rings. But this is added between the lines, suggesting
that it is an afterthought. Shakspere had no keepsakes from his
acting career such as costumes or other theatrical memorabilia.

Along with the absence of the valuable theater shares, Shakspere
makes no mention of the kinds of possessions that reveal a cultured
existence. He has no maps, odd for a dramatist who set plays in
foreign lands he evidently knew in minute detail, but to which he
never traveled.[15] There are no pictures, wall hangings, tapestries
or art works of any kind. Such items were prized heirlooms. The
poet John Donne bequeathed many paintings (called "pictures")
to beneficiaries in his will. If Shakspere's will is any indication, he
lived without what an archivist calls "the trappings of the civilized

man" (Vaisey 97). This is puzzling for a wealthy man whose life was supposedly one of great cultural achievement.

However, the most vexing lacuna of all is the lack of mention of education in the Stratford man's will. In wills of the time, bequests to minor children almost always included instructions for their education. For someone who supposedly received an excellent education at the Stratford grammar school, launching him on a career of unparalleled success, it is odd that he did not leave something for the education of his grandchild, Elizabeth Hall, or for any future grandchildren (though this is consistent with the fact that his daughters were illiterate). His granddaughter is named three times: first with a reversionary interest of £100 if his younger daughter Judith dies; second with "all my plate": and third as residuary legatee for all the "premises" that remain after the default of the heirs male enumerated through seven sons. How hard would it have been to add "for her education," or "to be brought up in learning," if, in fact, he was a man of learning who valued education?

This neglect of education is in stark contrast to many other testators of the time. People in every social class made the connection between education and quality of life for their family and people in their community. A yeoman of Rochford left an annuity to keep his son at "grammar school until fifteen and afterwards in one of the universities and after that in one of the inns of Chancery or Court for his better preferment and advancement." Although females were not educated as often as males, some did receive educational bequests. Tomas Collte, a gentleman of Waltham, left a hearty £50 annuity "toward the education and bringing up of my two daughters during their minority," and if they died without issue, this money was to go to the "setting up of a free school for ever for the teaching of poor men's children." Jacob Meade, a waterman of Surrey, provided for the education of his granddaughter. In a short will of less than a page, a clothier of Dedham included a bequest "to the maintenance of poor students at Cambridge that . . . sincerely seek God's glory."

Shakspere of Stratford left his godson twenty shillings in gold. A widow of Chingford left the same amount to her godson, but specified that it was "to buy him books." Had Stratford's Shakspere merely added those four little words, "to buy him books," it would have given the orthodox Stratfordians something to hang their hat on. As it is, they have nothing. How credible is it that many people provided for the education of their children and children in their communities, but "Shakespeare" did not?

It was not unusual for testators to leave endowments to schools and universities. A yeoman of Wivenhoe left money to St John's College, Cambridge, "for the maintenance of the scholars there and especially such as shall come out of the Grammar School of Colchester." An esquire left an annuity to the Free School of Chelmsford so that the school "may be better maintained and the youth and children may be better attended and instructed in learning and virtue." A clothier willed that after the death of his sister, "the tenement given to her [will go] to the governors of the public Grammar School in Dedham and their successors forever, to be employed for a dwelling house for a school master to teach children to read and write." Schoolmaster John Harte of Saffron Walden left a large bequest to pay "a discreet, honest and learned schoolmaster" to teach poor children of Great and Little Chesterfield "freely and without reward."[16]

According to Robin Fox of Rutgers University, "a mark of a man's success in business was that he should endow a school in his birthplace." Edward Alleyn did just that. Alleyn was born relatively poor, had a successful stage career, and became a wealthy businessman. But Alleyn founded Dulwich College and provided for its future perpetuation in his will (Honigmann 151-153). Traditionalists propose that Shakspere was successful as an actor, writer and a businessman. But he left nothing to the Stratford grammar school – the source of the putative education that allegedly set him on the path to success, and was the main institution of learning in the town in which future generations of his family would be educated.

Shakespeare the writer understood the importance of endowing a school, using the character of Lord Saye in *2 Henry 6* to speak of the benefits of education:

> Large gifts have I bestow'd on learned clerks,
> Because my book preferr'd me to the King,
> And seeing ignorance is the curse of God,

Knowledge the wing wherewith we fly to heaven.

(4.7.71-74)

In *Henry VIII*, the character Griffith praises Cardinal Wolsey for his contributions to the Ipswich Grammar School and Oxford University:

He was most princely: ever witness for him
Those twins of learning that he rais'd in you,
Ipswich and Oxford; one of which fell with him,
Unwilling to outlive the good that did it.

(4.2.45-47)

Is it credible that, with all his good fortune, Shakspere of Stratford took no interest in the school to which he presumably owed so much? As Fox states, "it was something almost required of a local boy made good." [17]

Shakspere's will was composed at a time when charitable giving reached its zenith in early modern England. In ten counties, a total of £3.1 million was left to charitable causes, reaching a peak of "incredible generosity which marks the years 1611 to 1640" (Jordan 243-245). Bequests for repairs of roads and bridges were common and might have been expected of a man who traveled often between London and Stratford. A typical bequest for this purpose is found in the will of John Wentworth who left an annual allotment of ten pounds "to the amending of the most needy places in the highway between St Anne's chapel and Braintree" (Emmison 1978:45). Shakspere's will contains none of this. Then as now, churches were frequent beneficiaries, and one might have expected that Shakspere would leave something to the Holy Trinity Church where he was to be buried. Bequests for repair of steeples, casting of bells, and general maintenance are frequent in wills of the time. He left nothing to this church or any other. Nor did he give to any hospital, almshouse, or prison.

Testators often forgave debts owed to them. Shakspere forgave none, and this is not surprising for a man who litigated over small amounts of money. He did leave a tersely worded bequest of ten pounds to the poor of Stratford, fulfilling a duty of testators for charitable deeds required by custom (Cox 24). In contrast, many testators showed genuine compassion, making elaborate provisions for the poor. A yeoman of Harlow set out legacies to the poor in eleven towns, as well as to the poor prisoners of Colchester, Newgate, the Marshalsea, the King's Bench, Ludgate and all London and Stortford [Hertfordshire]. Bequests such as these are not unusual even among ordinary testators.

Was Shakspere Wealthy?

Before looking into the legacies in Shakspere's will, his wealth needs to be addressed. By the standards of his time, he was a wealthy man. Shakespearean authorities would prefer to sidestep this issue, as the lack of bequests for education and philanthropy would not be so great a discrepancy had Shakspere not been wealthy. Honigmann shares this avoidance by stating, "we cannot tell from his will how rich he was." Perhaps not precisely, but we can learn a great deal from his will, especially when it is substantiated by his real estate purchases in the public record.

Shakspere owned five houses, and his primary residence, called New Place, was a mansion. From the sketches of New Place in George Vertue's notebook, the comments of Halliwell-Phillips, and various other records, we know that New Place was a large three-story structure with ten chimneys, five gables, a courtyard in front of the house, two orchards, two gardens, two barns and stables (Schoenbaum, *Lives* 14; Honan 236-237). It is estimated to have had at least twenty bedrooms. In the nineteenth century, Halliwell-Phillips examined the footings and found it to be sixty feet across and seventy feet along the side (Chambers 2:95-99). A J. Pointon estimates that Shakspere's estate was worth over £2,000, well over two million dollars in today's money (94). Historians categorize people as "middling rich" if their estate was worth between £200 to £500 (North 300). Collating this information, Shakspere was indeed one of the wealthiest men in his community.

What Is in the Stratford Will?

The Religious Preamble

With so much missing that one would expect an exceptional historical person to have in his will, the next matter is to ascertain what
Shakspere actually included in the document's three pages. Like
most wills of the time, Shakspere opened with a religious preamble
(Houlbrooke 123). The person who is regarded as the greatest poet
in England took his statement of faith right from a standard hand-
book. B. Roland Lewis was the first to note that it was a common
formula from William West's popular *Symbolaeographia*. Seemingly
embarrassed at saying such a thing, Lewis added that "One would
think that William Shakespeare virtually copied his *Notificatio* and
its exordium from William West's *Symbolaeographia* (1605), a volume
of typical legal forms widely used in his day" (482). In reading the
following, that is exactly what one would think.

West's *Symbolaeographia*	William Shakspere
Sick in body but of	in perfect health
good and perfect memory	& memory
God be praised	god be praised
do make and ordaine	doe make & ordayne
this my Last wyll and testament	this my last will and testament
In manner and forme following	in manner an forme following
that is to say	That is to saye
first I Commend my soule	ffirst I commend my soule
unto the hands of God	into the hands of god
my maker	my creator
hoping assuredly	hoping & assuredly beleeving
through the only merits	through thonelie merittes
of Jesus Christ my savior	of Jesus Christ my savior
to be made partaker	to be made partaker
of life everlasting	of life everlasting
And I commend my bodie	and by bodye
To the earth	to the Earth
whereof it is made	whereof yt ys made

If Shakspere was Shakespeare, why did he not take the opportunity to write, or dictate, a personalized preamble? Why did Shakspere use a banal formula derived from an almanac when many literate testators composed their own?

An example of a preamble written by a testator is found in the will of Edward Pudsey (Honigmann 92):

> I do wholly betake and Commit unto the infinite mercy
> of Almighty god meekly acknowledging both by original
> corruptions and by my many actual transgressions (in his
> Justice) damnation to be my due, yet assuredly believing
> by taking hold with the hand of faith upon the gracious
> promises of our merciful father to all repentant sinners in
> his holy writ delivered, And upon the merits of bitter death,
> and earnest mediation of our sweet savior Jesus Christ,
> That I am one of the elect before all worlds, for the holy
> and blessed spirit doth assure my spirit, That I am freed
> from all my infinite sins and transgressions and the punish-
> ment thereunto due, And so being justified by the merciful
> Imputations of Christ's righteousness, rest assured to be
> glorified both in soul and body. (spelling modernized)

The First Page

After the religious preamble, testators usually began with what was foremost on their minds, usually devising their real estate holdings or bequeathing personal property. These arrangements could be made in a single sentence or could be highly detailed. A gentleman of Romford chose to go the route of classic simplicity stating, "To my wife my lands and goods for life" (Emmison 1980:29). A gentleman of Wisdens began: "To Audrey my wife 6 silver spoons, a silver salt and such bedsteads, bedding, linen, brass, pewter, co-birons, spits and irons, dripping pans, trivets, pothangers, coffers, cupboards, presses, tables, stools, forms and household stuffe…" along with "a saw, a mattock, a shod shovel, a spade, a grinding stone, a plough, a coulter, an axe, a pitchfork . . . and my best black mare, six kine, ten sheep, half my hogs, poultry, tubs, barrels, trays and cheese motes, my malt mill, the weights and scales" (Emmison

1980:30). Considerately, the testator even sets out how Audrey is to select her half of the hogs.

In an overview of his bequests, Shakspere seeks to give all his real estate and most of his personal property to his older daughter Susanna. His intent is to give daughter Judith £300 pounds. Although he clearly favors Susanna with the more valuable real estate, £300 would be about $300,000 (US). He has made what appear to be reasonable provisions for his younger daughter. However, he encumbers the £300 in complex financial arrangements, apparently to keep the funds out of the hands of Judith's new husband, Thomas Quiney.

His concern seems justified. Judith married Quiney on February 10, 1616, at which point the will's new first page, dated January 25, 1616, had been drafted but before its final revision in March, 1616. It appears that these alterations reflect the changes in Judith's situation after her marriage, at which time it was discovered that her new husband had been brought up on charges of impregnating another woman. The woman died in childbirth, and Judith and Thomas Quiney were excommunicated for marrying during the Lenten season. In light of these circumstances, Shakspere's disapproval of his new son-in-law, indicated by these changes, seems well taken.

As a whole, the financial clauses reveal the shrewd mindset of the testator. In order for Judith to receive the first £50, she is required to surrender to her older sister "all her estate and right" in the copyhold manor of Rowington. This will keep one of Shakspere's houses out of the hands of Judith's wastrel husband. Ultimately the "stock" will go to Quiney (who Shakspere does not address by name) once he has settled upon Judith lands of equivalent value. But as Samuel Tannenbaum observed, the will is ambiguous on the amount that her husband must match in lands. Is it the £100 marriage "portion" interlined at the beginning of the will, or the £300 cash bequest in full? (98-103)[18] In any event, Shakspere's good intentions to provide income for Judith would be a high point of the will were it not for the problem that the garbled verbiage gave son-in-law Quiney grounds to challenge it. Tannenbaum remarks that "the matter might have proved a source of extensive litigation" (100). One wonders why a reasonably competent attorney (assuming Shakspere had legal advice) did not improve upon these conflicting instructions.

The language itself is curious. Not one word or phrase on this page or throughout the will seems Shakespearean. For example, the lump sums to Judith are called "stock," and before she receives these payouts she is to get what is termed "consideration" to be paid according to the rate of "two shillings in the pound." The words "stock" for principal and "consideration" for interest are terms from money-lending, an activity that Stratford's Shakspere is known to have pursued. A check in the *Harvard Concordance* reveals that these words are never used in a financial context anywhere in the Shakespeare canon in spite of extensive use of legal and financial terms in the works.

The Second Page

The second page might be called the "Property Page." Here Shakspere devises his houses and real estate to daughter Susanna and her husband John Hall, and enumerates personal property legacies. Nothing appears here for his wife Anne, but he provides for his sister Joan Hart, allocating one of his houses for her family at the nominal rent of 12 pence annually. In addition, he gives his sister Joan a monetary gift of £20 (approximately $20,000 today). His clothes also go to Joan, presumably intended for her sons who could wear them, and £5 ($5,000) to each of her three sons, though he names only two sons – so much for the "perfect memory" that he claims to have in the opening of the will.

Shakspere gives granddaughter Elizabeth Hall "all my plate" (with the exception of a silver gilt bowl), £10 to the "poor of Stratford," and his sword to Thomas Combe. After this, he launches into ten monetary gifts: money to the will's two overseers, money for rings to two Stratford friends, and three monetary gifts with no purpose specified. Among these bequests is the curious interlineation of money to his "fellows" Heminge, Burbage and Condell to purchase rings, the words jammed so tightly between the lines that the scrivener can barely fit them in. Why did Shakspere not add a bequest to the actors in a codicil at the end of the will, if indeed it was an oversight? According to Ralph Houlbrooke, additions could be made by a codicil "so long as it was not contrary to anything in the will." (89). Also, with this exception, all the other beneficiaries in the will are from the Stratford area. There is no mention of literary friends or any supposed patrons Shakspere might have had.

It has taken Shakspere a while to get to his most valuable property: his real estate. Having pressured Judith to surrender her rights in the Rowington house to her older sister, he now gives his remaining four residences and all of his land holdings in and around Stratford to Susanna as well. Shakspere is not following the trend in doing this, for by the early seventeenth century, gentry families were distributing the family assets more equitably among daughters and sons. In the chapter on "The Overall Distribution of Property" in *Women and Property in Early Modern England*, Amy Erickson concludes that "the allocation of parental wealth among offspring among the majority of the population was made upon a basis of remarkable equality" (78). An example of this can be found in the will of a gentleman from the town of Shelley who split up his property, giving a manor home to each of his five sons (Emmison 1980:44-45).

At this point in the will, Shakspere might have taken the opportunity to assign one of his houses to his wife for the duration of her life, something that most testators do at the opening of their wills. Instead, his thoughts turn again to Susanna with a long entail for the succession of his estate, going through seven male heirs "lawfully issuing" from Susanna's body. This is an unusual feature for two reasons. First, it is excessively long. This repetitious entail takes up eighteen lines, almost a fifth of the will. An entail could be set out in a sentence or two, as seen in the wills of other testators. Could not the greatest writer of the Elizabethan age have written more economically? Second, the seven sons were not yet born, and given Susanna's age, it was unlikely that she would have that many children. As it turned out, Elizabeth, born in 1608, was her only child.

The Third Page

Be that as it may, the thought of future generations of his family might have reminded him of his wife, for in an interlineation, as the will is coming to a close, he makes the notorious bequest of the *second best bed* to her. Generations of Shakespearean biographers have gone to great lengths to ameliorate the negative implications of this bequest. As Stephen Greenblatt notes, "Writers have made a strenuous effort to give these words a positive spin" (145).

Shakspere did not follow the usual practice of providing for his wife's maintenance in her widowhood, or allocating to her which of his five houses would be hers. He did not make her the executor or co-executor of the will, or his residual legatee with the household stuff. His neglect to address his wife by name is odd because he calls Susanna by name five times, Judith five times, granddaughter Elizabeth three times and sister Joan three times. These and other issues surrounding the second best bed bequest are examined in the following essay, "Alas Poor Anne."

After appointing his daughter Susanna and her husband John Hall to be his executors and naming his overseers, Shakspere closes his will with the standard instructions to discharge his financial obligations and pay his funeral expenses. But it ends with another odd feature. The preparer had originally written that Shakspere would put his "seal" to it. The standard wording is *hand and seal*. In

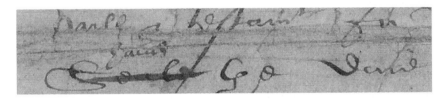

the last revision in March of 1616, the word *seal* is crossed out and the word *hand* written above it. That only the word *seal* was written in the earlier draft is an indication that the scrivener did not expect Shakspere to sign it.

Difficulties with the Construction

Stratfordian authorities have tried to explain how this miserable document could be the last words of an individual who possessed a great literary mind. From start to finish, it presents nothing but difficulties. It is a three page run-on sentence with no punctuation or paragraphs – though transcribers usually add these things to make it look a bit better. But even then, it is full of corrections, cancellations and interlineations, a "slovenly looking document made to do duty for the final will" (Tannenbaum 80). E.A.J. Honigmann compared it to other English wills and wrote that it is "a more heavily revised will than any I have seen" (*Selected Proceedings* 131). Even E. K. Chambers admitted in *Studies of Facts and Problems,* that the will has some "odd features" (175).

> The writing at the foot of sheet one is cramped and comes very near the bottom of the margin. That at the top of sheet 2 begins with two lines written higher up than one would expect from a comparison with the other sheets. And these are followed by a cancelled passage, with which they can never have had any sense-connection. This passage must originally have been the conclusion of something other than what now precedes it.

Chambers is on target with this explanation; a careful reading reveals that this page one was not the original page one. To this conundrum, Chambers offers a solution:

> In or before a January, probably of 1616, Shakespeare gave instructions for a will . . . Collins [his solicitor from an earlier land purchase] prepared a complete draft . . . it was not then executed, but on 25 March 1616, Shakespeare sent for Collins. The changes he desired in the opening provisions were so substantial that it was thought best to prepare a new sheet one. But he [the clerk] made, and afterwards corrected, the slip of transcribing January from the old draft. Then the opening provisions were dictated afresh . . . and proved so much longer than those they replaced, as to crowd the writing [at the bottom of sheet one] and necessitate the carrying of two lines on to the old sheet two, where they were inserted before a cancelled passage (175).

Schoenbaum in *Documentary Life,* concurs with Chambers' proposal that the first page was recopied: "Collins never got round to having a fair copy of the will made, probably because of haste occasioned by the seriousness of the testator's condition" (246). Yet Chambers' explanation does not account for the anomaly of the different inks. The first page is written in a darker ink and all of the

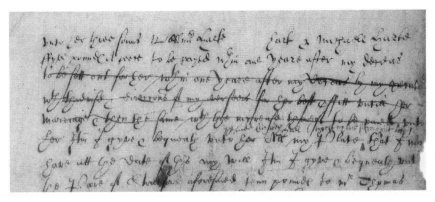

Top of the second page where the two lines from the first page were carried over from page one. The next three lines, originally at the top of this page, have been crossed out. The blank spot at the top line is where the name of Joan Hart's son would be, had Shakspere remembered his nephew's name was Thomas.

corrections and additions on all three pages are in the darker ink. (It should be noted here that the variations in ink are not as apparent in photographs available on the internet). It has been suggested that all of the revisions are in the same hand (Rogers 13).

But more mystifying are the lines crossed out at the top of the second page:

> To be sett out for her within one Year after my decease by my Executors with the advise and direccions of my over-seers for her best profit until her marriage and then the same with the increase thereof to be paid unto her.

These lines are directed toward Judith; Susanna had been married since June of 1607. But Shakspere does not seem to be anticipating an imminent marriage for his younger daughter. In these cancelled lines, he is providing for Judith's maintenance for an unknown interval of time until her marriage. It could be up to a year before this money is "sett out for her," and then "the increase thereof" will accrue from that point. When Judith marries, she will get the money, the "same" means the principal, with this "increase," which is the interest on the principal. It will take time for interest to be earned on the principal. This directly conflicts with the instructions on the first page in which the primary objective is to make provisions for Judith and her future children but keep the money out of the hands of her new husband.

Without a doubt, Shakspere's provisions for Judith and any children she may have are the best feature of his will. He understands that whatever he gives Judith will be snapped up by her new husband under the laws of "covert baron." But it is likely that the three cancelled lines at the top of page two came from a much earlier time, before he was alarmed by Judith's impending marriage to Quiney.

The date at the top right of the first page is also puzzling. It is strange that a scrivener would recopy the month *January* if this page was rewritten in March. That the word *January* is crossed out and *March* written above it indicates that the first page was composed in January and only corrected in March. Chambers' suggestion of a "little slip" seems unlikely. The opening words "Vicesimo Quinto die" translate as "twenty five day," so the day of the month is unchanged.

The next mistake occurs in the sentence "I give and bequeath unto my sonne-in-L" where the words "sonne-in-L" are crossed out and followed with "daughter Judith." The testator must have had something different in mind when he dictated the words "sonne-in-L" than what follows after these words are cancelled. This is a false start. Shakspere starts on one track and changes his mind mid-way. Why would this error be repeated in a re-copy of a document composed two months earlier?

The dark and light inks point to other anomalies. The scrivener was using the darker ink on the first page, both in *January* and in *March*. But pages two and three are in the lighter ink with emendations in the dark ink. The lighter ink is readily detectable in the signature of Francis Collins on page three. But what could be the meaning of these mistakes, corrections, and anomalies?

The original will probated in the Prerogative Court of Canterbury in June of 1616 can be viewed on the Folger website. I propose that page one originated as the dates at the upper right indicate: it was written out in January of 1616 and revised in March of 1616. Page one can be taken at face value. Pages two and three

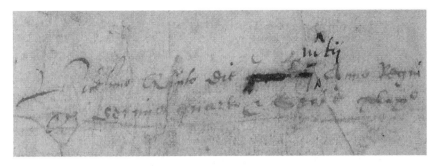

The word January *is crossed out and* March *is written above it.*

were taken from an earlier will and updated in January/March to fit circumstances of the testator's family at that time. However, pages two and three originated prior to January of 1616. Years earlier, before Judith's marriage was on the horizon, it was reasonable for Shakspere to give money directly to her. Also at an earlier time, Susanna had more childbearing years ahead, so the long entail to her seven sons yet unborn made more sense.

Additional facts support this proposal. Samuel Tannenbaun reports that each page of the will is from a different batch of paper. Each sheet is a different size, lending credence to the different "make" of each page (68-69). Curiously, only page two bears the Arabic numeral "2"; pages one and three are not numbered. Also, the watermarks on pages one and two are different (see illustration). There is no watermark at all on page three.

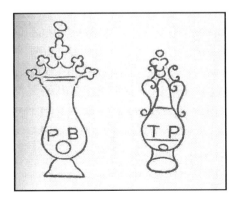

If the Stratford man had employed the services of an attorney, as orthodox biographers suggest, he was not a very good one. Not only is the will poorly composed, but whoever had a hand in it did not clear up ambiguities or reconcile inconsistencies. This can be seen in the bequest of "all my plate" to his granddaughter, interlined on page two. In Shakspere's residual clause on page three, his "plate" is listed along with the other "household stuff," a redundancy because all of the plate had been bestowed earlier in the will – there was no residual plate left to distribute.

Tannenbaum and other orthodox authorities believe that the different inks, differing watermarks, and dissimilar batches of paper, along with the mistakes, revisions, ambiguities, and contradictions, indicate the haste of preparation due to the illness of the testator (102-103). A better explanation may be that the lapse of time between the initial composition and the later alterations was more than just two months.

At what point in time could pages two and three have been composed? On page two, Shakspere gives his Blackfriars Gatehouse to Susanna. He purchased this property March 10, 1613, which indicates that page two could have been written as early as 1613 – a date that correlates better with Judith's single status and Susanna's remaining childbearing years.

Why should the time of composition matter? A last will and testament is an important document from anyone's life. But this will is crucial in determining how this particular historical person lived his life. In Shakspere's will, we see the people and possessions that were important to him. The will reveals someone who is tight-fisted, tough-minded, and somewhat mean-spirited. Even the excuse that his will was hurriedly thrown together as he lay dying hardly accounts for the issues it raises.

But it becomes more difficult to explain the deficiencies when Shakspere's will is considered in light of an earlier composition date for pages two and three. The bequest to the actors – the only theatrical connection in the will – looks dubious if this page was composed in the 1613 time frame. If the official story were true, in 1613, Shakspere was still writing plays. So why could he do no better than add, at a later date, an interlineation for rings for his fellow actors? Was not he at this time, supposedly a man-about-town in the London theater scene? But if he forgot about his fellows then, could he not have given them a bequest in a codicil at the end of the will, rather than a few words crammed between the lines?

If the will was composed over several years, then there is ample time to write a more sensible document. Wills were public documents, often read in open court, and it defies credulity that the author of *Hamlet*, among other masterpieces, would leave the world such a poor testament to show for his existence on this earth.

Conclusion

Nothing in the Stratford man's will indicates he had ever been a writer, led a cultured life, or possessed a cultivated intellect. There are no books, papers, writings, manuscripts, or related furniture. There are no musical instruments, art, tapestries, maps, or intellectual property of any kind. There are no shares in a theatrical company, theatrical attire, or memorabilia. He makes no provision for the education of his heirs or for anyone else. Nothing suggests a philanthropic spirit. There are no bequests to schools, colleges, almshouses, hospitals, or churches; there no mention of public projects such as the repair of roads and bridges. These kinds of benefices are missing despite the fact that he accumulated a large estate and died wealthy.

No wonder Reverend Greene was shocked when he discovered the will in 1747. No wonder the Prerogative Court of Canterbury prevented a full printing of it until 1851, and then only allowed a limited edition of one hundred copies. No wonder traditional biographers try to minimize or ignore the will. Nothing can redeem it. It is full of oddities and oversights, and downright silly in places. It's not what one would expect from the great-spirited man of enormous intellect who was William Shakespeare.

In 1590, Henry Swinburne published a monumental treatise that remains the most important compendium on wills of the era. He concluded with this thoughtful comment: "the mind, not the words, giveth life to the testament" (520). Reading through the Stratford man's Last Will and Testament, it seems inescapable that the mind that gave life to the greatest literary works in the English language is not to be found in this document.

Page One - Last Will and Testament - William Shakspere
(Courtesy of *The National Archives* of the United Kingdom)

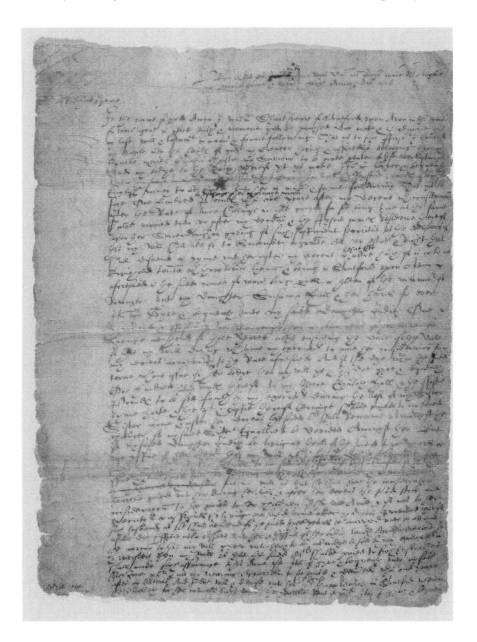

Page Two - Last Will and Testament - William Shakspere
(Courtesy of *The National Archives* of the United Kingdom)

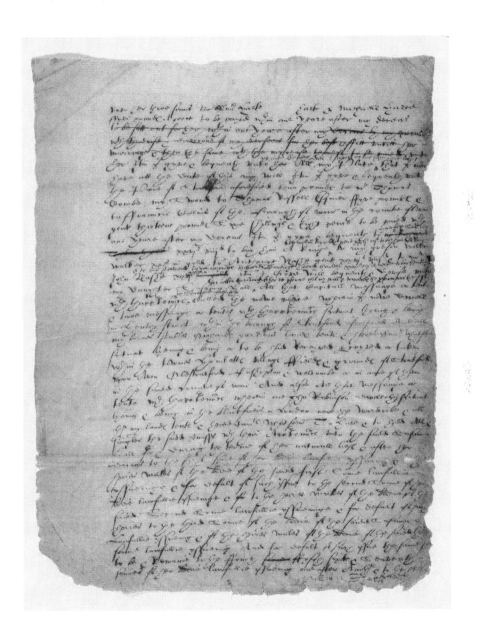

Page Three - Last Will and Testament - William Shakspere
(Courtesy of *The National Archives* of the United Kingdom)

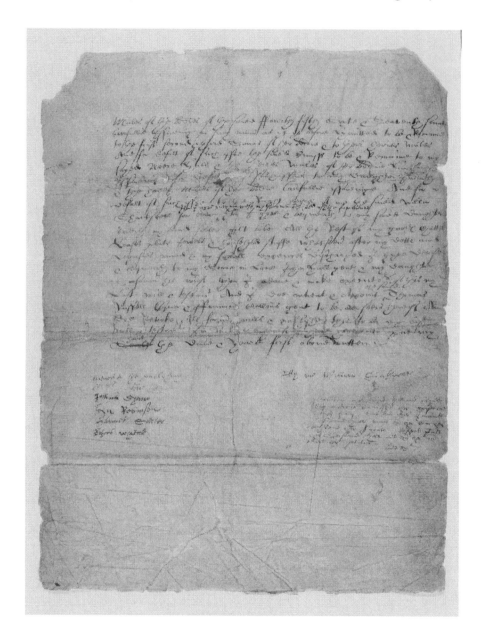

Notes

1. In *A Documentary Life*, Schoenbaum writes that "The copy mentioned by Vertue is very likely the one independently discovered by the Rev'd Joseph Greene in . . . Stratford a decade later." In *Shakespeare's Lives*, Schoenbaum believes that this copy, now called the Birthplace Copy, "was probably made shortly after the death of Dr. Hall in 1635" (92). Levi Fox, a chairman of the Shakespeare Birthplace Trust, reports on this copy in the *Shakespeare Survey 4*.

2. Other mistakes in Vertue's account are that Lady Bernard was Shakspere's great-granddaughter when she was his granddaughter. Vertue also credits Shakspere with the ownership of the Maiden Head and Swan Inns (presumably located in Stratford), but he owned no such property anywhere. Vertue wrote "a Copy of the original in poses (sic) of this Man [Shakespeare Hart] and may be seen in Doctors' Commons from whence they had it."

3. Allardyce Nicoll published some of Vertue's commentary in the *Shakespeare Survey 5: An annual Survey of Shakespeare Study and Production*. The article by Frank Simpson, "New place: The Only Representation of Shakespeare's House, from an Unpublished Manuscript," deals with Shakspere's mansion home in Stratford as it appeared to Vertue.

4. Honigmann and Brock concur with Vertue's discovery date of 1737 (108). They note that the first transcript was published in the posthumous edition of Lewis Theobald's *Works of Shakespeare*, 3rd edition, London 1752. Schoenbaum adds that "others have supposed that the original will was first printed in *Biographia Britannica* in 1763" (242).

5. His transcript, with a covering letter (dated 17 September 1747) to the Hon. James West, is in the British Library (MS Lansdowne 721, ff.2-6).

6. In his Preface, Halliwell credits a Mr. T. Rodd as the original copyist whose "tolerably accurate transcript" he reviewed and corrected.

7. In early modern England, wills were written in a variety of secretary hands, and even skilled paleographers have made mistakes in transcriptions. An amusing mistake occurred in the Stratford man's will, when the notorious bequest of the "second best bed" was first transcribed as the "brown best bed." This error, corrected at the end of the eighteenth century by Edmond Malone, unleased a storm of controversy within the orthodox community as it appeared that Mr. Shakspere disparaged Mrs. Shakspere (Schoenbaum, *Lives* 93, 120). More details are provided in the following essay, "Alas Poor Anne."

8. For more details, see Tannenbaum (100).

9. J. D. Alsop concurs: "It appears that a large number of wills in early modern England were written by professional notaries, scribes, clergy, family, friends and neighbors for both literate and non-literate testators" (20). Stephen Greenblatt concedes the point that testators dictated their wills (385).

10. See pages 146-147 for Prices' discussion of the Stratford will.

11. In dealing with the book problem, orthodoxy is divided into two schools of thought. The minimalist school holds that "Shakespeare" was a genius and imagination is all he needed to write great works of literature. Stephen Greenblatt in *Will in the World* and James Shapiro in *Contested Will* propose this solution. On the other hand, there is the maximalist approach in which the Stratford Grammar School is assigned a curriculum that would rival Renaissance studies at twentieth century Ivy League universities. Wherever orthodox commentators fall in this spectrum, no one is willing to concede that "Shakespeare" simply did not own any books, and the search for "Shakespeare's" library has been ongoing for centuries.

12. For more wills containing bequests of books and educational bequests, see Emmison 1978: 50-51, 73, 282-285.

13. For more information, see Erickson's chapter "Using Probate Accounts" in *When Death Do Us Part.*

14. The will and inventory of the Middlesex attorney Robert Swift also reveals this pattern: Swift makes extensive bequests of his books in the body of his will, but only the valuation is given in the inventory.

15. For an in-depth study of Shakespeare's knowledge of Italy, see *Shakespeare's Guide to Italy* by Richard Paul Roe.

16. For the complete wills from which these quotes are taken, see Emmison 1978: 45, 112, 184-185, 308, 315-316; 1980: 46, 48, 60, 62, 73, 84, 93-94, 124-125, 132. See Honigmann and Brock for the wills of Augustine Phillips and Jacob Mead, 72-75, 134-138.

17. Fox provides information on schools "endowed by tailors, brewers, mercers, drapers, skinners and goldsmiths… one of the most famous being the Merchant Tailors founded in 1560."

18. Chambers agrees that the language is ambiguous (178).

Chapter
3

Alas, Poor Anne
The Second Best Bed in Historical Context

In his last will and testament, William Shakspere's sole bequest to his wife of some thirty-three years was "my second best bed with the furniture."[1] These words, with their stark simplicity, take people by surprise. They are prompted to ask: "To whom did he leave his best bed?" Why did Shakspere bequeath his "second best bed" without previously referencing the best bed – or any other bed? The phrase "second best" occasionally appears in wills of the era, but it seems that these are words most testators prefer to avoid.[2] A study of several thousand contemporaneous wills reveals that this avoidance is pervasive. Most testators, perhaps instinctively, regarded these words as a disparagement of their beneficiaries.

Testators often bequeathed their "best" of a particular possession, and as beds were a major piece of furniture, bequests of "my best featherbed" or "best flock bed" appear frequently. Other examples of "best" items are articles of clothing or serving pieces: e.g. cloaks, doublets, petticoats, bowls, spoons, and, quite often, livestock.[3]

The customary way to identify bequests, whether the item was the best or not, was by a description or by its location in the home. A knight of Gosfield incorporates all of these approaches in his will. After giving his "best tester and ceiler" to his wife, he wills to another "the standing bed with the ceiler and tester… with cloth of gold and crimson velvet which is commonly used in the changer over the Old Parlour" (Emmison 1978:46-47). Another willmaker was adamant that his wife should have the "best" of everything, enumerating, among other things, the best joined bedstead, two best featherbeds, three best beasts (this usually meant cows), the best milk bowls, the best pewter platters, and even his best acre of barley (Emmison 1980:135-136).

According to Stratfordian authorities, William Shakspere's will was found in 1737 (Schoembaum, *Documentary Life* 242, Honigmann 108),[4] though it was not published in its entirety until more than a century had passed (Halliwell Preface).[5] However, an early transcript was published in the 1763 edition of the *Biographia Britannica*, and the bequest was transcribed as the "brown best bed."[6] Later that century, the Shakespearean authority Edmond Malone corrected the error, though Samuel Johnson and other editors still maintained that the bequest was the "brown best bed."[7] In any event, this transcriptional mistake postponed the impassioned debate that would eventually be generated by the words "second best" (Schoenbaum 93).

Another difficulty with the second best bed is that it is an interlineation. Worse still, the interlineation is on the third and last page of the will, giving it the appearance of an afterthought. Apparently Shakspere remembers his wife in the nick of time as the will is drawing to a close, not at the beginning as most testators do.[8] Most commentators believe that this interlineation was added along with the other changes on March 25, 1616, a month before Shakspere's death (Tannenbaum 96-97). Some suggest that Anne was just forgotten in the hastily revised will and bequests to her were in a discarded earlier draft.[9] However, the scrivener observed the convention of using the word *said* for someone previously mentioned, and this word does not appear before the words *my wife*. If Shakspere did include her in any way in an earlier draft, the scrivener was aware that the second best bed was the only item she was to get in this will, and one might expect the testator to know what was in his will when he signed it.

The fact that Shakspere left his wife only a bed is a problem whether it is the best or not (Greenblatt 145).[10] From medieval times, there existed in England a legal fiction known as the doctrine of coverture. By this doctrine, a husband and wife were considered to be legally one person – the wife was figuratively covered by her husband and had no independent legal identity (Erickson 237). She could not own property of any kind or participate in legal actions. She didn't even own the clothes on her back. Obviously, this put a woman at the mercy of her husband.[11] Since a woman owned nothing during marriage, it was uncertain what property would become hers in her widowhood; thus, it was morally incumbent upon her husband to provide for the maintenance of his surviving spouse if he had one. If a testator failed in this regard, there was a legal remedy that will be discussed shortly. Henry VIII added backbone to the moral obligation in a preamble to an act of 1529 (21 Hen. VIII, c.4). Aside from the irony that King Henry VIII, of all people, thought it fitting for men to provide for the "necessary and convenient finding of their wives," most willmakers, as a practical matter, did their duty and made provisions for their spouse early in their will (Cox 24).[12]

The Stratford man does not follow this pattern, but instead devotes most of the first page of his will to lengthy instructions for the maintenance of his younger daughter Judith. Though this is not a bad thing, it does seem odd that Shakspere expended great effort to provide for his younger daughter – and his older daughter Susanna is to inherit all of his real estate – but neglects to bequeath anything to his wife until the final lines of the will, and then only in an interlineation.

The Second Best Bed in Historical Commentary

The second best bed has remained a controversial bequest as it does not evoke the proper image of the cultivated, genteel poet/dramatist that is consistent with the Shakespearean iconography. Rather, it invites an element of ridicule. For this reason, generations of Shakespearean biographers have searched for ways to cope with its undesirable implications. One approach is to assume a posture of righteous indignation. No one does this better than E.K. Chambers. In his 1930 landmark *Study of Facts and Problems*, he laments the "sheer nonsense" and the "baseless theories of domestic discord or infirmity [that] have been devised to account for the absence of any further provision in the will for Shakespeare's wife" (2:176-177). The story that Mrs. Shakspere might have been "afflicted with some chronic infirmity of a nature that precluded all hope of recovery" was floated by Halliwell-Phillipps in his influential 1882 *Outlines* (185). He proposes that "in such a case, to relieve her from household anxieties and select a comfortable apartment at New Place, where she would be under the care of an affectionate daughter and an experienced physician, would have been the wisest and kindest measure that could have been adopted."

The normally prolix A. L. Rowse allocates only three paragraphs of his 1973 biography, *Shakespeare the Man*, to a discussion of the poet's last will and testament. He refrains from commenting on the second best bed, preferring to indulge in a sweeping overview in which he describes the will as "a very characteristic document, generous and neighborly," stating that "he left his widow to her daughter's care, who looked after everything" (270-271). In reality, the will is most uncharacteristic of wills of the time, and Shakspere makes no mention of entrusting the care of his surviving spouse to anyone.[13] However, the docents at the Birthplace in Stratford-up-on-Avon stick to the daughter story as it is promulgated by Rowse and Halliwell-Phillipps, though which of his two daughters had the duty of her mother's care varies. In *Shakespeare's Wife*, Germaine Greer posits that it was daughter Judith (328).

Methodology has been developed by Shakespearean biographers to promote a pleasant explanation for this unpleasant bequest. It usually boils down to two strategies: one is to make the bequest seem sentimental; the other to make it consistent with the legal standards of the era. To these ends, orthodox scholars have devoted a considerable amount of effort.

After Edmond Malone correctly transcribed the word *brown* as the word *second*, George Steevens tried to counter the damage of this apparent disparagement. Steevens floated the notion that "The bed he left her perhaps had peculiarly tender associations: it may, indeed, have been the bridal bed."[14] Others have followed Steevens lead. Schoenbaum supposes that the second best bed was "rich in tender marital associations" and gilds the lily with the idea that the "best bed was reserved for guests" (Schoenbaum, *Documentary Life* 248). With this suggestion, Schoenbaum also incorporated an idea from Halliwell-Phillips who opined that "the first best bed was reserved for visitors," the redundant "first best" being a Halli-well-Phillips invention (183). Another popular variation is that the best bed went to the son and heir (Fullom 319).

Anthony Holden masterfully combines all of the above, craft-ing a scenario of marital bliss in which:

> . . . the Shakespeares, like most well-to-do middle-class couples, would have reserved the best bed in their home, New Place, for overnight guests. . . . Far from signifying the rottenness of their marriage, the bequest suggests a specific (and rather touch-ing) vote of thanks from a grateful husband, aware of his own shortcomings for the long-suffering, dogged loyalty of a partner who had for years put up with a long-distance marriage. . . . It was the marital bed he had shared with Anne – on and off – for more than thirty years (and perhaps her own parents' bed before that) (322).

In all the scrambling for ways to ennoble the bequest, the most remarkable is the explanation put forth by Joyce Rogers, an Associate Professor of religious studies at the University of New Mexico. In her book, *The Second Best Bed: Shakespeare's Will in a New Light*, Rogers makes a staggering proposal. Apparently, in her pursuits of religious history, she ran across some terminology from feudal times in which a testator was required to give his best chattel to his liege lord and his second best chattel to the church to pay his mor-tuary or funeral expenses. The chattel was most often a horse, cow, or ox (78-86). From this ancient custom, she draws the analogy that the second best of something has "ecclesiastical connotations."

In support of this, Rogers treats the reader to small doses of the *Commentaries* of Blackstone (1766), the legal histories of Maitland and Pollack (1901), and the more recent common law history of Frank Thomas Plucknett (1958). Snippets from these authorities are inter-spersed with records from the medieval laws of Ranulf de Glanvill and King Canute (31-32, 62). Spanning a millennia of English legal history in a matter of pages, she makes some interesting observa-tions: for example, AEthelred and Canute agreed that the souls of the dead should be "rendered before the grave is closed" (85).

The objective of her book is to demonstrate that the second best bed bequest is a "parting tribute of profound meaning" (xvii). To support her theory, Rogers offers a collection of miscellaneous assertions. For example, "it is likely that Shakespeare himself was most singularly informed of the ancient laws that demonstrate the significance of the reconciliation aspect of mortuary law" (93). Taking free association to a new level, she writes: "Somehow in the consciousness of generations there seems to have developed a special significance for the 'second best' of a thing. It was something like a ritual word, as may be seen in its early usage in Jewish tithing law" (95). What Rogers is trying to say is that Mrs. Shakspere should have been pleased, even honored, with the bequest, as the second best of something has special meaning, even "metaphorical significance." She continues: "Shakespeare could have had in mind any or all of the meanings associated with the phrase." In a final flourish, she proposes that Shakespeare could have been "even expressing a desire for reconciliation as a final act of his life" (96). There is, of course, nothing to justify any of this.

Rogers has a right to put forth whatever she wishes, and this would all be well and good if no one took much notice of it. But what is troubling is that the main thesis of her book has found acceptance in academic circles since its publication in 1993. It was published by the academic publisher Greenwood Press as part of a series of "Contributions to the Study of World Literature," and appears on the library shelves of 140 state and private universities in the USA alone.[15] In her acknowledgements, Rogers thanks the important people who facilitated her studies, including the administrators at the Folger Shakespeare Library, academicians at Oxford University and the Bodleian Law Library, and the Keepers of the Public Record Office who granted her the privilege of viewing the will, a favor not often extended to the public at large. Furthermore, many Shakespearean authorities including Marvin and Helga Spevack of the *The Harvard Concordance of Shakespeare* gave her "ongoing encouragement" (xx).

Yet in spite of all this help from distinguished colleagues, she makes some factual mistakes. She notes that Dr. Hall "was buried in 1635 beside his wife" (101). In fact, Susanna Shakspere Hall survived him by fourteen years, dying in 1649. In Rogers' discussion of the early reports of the will, she states that Nicholas Rowe, the first modern editor of Shakespeare, thought the form of the will "somewhat disappointing" (14). This is another error. The will had not been discovered when Rowe composed his biography in 1709. It was discovered in 1737 by George Vertue, and Rowe was long dead.

Rogers seeks to base her hypothesis in the rights of inheritance in early modern England. In the final scheme of things, the argument that underpins the viability of the second best bed as a reasonable bequest – though in no way a considerate one – rests on what was known as dower rights. Rogers insists that "the brief history of this law will establish the validity of Anne's dower rights and thereby conclude my resolution of the major controversies in the light of testamentary law" (35). Peter Ackroyd and Michael Wood have agreed. Ackroyd notes that "Anne Shakespeare would have been automatically entitled to one-third of his [Shakespeare's] estate; there was no reason to mention her in an official document" (513). Wood treats the bequest as if Anne was getting a bonus, blessing it as the marital bed and "over and above the one-third of his estate that fell to his widow as a matter of course" (338).[16]

The dower rights explanation for the notorious bequest originated with a 19th century Shakespearean biographer, Charles Knight. A son of a bookseller, Knight followed the family trade, using his business acumen to make available to the general public works of literature that were wholesome, uplifting, and cheap enough for everyone to afford to buy. One of Knight's labors was *The Pictorial Edition of the Works of Shakespeare*, published in installments between 1838 and 1841 (Schoenbaum, *Lives* 273-274, 587). Editorializing on Shakespeare's will in his postscript to *Twelfth Night*, Knight made the following observation:

> Shakspere knew the law of England better than his legal commentators. His estates with the exception of a copyhold tenement, expressly mentioned in his will, were freehold. *His wife was entitled to dower* . . . She was provided for amply, by the clear and undeniable operation of the English law.

Before Knight published his discovery of dower, he ran it by an attorney friend whom he thought to be a "sound lawyer." After getting the lawyer's approval, he brought this idea to the attention of the Shakespeare Society where he was associated with John Payne Collier and James Orchard Halliwell (who became Halliwell-Phillips in later years). It met with immediate acceptance. With such auspicious backers, Charles Knight had succeeded in dignifying the ignominious bequest with a legal explanation. He thought he had found justification in the bedrock of the ancient common law of England. Knight's momentous innovation brings to the table two questions of great import: What are dower rights? And did Mrs. Anne Hathaway Shakspere have the expectation of financial support resulting from this law?

The dower was the right of a widow to a third of her husband's real estate.[17] Its genesis in the common law was sanctified in the Magna Carta of 1215 when the laws of dower were intended to protect the rights of the heir as well as to provide for the maintenance of the widow (Lewis 496-505).[18] But as dower rights evolved through subsequent centuries, their effectiveness was gradually eroded by the difficulties that widows endured in obtaining them. These issues will be addressed shortly. However, it was Henry VIII who dealt the most serious blow to dower with the implementation of the Statute of Wills in 1540. His Majesty, described in this statute as "being replete and endowed by God with grace, goodness and liberality," was supposed to be motivated by the desire "to relieve and help his said subjects in their said necessities and debility." Nevertheless, what Henry set in place in the Statute of Wills would be a terrible blow for future generations of women. With his statute 32 Henry VIII. Cap1., King Henry redefined how willmakers could allocate their real property, giving complete freedom of testation to men under most circumstances.

> That all and every person and persons, having, or which hereafter shall have, any manors, lands, tenements or hereditaments, holden in soccage, or of the nature of soccage tenure . . . shall *have full and free liberty, power and authority to give, dispose, will and devise, as well by his last will and testament writing,* or otherwise by any act or acts lawfully executed in his life, *all his said manors, lands, tenements or hereditaments, or any of them, at his free*

will and pleasure; any law, statute or other thing heretofore had, made or used to the contrary notwithstanding *(Important English Statutes* 40-44).

Most of the landowning classes in England held their property under soccage tenure – the kind of land ownership specified in this statute. Therefore, in most cases, this statute took away whatever protection a wife might have had through legal recourse if her husband did not provide for her in his will. Its ramifications reached far and wide. [19] The end result of this statute was that a willmaker could dispose of all his real property as he saw fit. He could cut off his wife with only a shilling (Erickson 27). [20]

In reading Shakspere's will, it is clear that he is taking advantage of the willmaker's full power of testation, leaving all of his property to daughter Susanna. Shakspere actually uses the word *all* four times in devising his houses and lands in Stratford-upon-Avon, Oldstratford, Bishopton and Welcome. To make sure he left nothing out, he adds "in any of them in the said county of War[wickshire]." He wills to Susanna the "messuage" at Blackfriars in London along with "all other my lands tenements & herediments whatsoever," and closes with the expansive phrase "all & singular the said premises with their appurtenances…"[21] As the entirety of the property identified in Shakspere's will matches the public record of the property that he owned, there is no other property that Mrs. Shakspere might have claimed or that he might have previously assigned to her use.

Simplistically, Charles Knight itemized the real estate that Shakspere devised in his will, and was confident that his widow would get an interest in these properties, due to the laws of England (Schoenbaum *Lives* 275)."[22] But he had no idea what these laws were. He did not know that a widow had to claim dower and the rigorous legal ordeal this entailed. Moreover, he could not possibly have known how complex the laws of property and inheritance were in the late sixteenth and early seventeenth centuries. Another century would pass before England's legal historians would begin to unravel the complexity of the four legal systems functioning in early modern England: the Common Law, the Law of Equity, Ecclesiastical Law, and Manorial Law.

Inheritance disputes in real estate, tenures, and moveable property came under these competing jurisdictions and their respective courts (Erickson 23-25, 27, 30). To make matters more confusing, manorial law dominated the will-making process, and these laws changed from town to town as the "custom of the manor" dictated (Stretton 30).[23] Wills were probated under ecclesiastical law in the church courts, but if a widow wished to claim her dower – something that rarely occurred after the 15th century – the suit had to be filed in the common law courts, though occasionally the court of equity came into play (Stretton 109).[24]

Nevertheless, Knight's erroneous proposal of the dower rights excuse for the second best bed bequest has had lasting influence in Stratfordian biographies. Therefore, it is time to exert due diligence and drill down on this point.

The Demise of Dower Rights in England

From the time of the Magna Carta in the early thirteenth century, women did not automatically receive their dower interest. A woman had to go to court to claim what she thought was rightfully hers; in short, she had to become a plaintiff and litigate. It can be assumed that some widows obtained their rightful dower without filing a writ in Chancery; but Sue Sheridan Walker notes that dower was a popular plea, indicating that "some persons, then as now, never yielded anything undemanded"(85).[25] Walker continues that once the common law action was initiated, "the legal process required determination, knowledge, persistence, and probably hired expertise" (84). It would be miserable and expensive, but the stakes were high, and with her economic survival in the balance, many women took to the law in the thirteenth and fourteenth centuries to seek redress from the courts (83-85).

If a woman chose to take her chances in the courts and sue for her dower thirds, she had to file a writ in the Royal Courts within forty days of her husband's death. This meant a trip to London to see an attorney and get the proper documents filed in the Court of the King's Bench. In addition to the time element, a new writ was required for each parcel in which she wished to establish a claim (Walker 85). Her presence, or that of her attorney, was required at all stages of the litigation; some women lost simply because she or her representative could not show up at some point in the process. If she lost, she had to pay a monetary penalty known as an amercement – something akin to today's court costs (Walker 92).

Besides the logistical considerations, the widow could expect to confront a number of legal objections once she filed her dower claim. It was the duty of the heir to assign to her the portion of her deceased husband's property in question, and a legal battle ensued if the heir was of a mind to deprive her. According to Walker, "The lawsuit often brought opposition, which revealed facts or allegations that were potentially deleterious to the success of the dower claim. The contest between the claimant widow and the defendant denying the obligation to grant her dower is valuable in understanding what it meant, in personal terms, to sue for dower" (84-85).

It was fertile ground for interfamilial struggles. At a time when many women died in childbirth, the heir was often the son from a previous marriage. In addition to a son, an heir could be a collateral male such as a cousin or nephew, or in some cases the tenant of the property. Even a female heir could put up stout resistance, as the income from the disputed property may have been crucial to a daughter's survival too.

There is more to overcome in the litany of difficulties if a woman sued for dower. She would find that she had to prove that her marriage had been valid to start with, and this could be problematic if the marriage had been arranged privately. Moreover, record keeping was not what it became in the modern era. Next, the type of land tenure would be questioned. Some tenures were bars to dower, and tenures became more complex as the centuries rolled by. Walker reports on these issues: "The objections to granting dower to the plaintiff based on the nature of property holding reveal the incredible complexity of the medieval law of tenures and estates, and the relish with which freeholders exploited the nearly infinite possibilities to rent, grant, sell and resettle the property, even though feudal tenures could not be willed" (93).

Additional uncertainties came from identifying which property her husband was "seized of" (owned) at the time of his death. Again, Walker points out that "dower was not a static concept but rather, evolved over time; a crucial issue was that of defining what measure would be used to determine which of the husband's land would provide dower" (8).

The list goes on. If a husband died overseas as a casualty of war, a widow could have difficulty proving his death (86, 91). Dower rights were extinguished by felony convictions, and these, sadly, could result from minor incidents.

Worst of all, adultery was considered a bar to dower. Not long after the Magna Carta allocated dower, a statute was passed that put a widow in the precarious position of having to defend her character. Under this statute, if a charge of adultery was made, a widow would be subjected to a jury of her neighbors to determine the validity of the accusation (Walker 8, 88-89).[26]

With many impediments to dower, it is surprising that widows did indeed press their claims in the thirteenth and fourteenth centuries. It could be hoped that a more equitable system might have evolved in subsequent centuries. Unfortunately this was not the case. Richard Helmholz discusses the fifteenth century, describing it as a watershed time in which women's rights were greatly diminished (169-170).[27] By the sixteenth century – the Tudor century – the upper classes and land owning families had traded dower for jointure (Erickson 25).

A jointure was a settlement that a man or his father made on the prospective bride, usually before the marriage. It was an early English equivalent of a marriage contract. In the jointure contract, the groom (or his family) specified the income that the woman would receive if she survived her husband, and specified the lands from which this income would be provided. In describing the advantages of jointure over dower, Attorney General Edward Coke commented that jointure was "more sure and safe for the wife" (Spring 49). At least jointure was relatively automatic, whereas pursuing dower in the court system was not. But jointure had a downside: once in place, it was a permanent bar to dower, even if, as Eileen Spring notes, the husband "inherited half a county" (47-49).

Another drawback to jointure is that it was based on the amount of money that the woman's side of the family paid as her marriage portion (Spring 50-56). The jointure deal was rooted in the value of the land-holdings of the eventual husband. The ratio was usually 10%. This means that if the bride's family paid the groom (or his family) £1,000, then the groom would settle on the bride a jointure of £100 in annual income from the property owned by the groom's family – with payments to begin during her widowhood (50).

It's easy to see that this was a lopsided deal to start with: the groom's family received the money at the beginning of the marriage, and the bride would receive her jointure payments if she outlived her husband. The bride would break even, so to speak, only if she outlived her husband by ten years (Stretton 32).

King Henry VIII spurred the decline in the economic position of women. The jointure/marriage portion arrangement which favored the groom's side over the bride's became even more disproportionate when Henry passed his Statute of Uses of 1535. Ostensibly, this statute was intended to prevent a man from hiding land ownership through a device known as a "use;" i.e. the transferring of his land to trustees to avoid his feudal dues to the king. If the Statue of Uses had actually made land ownership more transparent, it might have facilitated a widow's claims to dower. But this did not happen. The Statute contained a provision that *established jointure as a bar to dower.* It was a final blow to the vestigial remains of a widow's dower rights. Eileen Spring sums it up: "The very statute whose preamble speaks of the wrongs done to widows proceeds to give statutory embodiment to those wrongs. Henry had shed crocodile tears for the widow" (47). No surprises there.

Anne Shakspere and the Laws of Property

As we see from this discussion on the legal position of women in early modern England, if Anne Shakspere had been depending on the English laws to provide for her maintenance (as Charles Knight put forth and some modern biographers still tell us), she was in for a disappointment. There is no evidence to indicate that William Shakspere made any financial arrangements for the pregnant Anne Hathaway before their marriage, nor are there any documents to lead us to suppose that he did so at a later time. Suggestions that he might have given her property that posterity does not know about are frustrated by the conveyance records of his land and house purchases which, as previously noted, square with the property accounted for in his last will and testament. Had Anne had property from her own family – what in today's world is called "separate property" – then she lost it all to him by the laws of coverture at the time of their marriage. In cases where a wife brought property to the marriage, her husband usually bequeathed it back to her in his will. This is something else that Shakspere does not do.

How wealthy was the Shakspere family? Certainly William expanded the family holdings that he inherited from his own father, and, by the time of his will, was living in affluence. This assessment is based on his two large land purchases and his five houses, one of which was a mansion. Christine North defines the middling rich as those with an estate valued between £200 and £499 (300). Shakspere undoubtedly qualifies by this definition. Though the final valuation of Shakspere's estate is unknown, from Shakspere's real estate holdings and the £370 in cash bequests in his will, his estate can easily be valued at more than £500, putting him at least in the category of middling wealthy.[28] Erickson writes that it was the practice of the middling rich to provide the widow with a lump sum settlement in the testator's will (138). She also comments that "the principal piece of property a man had to give to his wife was usually his house and land" (163). This practice is borne out in many wills of the Elizabethan time.[29]

Obviously, Shakspere is not among the majority of will makers of his class who provided for the maintenance of their surviving spouses. But the question remains: what were his intentions in allocating only a bed to his wife? Bequests in wills are a major resource used by historians to gain insight into the testator's "personal intentions, as opposed to the impersonal operation of law." Testators could be driven by many things, including "convention, affection, guilt, need, and duty" (Erickson 32-33). To ascertain Shakspere's intent, other aspects of will making must be considered.

In early modern England, women were appointed the sole or co-executrix of their husband's estate approximately 75% of the time (Houlbrooke 136; Erickson 158).[30] In her article on middle class widows, Mary Hodges states, "the prevalence of women as executors seems to indicate that most men were willing to leave this important and demanding task to women" (309). Noticeably,

Shakspere does not make his wife his executrix. Some Shakspear-ean biographers believe that he may have wished to spare his aging wife a troublesome burden, but had Shakspere felt her advancing years a hindrance to performing the duties of an executrix, he could have appointed her co-executrix along with his daughter Su-sanna and her husband John Hall. As a practical matter, the widow often shared this duty with one or more of her grown children. There were other options as well. A widow could renounce the position of executrix in favor of an adult child or even an overseer of the will. Besides, it seems that Shakspere's son-in-law bore the brunt of the work as executor of his will, so appointing Mrs. Shak-spere a co-executor would have been a gesture of goodwill (Honan 398). It would have been a token of respect that would have cost Shakspere nothing. Ralph Houlbrooke concurs that the custom of making the wife the executrix was "clearly regarded by many testators as a mark of favor as well as trust" (136). It leads to the suggestion that Shakspere did not want his wife to have any part of his property, for, as Amy Erickson observes, once appointed, "a widow had virtually complete control over her former husband's estate" (161).

Additional omissions indicate that Shakspere deliberately de-nied his wife ordinary means of support. During this time, the wife was almost invariably designated by her husband as the residual legatee (Erickson 162). This meant that she would receive what remained of the "household stuff" after the special bequests were distributed (Hodges 309).[31] The contents of the household could include the crops and foodstuffs as well as household items neces-sary for everyday life. A residual clause appears in the closing para-graph of Shakspere's will – as it does in most wills of the era – and along with the household stuff Shakspere specifies chattel, leases, plate, and jewels. The residual property is to go to daughter Susanna and her husband John Hall. If Stratfordians try to argue that Shakspere was following the usual pattern in making his daughter and son-in-law the executors and residual legatees of his will, they would be misinformed.

Rarely did a testator entirely cut off someone significant in his life, and when he did, the practice was to give the person to be excluded an item of little value, most often a single shilling

(Erickson 162; Greenblatt 146). It was appropriate to give an insufficient bequest because this supported testamentary capacity – the will maker did not simply forget about this person. It also strengthened the testator's intent that a small item was all that this individual was to receive (Houlbrooke 94). Although highly unusual for a testator to withhold spousal support, Shakspere is not the only one to do this. Thomas Crawley, a man from Wendon Lofts, left many bequests, but "To Frances my wife the household stuff *which she brought me* and *one featherbed*"(Emmison 1978:73-74). He returned to her what was hers to start with, but the only item he gives her from his lands and goods is the featherbed.

That Shakspere does not address his wife by name is another oversight. It is a rare will maker who does not give his wife's name. This neglect is further compounded by the absence of a respectful term of address such as "my loving wife" or "my welbeloved wife." This is routine language, and similar phrases often occur when testators acknowledge extended family; for example, "my well beloved son-in-law," or "my well-beloved cousin" (Emmison 1980:37). Overseers were often described as "trusty and well beloved friends" (Erickson 161). Such phrases were formulaic, indicative of trust and respect, and not necessarily terms of endearment.

Conclusion

There is no perspective from which the bequest of the second best bed can be viewed that speaks well of this testator. Shakspere did not make provisions for the maintenance of his wife in her widowhood, but left her only one item that was insufficient for her survival. He did not appoint her the executrix of his will, nor did he make her his residual legatee. He did not address her by name or use a form of address indicating at least respect, if not affection. When all of these elements are taken into consideration, it is difficult to escape the conclusion that it was Shakspere's intent to disparage his wife as well as to deprive her of adequate maintenance. Orthodox scholars try to minimize this by shifting the blame onto the shoulders of Shakspere's attorney, Francis Collins. However, Collins provided for his own wife in his own will (Honan 397).

The Stratfordian excuse that Shakspere expected one of his

daughters to care for his wife is not acceptable. Other testators had children too, and they routinely allocated adequate resources for their widows to live on. Besides, Judith could die, a possibility Shakspere himself notices twice on the first page of his will, but it escapes him that Susanna could also predecease her mother. In this case, John Hall would be in possession of Shakspere's mansion home of New Place along with the rest of his real estate. Hall could remarry and have another family. A second wife might not be pleased to have her husband's former mother-in-law under foot. As Shakspere owned five residences at the time of his death, it would seem that the least he could have done for his wife was to leave her his second best house.

Please also see Appendix A: Text of the will of William Shakspere.

Notes

1   The term "furniture" means the bedding, pillows, covers, sheets, and bed hangings that went with the bed, and did not include any additional household furnishings. Occasionally, Shakspere's biographers attempt to increase the scope of the bequest to include a "bedstead" to make it seem a bit more impressive.

2   Orthodox scholars have trawled through early English wills in search for examples of other testators who bequeathed the "second best" of an item. In her book *Second Best Bed*, Joyce Rogers has a paragraph with the usual examples (72).

3   In Emmison's transcriptions of wills published in 1980 by the Essex Record Office, a gentleman of Prittlewell left "my best cloak" to his brother, other "best" articles of clothing to other friends, "a silk grogram doublet" to another, and the "rest of my apparel" to another (51). A gentleman of Halstead left "my best gown" to his brother-in-law and "my frize gown" to a friend. This same individual leaves to his wife Dorothy "my best featherbed," and his "next best bed" to his son (47). A yeoman of steeple Bumpstead leaves his wife "my best bed and bedstead in the chamber over the kitchen" along with all her apparel (126). The term "next the best" is often found after "the best" item is bequeathed (70, 135). A widower of Sible Hedingham infused his will with many "best" items that would go to his daughter, including the "best bed in my parlour," and a servant was to have the "ceiled bed aloft of the folks' chamber" (104).

4   Schoenbaum states that George Vertue "noted a copy" in 1737 and that the Reverend Joseph Greene "independently discovered it" a decade later in 1747. In their invaluable book *Playhouse Wills*, editors Honigmann and Susan Brock accept the 1737 date for the discovery of the original will now in the National Archives at Kew.

5. In 1851, after many requests, the Prerogative Court of Canterbury allowed J. O. Halliwell to publish a limited edition of 100 books in which the interlineations and canceled passages (called "corrections") were shown in type. The notorious bequest is clearly transcribed as the "second best bed."

6. Malone attributed the mistake to Louis Theobald, but, as Schoenbaum notes, Theobald had died three years before the will was discovered. The rapscallion who offered the erroneous transcription is unknown, but Philip Nichols signed off on the 1763 *Britannica* entry, and at a minimum is a responsible party.

7. This will is written in facile secretary hand (Honigmann), and when the word "second" is closely studied, it does bear a resemblance to the word "brown," making it possible to excuse the mistake as part of the difficulties of deciphering secretary hand. Nevertheless, the "brown best bed" is nonsensical, though maybe this, too, is understandable given the suspension of common sense that accompanies examinations of the Stratford man's will.

8. With rare exception, wills of the era bear out that men provided for the maintenance of their wives, and usually did so at the beginning of the will, immediately following the religious preamble. It is clear from the language that many will makers were sincere in their desire to provide for their widow and were not simply accommodating customs and laws. After allocating to his wife what he regarded as adequate bread and board, a yeoman of Harlow wanted her to have "a sufficient servant to serve her at all needful times for a woman of her age and calling..." (Emmison, 1980:122.)

9. Dr. Samuel Tannenbaum proposed this ingenious solution to the interlineation problem. Following the proposal of E. K. Chambers and others, it is accepted by scholars that the first page of the will was recopied. In an effort to suggest that Shakspere did his duty "up front" like most testators, Tannenbaum offers that Mrs. Shakspere was provided for in this previously written and later discarded first page. Still, it remains to be seen

how the testator or the scrivener or the attorney (who served as one of the witnesses) simply forgot to include appropriate provisions for his wife's maintenance in the final draft.

10. Greenblatt accepts the absence: "It is as if she had been completely erased."

11. A dichotomy existed between real and personal property with different legal systems governing how various types of property could be distributed. The common law applied to real estate; ecclesiastical laws dealt with movables. As early as 1500, in the province of Canterbury, "a man had complete freedom to disinherit his children and leave his wife penniless" (Erickson 28). By 1600, even the ecclesiastical laws that protected widows' rights to a third of her husbands' movable goods had given way to customs and manorial law. In the seventeenth century, the ecclesiastical laws remained in the province of York, Wales and the City of London. These laws were eliminated by laws in 1692, 1696, and 1725 respectively (Erickson, 246). E. K. Chambers avoids the issue of the custom of Stratford-upon-Avon, noting, "Whether the widow was entitled to a third of personalty similarly depended upon local custom: the Warwickshire custom is unknown" (*Study of Facts and Problems, Vol II*, 177). As Erickson sums it up: "Most women, even those with a marriage settlement, were largely at the mercy of their husbands' good will, both during and after marriage" (151).

12. In addition to spousal provision, the testators' three remaining obligations were to pay their debts, support their minor children, and make charitable bequests "for the Health of their Souls."

13. In his Introduction to *Playhouse Wills*, Honigmann states that "Here, as in other things, Shakespeare stands out as different and deserves a short digression." The editors give an account of Shakespeare's property (8), the laws involved with property and inheritance (14-15), and an accurate transcription of Shakspere's will (105-109).

14. Citing Malone's *Supplement* in *Shakespeare's Lives*, Schoenbaum

provides an overview of the dispute between Malone and Steevens over the interpretation of the second best bed bequest (120, 578).

15. Among the notable universities are Harvard, Yale (and the Yale Law Library), Princeton, Auburn, Brown, Columbia University, Georgetown University Law Library, Duke, Cornell, Purdue, Rice, Notre Dame, Pittsburgh, Pennsylvania, Texas, and UCLA. Not to belabor the point, but this is truly an achievement for a book with a hypothesis based on sheer speculation.

16. In all fairness to orthodox scholars, many of them, including Schoenbaum, are aware of the difficulties associated with the dower rights explanation. Include in this group are Park Honan (*Shakespeare: A Life*, 397); Richard Wilson (*Will Power*, 210); Stephen Greenblatt (*Will in the World*, 146); and Scott McCrea (*The Case for Shakespeare: The End of the Authorship Question*, 47). Dennis Kay implies that Anne was provided for, though noting that "the Stratford view of the so-called 'widow's portion' has not been identified" (*Shakespeare: His Life, Work and Era*, 348).

17. Spring discusses the variables in the law (46). If the land were held by "soccage tenure," the widow could claim a half interest. The widow of a villain (serf) could succeed to all of her husband's property. As a rule, the larger the estate, the smaller the proportion was that went to the wife. Obviously, the wife of a poor man who worked a small plot needed all of her husband's property to eke out a subsistence. According to Erickson, the majority of the population owned only a few household goods and a cow, and had a lease on a cottage (18).

18. Lewis offers a lengthy explanation of the history of dower from its origins prior to the Magna Carta. Initially, the concept of dower thirds was a limitation on the rights of the widow, i.e. she could not obtain more than a third as her dower interest. "The history of English law, as it applies to dower, is not that of requiring or obligating a husband to grant his wife such dower but, very largely, a matter of limiting the amount of landed estate that may be given a wife" (496). Lewis' overview is infor-

mative, but suffers from some contradictory statements as he discusses the development of dower through the centuries and reviews information in Blackstone and Holdsworth, giants of English legal history. Lewis acknowledges that in Stratford-up-on-Avon, "local custom did not prescribe a three-part division of the husband's estate, one of which was to be devised to the wife" (503).

19. Royal entitlements were still attached to property held by knight service; the burdens engendered by this tenure are discussed in the essay "Evermore in Subjection."

20. For the average citizen of the era, manorial customs determined how a will maker could devise his real estate, but both "the common law and manorial customs of inheritance only operated in cases where no previous arrangement had been made." In other words, the testator could dispose of all of his real estate by will. Christopher St German, an early 16th century commentator, noted the "ability of a husband to cut his wife off with a shilling by will." This source is cited by Erickson (246) and referenced in Baker's *English Legal History* (164).

21. For a modernized spelling transcript of these passages, see Appendix A. For a transcription in original spelling, see Honigmann and Brock, 105-109.

22. Schoenbaum understands that Knight had overreached by wading into English legal history and attaching dower law to the exasperating bequest. Shakespearean biographers who haven't gotten the memo would do well to read Schoenbaum's discussion in his book, *William Shakespeare: A Compact Life*, 1987 (301).

23. Stretton explains that in "grassroots England," local custom prevailed. "It is difficult to generalize about custom because it was local, differing from town to town, manor to manor, and sometimes even from tenement to tenement."

24. Although jointure actions were tried more often than dower in the equity courts, widows could sometimes gain access to

the equity Court of Requests, and potentially receive a more favorable hearing on disputes over dower. The Requests was considered the "poor man's Chancery." According to Stretton, "in theory it was a court for poor litigants" and heard "poor miserable persons causes" which included widows and orphans.

25. In her article, "Litigation as Personal Quest: Suing for Dower in the Royal Courts, circa 1272-1350," Walker indicates that it is unknown what percentage of widows received their dower in the 13th and 14th centuries without "going to law." If the dower was yielded in a timely manner, then of course nothing will be in the court records. Walker posits that the number of court cases left for posterity to see is an indication that many defendants still waited for the widow to sue, even "if the defendant had no substantive objection to giving the woman her dower" (85).

26. Note *Statutes of the Realm*, 1:87.

27. Helmholz discusses the rights of medieval women to make wills in order to dispose of personal property. Dower laws dealt with the portion of a man's real estate holdings to which his widow was entitled. However, the erosion of the legal status of women in the 15th century runs parallel in both the areas of property and inheritance. The decline of the legal position of women in the 15th century is further addressed by Martin Sheehan in his study on medieval wills. Walker provides additional comments (10).

28. The Prerogative Court of Canterbury (where Shakspere's will was probated) did not routinely keep the final probate accounts in which this figure would have been recorded.

29. In addition to the collections of Essex wills transcribed by F. G. Emmison, other collections that are readily available are: *Wills and inventories from the Register of the Archdeaconry of Richmond*, edited by James Raine; *The Publications of the Surtees Society*, Vol. CXLII; and *Wills and Inventories from the Registers of the Commissary of Bury St. Edmunds and the Archdeaconry of Sudbury*, edited by

Samuel Tymms.

30. In fourteen geographical areas throughout England, Erickson shows that the percentages where the surviving spouse is the executrix varies from 63% to 96% depending on the jurisdiction. Only one entry is 46%, and this information was collected from 1372-1540, an earlier era (158).

31. Hodges writes that "the great majority of men left their surviving spouses either all their moveable property or the unbequeathed residue thereof."

Chapter 4

Let the Punishment Fit the Crime
Censorship in Early Modern England

Many laws were on the books in Tudor England to control the spoken and written word. These laws empowered the Elizabethan and later, the Jacobean authorities to censor writing that was critical of government officials and their policies. The eminent Annabel Patterson opened the door to academic discussion of the relationship of politics and art in early modern England – in *Censorship and Interpretation* – when she explored the strategic approaches used by writers to circumvent the restrictions on freedom of expression (44-75). In *Art Made Tongue-tied by Authority*, Janet Clare provides more details on the harsh enforcement measures used in the late sixteenth and early seventeenth centuries to punish writers who went too far with politically sensitive commentary in plays, books, or pamphlets. However, the subject of censorship as it relates directly to the Shakespeare canon receives only peripheral attention from academics, a disinclination that is understandable in light of the questions that it raises in the Shakespeare authorship discussion.

That the man from Stratford-upon-Avon went unnoticed by the Elizabethan government is a stark reality. Nowhere in the many biographies of William Shakspere is there anything to indicate that the authorities of state were aware of his existence as a writer. So far as the record shows, he was never interviewed by the Privy Council or any legal enforcement entity. If any scholars or members of the London literati met him, corresponded with him, or even visited him during his affluent retirement in Stratford-upon-Avon, there is no mention of it (Price 302-305). Nor is there anything to connect him in a personal way with a patron or an important government official, as Charlotte Stopes, the industrious Shakespearean researcher, noted regretfully in the preface of her 1922 biography of the Earl of Southampton (v).

Even if Shakespeare's plays had been apolitical, it is odd that the man from Stratford was not seen by the watchful eye of the government. After reviewing the punishments meted out to other writers in early modern England whose words were thought seditious, we will examine the politically dangerous material in the Shakespeare canon. If the author behind these works was in the habit of commenting on politics, then how did he escape the penalties imposed regularly on less reprehensible, less prolific, and considerably less talented Elizabethan writers?

This leads to a bigger question: how could anyone have written the Shakespeare plays and remained untouched by government authority?

Censorship in Early Modern England

In the last decades of the 16th century, the Revels Office and the Stationers Company controlled what the public could see and hear through the power of licensing. Exhibitions of the spoken word, i.e., theatrical performances, required the approval of the Master of the Revels. Books, pamphlets and other publications were licensed by the Stationers Company. Officials of the Revels Office and the Stationers Company were on the lookout for two kinds of subversive material: satire directed toward an important individual and subject matter critical of governmental policy. Both the written and spoken word could be used to promote dangerous political commentary; of the two, the written word was regarded as a more enduring weapon of propaganda. The authorities recalled parts of the second edition of Raphael Holinshed's 1587 *Chronicles*, as the historian had included a "reporte of matters of later yeeres that concern the State, and are not therefore meete to be published in such sorte as they are delivered" (Clare 38-39).

Books on historical subjects were scrutinized for contemporary political satire disguised in historical settings. An example was made of Sir John Hayward, a scholarly historian whose book, *The Life and Reign of King Henrie IIII*, met with a harsh reception when it was published in February 1599. Henry IV's usurpation of the throne of England was a touchy subject in the closing years of Elizabeth's reign, and the authorities were quick to spot a treasonable subtext in Hayward's book. Unwisely, Haywood dedicated the work to the Earl of Essex (Patterson 47-48).[1] Essex was thought to be positioning himself as the successor to the Tudor queen and the dedication further strengthened the analogy of the earl with the usurper Bolingbroke (Hazard 191). Although Hayward's book preceded the Essex Rebellion by two years, the offending inference brought him imprisonment in the Tower. At his trial, Attorney General Edward Coke didn't mince words in characterizing it as "a storie 200 yere olde . . . intending the application of it to this tyme" (Hammer 6). The furor over Hayward's book reveals how aggressively Elizabethan officials responded to writing that was thought to mask current events in a historical context. Moreover, in the aftermath, the Archbishop of Canterbury stipulated that all histories be approved by the Privy Council, a startling measure which gave the elite in the Queen's government direct authority over the writers of the era in matters pertaining to England's history (Clare 83).

Though treasonous intent could be embedded in the written word, the theater was considered a more immediate danger, as seditious dialogue could rouse an audience. A play that incited riot or, worse still, open rebellion could pose a direct threat to the peace of the realm. The risk increased as the population of London surged during Elizabeth's reign. As early as 1573, William Cecil, Lord Burghley, tightened the government's grip on "playmakers and plaiers" with a document designed to increase the authority of the Revels Office. Another document prepared for Lord Burghley in 1581 implemented even closer state surveillance of the theaters and reinforced the penalty of imprisonment for those who violated government restrictions.[2] By the early 1580s, the Queen's Privy Council was regularly issuing orders to Justices of the Peace, the Lord Mayor of London, and other authorities to permit only those plays which yielded "honest recreation and no example of evil" (Clare 30-31).

These increasingly severe measures were underpinned by legislation passed by Parliament in 1581. An "Act against seditious words and rumours," recorded as 23 ELIZ CAP II, became known as the "Statute of Silence" (Patterson 25-26). The statute came in the wake of the punishment of John Stubbes, who wrote a pamphlet, *The Gaping Gulf*, in which he disapproved of Lord Burghley's policy supporting the Queen's proposed marriage to the French Duc d'Anjou. Stubbes was charged with disseminating seditious writings and found guilty. As punishment, his right hand was cut off with a butcher's knife and the wound seared with a hot iron. His publisher suffered the same fate. Stubbes was imprisoned for eighteen months; the publisher died of his wounds (*DNB* 19:118-119). If the "unhanding" of Stubbes was meant as an object lesson to stifle public criticism of government policy, it succeeded. The subsequent Statute of Silence clarified just what kinds of writing would constitute a libelous crime and specified even harsher penalties for disobedience.

The Playwrights

Christopher Marlowe was a successful playwright whose work brought him unwelcome attention. In May of 1593, he was summoned to London by the Privy Council. Charges had been brought against him by one Richard Baines (Nicholl, *Reckoning* 46, 352). In correspondence with Lord Burghley, Baines wrote that Marlowe "persuades men to Atheism . . . scorning both God and his ministers" (Riggs, *Marlowe* 329-336). In spite of the fact that Baines was an insidious informer in the Elizabethan secret service, these charges were serious enough to be punishable by death.

In building the case against Marlowe, on May 6, 1593, government officials arrested his roommate Thomas Kyd (Riggs, *Marlowe* 319-320).[3] Kyd's lodgings were searched and his papers confiscated by order of the Royal Commissioners.[4] He was incarcerated in Bridewell Prison, interrogated on May 11, and, in his own words, withstood "pains and undeserved tortures (Miles 27)."[5] Bridewell was known for a method of torture called "the scavenger's daughter." This mechanism consisted of an iron ring, tightened by turning a screw to bring the head, feet and hands together until they formed a circle. With this incentive, Kyd wrote two letters to Thomas Puckering, the Lord Keeper of the Privy Seal, in which he confirmed that Marlowe had committed religious heresies.[6]

These letters are still extant, but scholars, quite sensibly, discount their credibility since Kyd composed them under the duress of "being crushed alive at Bridewell" (Riggs, *Marlowe* 320-322). It is thought, not unreasonably, that this treatment hastened his death a year later. Historian Rosalind Miles summarizes this unfortunate situation: "Ignorance, innocence even, was no defense for a suspected playwright against the might of a suspicious state" (27).

Although Marlowe's associates accused him of heretical religious views, his works are ambivalent toward religion, suggesting that it was the sheer popularity of his plays that brought him to the attention of the Royal Commissioners and the Privy Council. His plays: *Tamburlaine*, *The Jew of Malta*, and *The Massacre at Paris* had played to packed houses (Riggs, *Marlowe* 319). By the spring of 1593, *Doctor Faustus* may have been underway (Clare 50), and the material dealing with the unorthodox Catholic philosopher Giordano Bruno could have been a factor contributing to Marlowe's downfall (Riggs, *Marlowe* 248-249). Bruno became known in England when he lectured at Oxford University in the 1580s. He later spent some time in France, where Sir Francis Walsingham used him as an "intelligencer" (a spy) within the French embassy (Nicholl, *Reckoning* 202-210). The details are beyond the scope of this paper, but it is clear that the Bruno material in Marlowe's play had, according to Clare's *Art Made Tongue-Tied by Authority*, "disquieting implications for the Elizabethan government" (49). That the Bruno scene was problematic can be inferred from the delay of twenty-three years before the scene was published in the 1616 edition of Marlowe's *Doctor Faustus*.[7]

Although it remains unclear exactly what alerted the authorities to Marlowe's writing, once activated, they moved swiftly. On May 18, 1593, the Privy Council issued a warrant for his apprehension. Henry Maunder was sent "to repair to the house of Mr. Thomas Walsingham in Kent" to bring Marlowe to London. Marlowe was questioned by the Council on May 20 and released on bail with the command "to give his daily attendance on their Lordships" –

which meant that he had to report every day to Greenwich Palace where the Council resided. Marlowe was on a short leash (Riggs, *Marlowe* 333; Nicholl, *Reckoning* 46-47). It is instructive to note that it took only two days for the Privy Councilors to locate Marlowe and reel him in for questioning. By May 30, only ten days later, he was dead.

Thomas Nashe was another writer making a name for himself in the 1590s, by which time he had established a reputation for catching "the intellectual pulse" of the urbane London intelligentsia (*ODNB* 5:40, 240). He was arrested and imprisoned in 1593 for his apocalyptic religious lament *Christs Tears Over Jerusalem*, and was released through the good offices of his new-found patron, Sir George Carey, to whose wife the work was prudently dedicated (*ODNB* 5:241). In the summer of 1597, Nashe collaborated with Ben Jonson on a play, *The Isle of Dogs*. It was performed at the Swan Theater. Records of the Privy Council and other literary sources reveal the fierce response it elicited from the authorities (Clare 72). It is reported that Queen Elizabeth was greatly angered, and the matter was handled by the highest officials in her court (Miles 31-32).[8] In an order of July 28, 1597, the Privy Council closed down all the London playhouses. Jonson and several actors were imprisoned immediately (Miles 32). Most tellingly, the investigation was turned over to none other than the Queen's notorious torturer, Richard Topcliffe (Clare 72-76). Topcliffe was further empowered by the Council to "peruse such papers as were found in Nashe's lodging" and to discover how many copies of the play had been distributed and to whom (Nicholl, *Nashe* 244). As no copies of *The Isle of Dogs* survive, it is reasonable to assume that Topcliffe did his job thoroughly (Hibbard 235).

Known as a "monster of iniquity," Topcliffe tortured confessions from the Jesuit missionaries in England during the last decades of Elizabeth's reign (*DNB* 19:979-980). He had a rack and other demonic machines of his own invention in his home, and was given the authority to bring prisoners there for questioning. He reported directly to the Queen (Nicholl, *Reckoning* 110-112).

Henslowe wrote in his Diary that he "paid this 23 of August 1597 to Harey Porter, to care to T Nashe now at this in the Fleet, for writing the Isle of Dogs ten shillings, to be paid again to me when he can." Twentieth-century historians have come to question the authenticity of this entry (Freeman 206, 415),[9] though a woodcut published in 1597 shows Nashe in leg irons. It is accepted today that somehow Nashe made a getaway to the country (*DNB* 14:107-109),[10] perhaps having recovered from the ministrations of Topcliffe. It is unknown when, where, and how Nashe died (Miles 65; Nicholl, *Nashe* 269). The earliest reference to Nashe as deceased was in 1601.

Nevertheless, according to the official story, Nashe supposedly wrote *Lenten Stuffe* the next spring when he was on the lam, and it was entered in the Stationers Register in early 1599 (Hibbard 236-237).[11] Again, the hammer came down swiftly. Soon after, the Archbishop Canterbury and the Bishop of London ordered that all of Nashe's writings be collected and destroyed (Arber 677-678). Nashe had suffered quite a fall from the days when his play, *Summers Last Will and Testament*, was performed at the Archbishop's summer lodgings at Croydon (Hibbard 88-89).[12]

That all NASSHES bookes and Doctor HARVYES bookes be taken wheresoeuer they maye be found and that none of theire bookes bee ouer printed hereafter /

That thoughe any booke of the nature of theise heretofore expressed shalbe broughte vnto yow vnder the hands of the Lord Archebisshop of CANTERBURYE or the Lord Bishop of LONDON yet the said booke shall not bee printed vntill the master or wardens haue acquainted the said Lord Archbishop, or the Lord Bishop with the same to knowe whether it be theire hand or no /

Jo[HN WHITGIFT] CANTUAR
Ric[HARD BANCROFT] LONDON

Suche bookes as can be found or are allready taken of the Argumentes aforesaid or any of the bookes aboue expressed lett them bee presentlye [*i. e. immediately*] broughte to the Bishop of LONDON to be burnte

Jo[HN] CANTUAR
Ric[HARD] LONDON

Sic examinatur /

III. 677

Nashe was not the only writer whose work was consigned to the
"All Nasshes bookes and Doctor Harveyes bookes . . ."
Excerpt from the Bishops' Ban.
[June 1599] [41 Reginae Elizabethae]

flames. Included in the Archbishop's instruction "to be burnt" were works of John Marston, Thomas Middleton, Gabriel Harvey, Sir John Davis, and several writers who were less well known (Arber 677).

In 1599, John Marston was new on the London scene, having made his debut the year before with a satirical book, *Pigmalion*. This, and his subsequent *Scourge of Villanye* were at the top of the list of books set for destruction by the Bishops' Ban 1599. With his total literary output condemned, Marston might have taken the hint that he did not have much of a future in the London literary world. But in case he needed further prompting, two years later he was satirized by Ben Jonson (along with Thomas Dekker) in Jonson's play *The Poetaster*. Jonson was in trouble as well for *Poetaster* (Patterson 49). Brought up on charges before Lord Chief Justice Popham, Jonson "lawyered up" – a novel approach for that day and age. His attorney, Richard Martin, defended him successfully, and Martin's advocacy is credited with saving the play, although it was highly censored upon its publication the following year (Riggs, *Jonson: Life* 80, 87; Clare 107-111).

The bone of contention between Marston and Jonson is unclear, but several years later, their enmity forgotten, they collaborated (along with George Chapman) on another dangerous undertaking. That play, *Eastward Ho*, was performed in 1605 and reportedly mocked the new King and his courtiers. Jonson and Chapman were imprisoned (Clare 119-172).[13] According to the *Dictionary of National Biography*, Marston was incarcerated as well, though recent historians are uncertain on this point (*DNB* 12:1142; Miles 96).

The offense provoked a serious response. It appears from Jonson's letters that the playwrights were to have their ears and noses cut (Clare 141,169). Pleading for clemency, Jonson wrote frantically to highly placed individuals including the Earls of Salisbury, Suffolk, Pembroke, Montgomery, the Countess of Bedford, his patron Esme Stuart Lord D'Aubigny, and the King himself (Salgado 180).[14] Even though Jonson was still at a fairly early point in his career, he had established a remarkable network of acquaintances he could call on directly. Apparently this lobbying effort secured his release with his ears and nose intact.

Reliable information about Marston and his literary career is difficult to come by. Much of his work was published anonymously, and some with only his initials I. M. In *Scourge of Villainy*, he adopted an odd pseudonym, "W. Kinsayder," and he dedicated *Scourge* to "Oblivioni Sacrum." Translated as "everlasting oblivion," this motto must have been meaningful to him as it appeared on his funeral monument decades later (*DNB* 12:1141-1142).

In 1608, three years after the *Eastward Ho* debacle, Marston was imprisoned with George Chapman. Marston continued to operate in the shadows and his later offense is unclear, but after his release from prison, he was put out to pasture. He took holy orders and was given the living of Christchurch in Hampshire, a post he held until shortly before his death in 1633. Still, he may not have disappeared entirely from the literary scene, as he is suspected of writing anonymous satires from time to time. It is thought he was responsible for criticism of the Duke of Buckingham shortly before the Duke's assassination in 1628 (*DNB* 12:1143).

The Earl of Essex continued to be a sore subject long after the Earl and his eponymous rebellion had come and gone in 1601. In 1605, Samuel Daniel brought the wrath of the Privy Council down on his head when he published a milquetoast play *Philotas (DNB* 5:477-478).[15] The Council was disturbed by what they thought were sympathetic allusions to the now quite late Earl of Essex (Clare 148, 169-170).[16] Daniel has been described as "a workman-like man of letters" who "edged his way from one noble family to another in precarious feats of survival" (Parry 209). By this time, he had worked his way up to a cushy court job as the director of the Children of the Queen's Revels. But the allegations against him could end his upward mobility, and when he turned to his patron, the Earl of Devonshire, for a word in his defense, the Earl sought to distance himself from Daniel. This incident reveals how hypersensitive the government elite could be to the slightest hint of sedition. It is odd, too, that a small misstep nearly ruined the career of the politically savvy Samuel Daniel. Janet Clare brushes off the situation with the mild assessment that "its scholarly use of classical material failed to deflect interest in its topicality as political drama" (148). More to the point, the damage done by the Earl of Essex had a strangely long shelf life.

Ben Jonson was one of the best-known playwrights of the English Renaissance. Characterized as the dictator of the London literati, his turbulent career spanned almost four decades. He was imprisoned four times (though two were in connection with murder and do not concern us here (*DNB* 10:1070-1071; Riggs *Jonson: Life* 32-35, 80, 105-106, 122-126). Three of his encounters with the law have been previously discussed: his imprisonment over the *Isle of Dogs*, his appearance before Chief Justice Popham over *The Poetaster*, and his incarceration with Chapman (and possibly Marston) as a result of *Eastward Ho*. Though other troubles were in his future, one more incident is especially noteworthy. This time he was called to report to the Privy Council on a charge of treason. The penalty for treason was death, so it is safe to say Jonson found himself, once more, in a rather serious situation.

Sometime in 1603, *Sejanus* was performed at the Globe by the King's Men. This play was suspected of depicting parallels between the careers of the historical Sejanus and the recently executed Earl of Essex, another instance of ancient history being used to disguise contemporaneous satire (Patterson 50; Clare 134).[17] Jonson responded to the charges brought before the Privy Council by marshaling the support of his influential friends, and turned to his patron Esme Stuart, Lord D'Aubigny (Riggs, *Jonson: Life* 369). Although the details are not known, it appears that D'Aubigny used his status as a favorite with King James to get Jonson off the hook from the treason charge (Clare 133). When the play was published two years later, Jonson smartly added what has been called an "ideological gloss," i.e., elaborate annotations to give the play more historical context and lessen its contemporary relevance (Patterson 49-50).[18] Remarkably, the disingenuous Jonson asserts his innocence of historical parallelism, even as he puts forth his "less-than-innocent critique of contemporary English authorities" (Donaldson 187-189, 437). But the literary gambit worked, and Jonson's ostensible exposition on the heinousness of tyranny, for some reason, satisfied the authorities. Jonson makes it clear, however, that the printed quarto is "not the same as that which was acted on the public Stage."

The *Sejanus* affair has an additional significance: this is the second time that Jonson's path supposedly crosses Shakespeare's (Riggs, *Jonson: Life* 105). Orthodox scholars often note that Shakespeare acted in two of Jonson's plays, *Every Man in His Humor* and *Sejanus*, performed in 1598 and 1603 respectively. Jonson biographer Ian Donaldson goes so far as to suggest that "[w]ith Shakespeare possibly playing the part of the emperor Tiberius, this [*Sejanus*] would have been the hottest ticket in town" (186).[19] It is seldom noted that these two references to Shakespeare as an actor are found in Jonson's *Works*, published in 1616. Doing the math, this is a delay of eighteen years for *Everyman* and thirteen years for *Sejanus*. Coming so long after the fact, Jonson's reference to Shakespeare suggests that the clever Jonson has done some bootstrapping. That inference is supported by a legal test known as *res gestae*. *Res gestae* means that for evidence to be reliable, it must be "so spontaneous and contemporaneous with the circumstances as to exclude the idea of deliberation or fabrication" (Miller 376). In other words, evidence cannot appear to be contrived.

In his biography of Ben Jonson, David Riggs discusses how Jonson used his 1616 folio as an opportunity to reinvent himself:

> Jonson was not content merely to revise his early quartos: by dating the folio texts from the time of their original performances, he also fostered the illusion that he had not revised them . . . Jonson's pretense of total accuracy is exceedingly disingenuous. (225)

Riggs gives examples of statements that are misleading, and notes that Jonson "also expunged various clues about his own changing circumstances" (225). Riggs' suggestions lead to something beyond mere embellishment. While Jonson was reinventing himself, might he have taken the opportunity to invent a paper trail for someone else?

The lack of real-time references to Shakespeare as an actor in *Sejanus* are all the more bizarre in the historical context when, as noted, the play kicked up some trouble when it was originally performed in 1603. Bearing in mind that Jonson was called before the Privy Council on charges of treason, does it not seem a bit odd that no one thought to have a word or two with Shakespeare? (Chambers, *Stage* 4: 168).[20] In his book *Contested Will*, James Shapiro labors to tell the readers that Shakespeare was a phenomenal observer (275). If Jonson's belated reference in 1616 can be trusted, then Shakespeare was right there on the scene in 1603. If so, here was the perfect witness to report to the Privy Council on Jonson's theatrical intent. After all, by 1603 (if the Stratford man was truly the author of the Shakespeare works), he was a well-established playwright with a long list of masterpieces under his belt. Both his narrative poems, *Venus and Adonis* (1593) and *Lucrece* (1594), had been republished several times, indicating broad public awareness of Shakespeare's poetry. Is it not strange that the Privy Council let this golden opportunity for a firsthand account of *Sejanus* from an individual so articulate (not to mention one with such great powers of observation) slip through their fingers?

The Shakespeare Canon and Censorship

Falstaff – Oldcastle

In a controversy affecting Shakespeare directly, it seems the dissipated character Sir John Falstaff in *1 Henry IV, 2 Henry IV,* and *Henry V* was initially named Sir John Oldcastle (*Riverside* 930, 972). A commentator later wrote that the Cobham family was offended by the "buffone" in *Henry V* using the name "Oldcastle" (Clare 97). The historical Sir John Oldcastle held the title of Lord Cobham, and the Brooke family, who had the Cobham title during Elizabeth's reign, apparently regarded Shakespeare's use of this name for a crass, debauched character as a denigration of their family dignity. In the words of Janet Clare, "we can only surmise whether he [Shakespeare] set out deliberately to travesty the House of Cobham" (98). It gets worse. What escapes Clare's notice is that Lord Cobham's daughter, Elizabeth Brooke, was the wife of Robert Cecil; therefore, the House of Cecil might have taken notice of the slight as well (Handover 67-69). That any writer of the era could get off scot-free with a travesty of these two families – and could keep the offending name going through three plays before it was imperfectly removed from the published versions – should raise questions about the author's identity.

Polonius – Lord Burghley

First broached in 1869 by George Russell French, it became accepted in the twentieth century that the character Polonius in *Hamlet* is modeled on William Cecil, Lord Burghley. Orthodox Shakespearean biographers shriek with dismay, but the identification has been recognized by established historians including Lawrence Stone, Joel Hurstfield, and Alan Gordon Smith. In an innocuous comment, a historian refers to Lord Burghley as "the canny Polonius," an indication that the theatrical representation is well accepted (James 387).

   Pushing back as best he can on behalf of Stratfordians, James Shapiro has grasped that the stakes are high, purporting that those who concur with the Polonius-Burghley connection "betray a shallow grasp of Elizabethan dramatic censorship" (177).[21] How ironic a position for an academic to take, especially in light of the stature of the historians who accept the identification. But more to the point, the identification is ironclad. The character was named Corambis in the first quarto, an unflattering take on Lord Burghley's motto, *Cor unum, via una* (One heart, one way). Polonius's precepts to his son Laertes resonate with Burghley's "Precepts to a Son," published after the Stratford man's death.[22] Knowledge of the unpublished "Precepts" and other parallels between the character Polonius and Lord Burghley indicate that the author of *Hamlet* had inside information about the Cecil family, as well as a lot of nerve.

Robert Cecil – Little Crookback

And what of the canny Cecil's hunchback son, Sir Robert Cecil? The younger Cecil's gift for strong-armed tactics was first apparent in 1592 in his recovery of pilfered goods from the Spanish ship the *Madre de Dios*. As he reported to the Queen, "I must be offensive to the multitude and to others that may be revengeful..." Unsurprisingly, the younger Cecil soon earned the moniker "*Robertus diabolus.*" Biographer P. M. Handover accepts that "to attain his ends he has ignored the moral distinction between good and evil." Cecil himself commented that "By my rough dealing I have left an impression" (1, 85-88).

The outpouring of pent-up revulsion that followed Robert Cecil's death in 1612 reveals the extent to which he was hated (Dickinson 76; Handover 145).[23] According to G. P. V. Akrigg in *Jacobean Pageant*, "Men who had been afraid of him and his spies while he lived now spoke freely" (109). Cecil's distinguished cousin Francis Bacon published an essay, titled "On Deformity," that was widely thought to be modeled on him. Of this essay, the busy correspondent John Chamberlain wrote that "the world takes notice that he [Bacon] paints out his little cousin [Cecil] to the life" (du Maurier 61). Among the more unkind epitaphs is an anonymous verse comparing Cecil to Richard III: "Here lies little Crookback/ Who justly was reckon'd/ Richard III and Judas the second" (Akrigg 110).[24] It would be far too bold for historian Akrigg to associate the hunchbacked Cecil with the despised Plantagenet king in the popular play, yet this libel demonstrably shows that someone connected the dots.

Tellingly, the occupant of the mansion home in Stratford-up-on-Avon was never asked by the authorities to explain if the character Richard III was a thinly veiled dramatic representation of the eminent Tudor official with whom he shared conspicuous physical attributes (Clare 42).

Richard II and the Essex Rebellion

The most puzzling failure of Elizabethan censorship was Shakespeare's *Richard II*. It is known that this play was publicly performed the day before the Essex Rebellion.[25] It is also known that this play had already acquired a clear association with the Earl of Essex. In a letter from 1597, dealing with Essex's military campaign to the Azores four years earlier, Walter Raleigh wrote that "the conceit of *Richard II* hath made the Earl of Essex wonderful merry" (Handover 155, 162). Two years later, John Hayward's dedication of *The Life and Reign of King Henrie IIII* to Essex reinforced the comparison between the Earl and Bolingbroke (Lacey 218, 300; Donaldson 187-188). One wonders how Essex kept his head on his shoulders as long as he did. But whatever his eccentricities, when his literary interests are taken into consideration, it does seem odd that Essex never extended an invitation to the author of the play he so admired to join with his clientele of scholars, statesmen and soldiers who gathered around him for many years at Essex House (Dickinson 100-102).[26]

Moreover, on the fateful weekend of February 7, 1601, the performance of *Richard II* at the Globe Theater was intended to embolden the followers of Essex and Southampton and rouse the populace in support of their uprising – exactly what the Queen and her royal administration feared the most from the public theater. Historians are uncertain whether this was the first time the deposition scene was played on the public stage; the three quartos published prior to the rebellion do not contain it (*Riverside* 837-838).[27] Yet it seems that this scene had to have been a focal point in the performance, as the play is referred to in the legal aftermath as "the killing of Richard II" (Chambers 2:322-327).[28]

Essex and his leading adherents were quickly apprehended, tried and convicted, but the actors themselves were handled gently. Ten days elapsed before one actor from the Lord Chamberlain's Men, Augustine Phillips, was tapped for questioning by the Privy Council, and he was not even placed under arrest. In his deposition, he stated that *Richard II* was an old play and nobody would come to see it (Chambers 2:323). The actors, he said, were paid an additional forty shillings for their efforts, ostensibly to compensate them for the loss at the box office (Handover 192-194, 222, 229). For whatever reason, the actors were readily forgiven and, strangely enough, the company was performing for Elizabeth's court just days later on February 24, the day before the Earl of Essex's execution.

As noted, the theaters were kept under government surveillance for the very reason that they could be cauldrons for public disturbance, leading to riot and rebellion. It has also been noted that historical subjects were considered especially dangerous. The Essex Rebellion was the most serious threat to Elizabeth's reign since the Spanish Armada in 1588 and the most dangerous civil uprising in thirty years. Worse still, discussion of the royal succession was expressly forbidden. Yet *Richard II* deals with not one, but three, explosive subjects: the deposition of a reigning monarch, the succession of the next, and the Royal prerogative (Gohn).

Shakespeare and Richard II

It is instructive to review how many Shakespearean elements coalesce in this performance of *Richard II*:

- Shakespeare's play is used for sedition and inciting rebellion (Dean 55).

- It is performed by Shakespeare's company, the Lord Chamberlain's Men.

- The performance takes place in Shakespeare's theater, the Globe.

- Shakespeare's patron, the Earl of Southampton, is a principal leader in the uprising (Handover 224).[29]

In his introduction to the *Riverside Shakespeare*, G. Blakemore Evans writes of the eminence of Shakespeare in his company, a position undisputed by the orthodox (28). However, if that is true, it is all the more odd that the authorities chose to question Augustine Phillips rather than Shakespeare, the individual whose associations with the play, the company, the venue and the leader of the rebellion should have been readily apparent, again assuming that the traditional attribution of authorship is true.

It seems that only the author of the Shakespeare works could insult important families, write about the deposition of a monarch, have his work performed as part of a treasonous enterprise, and still remain unseen (Akrigg, *Southampton* 248-253).[30] Shakespeare was free of governmental oversight when transgressions far less serious brought consequences to other writers of the time, ending their writing careers if not their lives. But as far as the record shows, Shakespeare never had to explain himself. He inhabited a very special place in the Elizabethan world. He was exempt from retribution – and untouchable.

Notes

1. Hayward's biography was published at a time when the Earl of Essex was challenging the Queen's authority, and the dedication to the Earl sent a provocative signal to the readers that there was a contemporary subtext in his history book.

2. Clare, 32-33. The document is printed in Albert Feuillerat's *Documents Relating to the Office of the Revels in the Time of Queen Elizabeth* (Louvain, 1908), 51-52.

3. Riggs notes the attentiveness of Queen Elizabeth to the libels posted at the Dutch churchyard on May 5, 1593. Though there is nothing to indicate that Marlowe was involved with these libels, references were made to several of his plays. The Queen expressed her "vexation" with this matter to the Royal Commissioners on May 11, 1593, and seven days later, Marlowe was ordered to report to the Privy Council.

4. The Royal Commission (also known as the High Commission) was a multifaceted apparatus used directly by the Queen and her Privy Council. It could be used to enforce royal statues as well as a means to investigate and respond to matters that might endanger the Queen's safety. It could also operate as a court in which ecclesiastical disputes were resolved. For additional information, see Arthur J. Klein, *Intolerance in the Reign of Elizabeth the Queen* (1917; rpt. NY: Kennikat Press, Inc., 1968), 71-75.

5. Miles cites Fredson Thayer Bowers's article published in *Studies in Philology*, xxxiv (1937) for Kyd's account of the torture.

6. Documents of the charges against Kyd are preserved among Thomas Baker's manuscripts (MS Harl. 7042, f. 401). *DNB* 11, 351-352; Riggs, *World*, 329.

7. Clare, Patterson, Nicholl and Riggs do not speculate if the Bruno scene was included in this 1594 production. It is possible that

it was for two reasons. First, it contained a strong anti-Catholic message which should have been popular with audiences at the time; and second, Bruno's connection to the Pembroke faction (as verified by Bruno's dedication of his 1584 *Spaccio de la bestia trionfante* to Sir Philip Sidney) indicates that he had powerful patronage (Patterson 109).

8. Those present to consider the matter included the Lord Treasurer, the Lord Chamberlain, the Chancellor of the Exchequer, the Comptroller of the Household, and Sir Robert Cecil, who at this time was the Queen's Principal Secretary.

9. It has been suggested that the entry in Henslowe's Diary concerning Nashe's incarceration in the Fleet prison is a John Payne Collier forgery. But the Freemans do not make the reasons for this clear in their two-volume study of Collier's forgeries.

10. According to the *DNB*, Nashe was "banished" from London after his release from Fleet Prison. The engraving of Nashe in irons in the Fleet Prison appeared in Richard Lichfield's 1597 pamphlet *Trimming*, and was republished in Harvey's *Works* edited by Grosart, iii. 43.

11. See Hibbard for a discussion of *Lenten Stuff* with the "red herring" in the title and a text disclosing to the reader that there is "one red herring after another." The notice of false scents indicates that there is misdirection in *Lenten Stuff*.

12. Hibbard concurs with E.K. Chambers and R.B. McKerrow that the play was performed at the Archbishop's summer residence of Croydon.

13. In her chapter on "Drama and the new regime," Clare observes that "literary censorship often arose from the King's personal disapproval of particular books...." The astute contemporaneous commentator Sir Robert Wilbraham wrote that "The Queene [was] slow to resolution, and seldom to be retracted: his majestie quick in concluding indecorous and

libelous in their satire; but when the critique touched on issues which he cherished, such as the projected union between England and Scotland, he was irascible and quick to act" (121). Robert Ashston, *James I By His Contemporaries* (London: 1969), 6,7.

14. Of particular interest is the letter written by Jonson to Robert Cecil. From this letter it appears that writing a satirical play was a serious offence.

15. According to the *DNB*, the "play excited groundless suspicions at court." Daniel's sympathetic treatment of the historical Philotas—who suffered for a treasonable conspiracy against Alexander the Great—suggests a parallel with the Earl of Essex, raising the suspicion at the time that Daniel might be making an effort to rehabilitate the fallen Earl.

16. Additional details of the problems generated by Philotas can be found in Lawrence Michel's edition of the play, and in Stirling Brents's article "Philotas and the Essex case" in *Modern Language Quarterly 3* (1942).

17. Jonson's source was the Roman historian Tacitus. Tacitus was a favorite of Essex and his circle, pointing to a connection between the murderous Sejanus and the Essex conspiracy. It even seemed to suggest that the recently deceased Queen Elizabeth was a Tiberius, something that should not have terribly distressed her successor King James. Nevertheless, Jonson was hitting a nerve; treason was not a trivial matter.

18. Patterson furnishes a concise overview of Jonson's "sociopolitical difficulties," and notes that Jonson "incorporated them into a political and social theory of literature" which he develops in his later epigrams.

19. It is disheartening to see a scholar of Donaldson's stature join the undiscerning who accept the belated 1616 list. Moreover, there is not a scrap of evidence to suggest any part that "Shakespeare" might have played in any play.

20. According to E.K. Chambers in *The Elizabethan Stage*, the Kings Men performed at court December 26-30, 1603. Though there is no record of what was performed, Chambers reasonably concludes that one of the plays was *Sejanus*. If it is true that "Shakespeare" was indeed among the cast, it is strange that King James gave him no recognition (Riggs, *Life* 105, 367).

21. Shapiro amplifies his position with the argument that the Master of the Revels would have lost vital parts of his anatomy had he allowed a play to be published that caricatured the Queen's leading statesman. It is true: Lord Burghley would hardly have stood for it, nor would his son and political successor. In an account of Burghley, his biographer remarks "Throughout his life he was, for a veteran politician, exceptionally sensitive to personal attacks." Conyers Read, *Lord Burghley and Queen Elizabeth* (London: Jonathan Cape, 1965), 96.

22. Mark Alexander provides a comprehensive study of the parallels between the character Polonius and William Cecil, Lord Burghley. (www.sourcetext.com/sourcebook/essays/polonius/corambis.html)

23. Court circles did not necessarily wait until Cecil's death in 1612. In her recent explication of Essex and his clientele, Dickinson notes pejorative allusions to Robert Cecil's spinal curvature in correspondence between Francis Davison and his father. In these letters, written in 1596, Cecil is called a "pygmy" and "St. Gobbo," the latter a reference to the statue of the hunchback St. Gobbo in the Rialto in Venice.

24. The epitaph (whose author smartly chose to remain anonymous) is archived in the Folger Library, MS. 452.1.

25. In his 2008 article Paul Hammer responds to a proposal by Blair Worden that the play performed the day before the Essex Rebellion was an adaptation of John Hayward's book. Hammer cites facts to support the long-standing assessment that the performance was the Shakespearean *Richard II*.

26. Orthodox historian Janet Dickinson's work is supported by Martin Green in his book *Wriothesley's Roses: In Shakespeare's Sonnets, Poems and Plays* (Clevedon Books, 1993), pp. 129-136, 156-160, 323, 325, 350-351. Green has amassed a wealth of information about the literary men who were directly associated with the Earl of Essex. Green examines the possible connections through which "Shakespeare" may have had access to Essex House, and attempts to connect "Shakespeare" to the Essex clientele. In spite of Green's herculean effort, there is still no tangible evidence of "Shakespeare's" supposed presence in the Essex House Group.

27. In his introductory notes, Herschel Baker covers the well-trodden ground of the *Richard II* QI (1597) and Q2, Q3 (1598). The deposition scene was added in Q4 of 1608 but, according to Baker, it "strongly suggests a memorially contaminated text."

28. Sir Gelly Meyricke's deposition was taken on February 17, 1601 (two days before the Essex trial) and he stated that "the play was *King Harry the iv*, and *the kyllyng of Kyng Richard the second* played by the L. Chamberlen's players." Augustine Phillips's testimony was taken the next day, and he called it "the play of the deposyng and kyllying of Kyng Rychard the second."

29. In a shocking, candid letter written on February 10, 1601, Robert Cecil states that "by the time my letters shall come unto you, both he [Essex] and the Earl of Southampton, with some other of the principals, shall have lost their heads" (Camden Society, 66).

30. In his chapter on "Shakespeare and the Essex Rebellion," Akrigg admits that "Southampton's surviving letters make no mention of Shakespeare and contain no allusion to any Shakespearean play or character."

Chapter
5

Evermore in Subjection
Wardship in 16th Century England

When Henry Tudor ascended the throne of England as Henry VII in 1485, he found his royal coffers empty and set about to remedy this by asserting his right to feudal dues. Even as England was evolving past the feudalism of the Middle Ages and looking toward a more enlightened era, Henry was taking a hard look at the medieval customs from which revenues for his royal administration could be extracted. The newly-minted monarch wasted no time, and within the first year of his reign, his ministers were working to revive the moribund medieval system known as wardship (Hurstfield 7).[1]

It is difficult for modern society to fathom what feudal dues and the wardship system it fostered were all about. Feudalism was a form of social order based on land tenure. *Tenure* is a term for how land is owned; feudal tenures were built on the relationship between a property owner and his overlord. From the time of the Norman Conquest, if not before, it was understood that every man who held land owed service to someone of higher social standing. The *tenant* was at a lower rung of the ladder; the individual at the higher level was a *lord*. The king stood at the top of this hierarchy as the supreme landlord of the entire country (Bell 1-5).

In medieval centuries, most of the land of England that was not in royal possession was held by barons. They had initially been given their lands and titles by the monarch, often as a reward for military service. A baron was to continue to provide military service – called *knight service* – to the king in return for the title and property that the king bestowed on him. The king expected his barons to be at the ready to render knight service when he had a war to fight or needed to defend his kingdom from an enemy. At this time, the barons put on their armor, got on their horses, gathered together the men who lived and worked on their properties, and led their men into the fray to support king and country.

This scenario may have worked well enough with an able-bodied father in the household, but if a baron died while his heir was still a minor, then his child was not physically able to give the required knight service. When this happened, the king felt entitled to compensation that came in the form of income from the lands that the child would inherit. The revenue generated from wealthy estates could include rents from the cottages, sales of crops and livestock, wool from the sheep, wood from the forests, and control of any minerals on the land. But there was more. The king assumed the right to the custody of the child in order to supervise his upbringing and ensure that he would be a loyal tenant in adulthood. Furthermore, it was considered morally justifiable for the king to direct the child's eventual marriage so the property – which at an earlier time was regarded as crown property – would stay in friendly hands. Thus the king had, as a feudal right, the physical custody of the heir along with the income from the heir's property during his minority. Moreover, with the right to bestow the ward in marriage, the king controlled the ward's future – a future that could encompass the destiny of the ward's family. Indeed, the right of marriage came to be considered the greatest of all the evils that the ruling class visited upon the less fortunate of the monarch's subjects (Bell 125; Hurstfield 134).

Cold Blooded Profiteering

If a modern reader chances to pick up H. E. Bell's 1953 book on wardship or Joel Hurstfield's 1958 book *The Queen's Wards*, they would find it hard to believe that so outrageous a social system could have existed in a nation on the eve of a great humanistic renaissance. One might even be tempted to doubt the existence of the feudal wardship system, especially since most histories of early modern England treat the subject lightly if at all. But in spite of historical neglect, wardship was a reality in which the custody of children, the income from their lands and the right to direct their marriage were auctioned off to the highest bidder (Bell 119). Hurstfield has summarized wardship as "a squalid organ of profiteering from the misfortunes of the helpless" (Hurstfield 241). In 1549, the clergyman Hugh Latimer exclaimed against it. Sir Thomas Smith wrote that it was "unreasonable and unjust, and contrary to nature that a freeman and gentleman should be bought and sold like an horse [sic] or an ox."[2] Sir Nicholas Bacon wrote that wardship was "a thing hitherto preposterously proceeding," a peculiar statement coming from a man who was the attorney for the Court of Wards, and one who benefitted from its very existence. Yet proceed it did, gaining strength as the 16th century marched on – a phenomenon that Bell credits to the administrative proficiency of the Tudors (133-149).[3]

Henry VIII showed his Tudor aptitude for administration by setting up a court in 1540 to handle the workload engendered by the business of wardship. Called the Court of Wards and Liveries, it brought a legal and judicial underpinning to what had previously been a societal custom, giving it the trappings of social justice (Bell 13; Hurstfield 12). Using a Court to oversee the buying and selling of wards facilitated the Tudor objective to centralize authority in the Crown, shifting the balance of power from the old aristocracy to the monarchy (Stone, abr. ed. 97, 131-134). It also contributed to furthering a bureaucracy filled with new men who were loyal to the Tudors (Hurstfield 16-17). It was a brilliant innovation on the part of the Tudor monarch.

With the dissolution of the monasteries in the late 1530s, vast tracts of land were purchased by members of the king's elite court circle who were in a position to buy property, bringing an estimated £90,000 a year to the royal coffers (Hurstfield 11). Even so, the wily king had something more in mind than just immediate profits. Unbeknownst to the purchasers, the seized church lands that would enrich them came with a Faustian twist: to the monastic lands, Henry VIII attached the feudal tenure of knight service.

It mattered not a whit to Henry that the lands of the church had not the slightest connection to the feudal duties of knight service. But it would eventually matter a great deal to the buyers, for it meant that the children of those who had participated, often zealously, in the seizure and acquisition of monastic property would be subjected to the charges of wardship in the event of the father's death before the heir reached his majority. Since this happened in one of three well-to-do families, it was certain that subsequent generations of the king would continue to reap profits from subsequent generations of his courtiers' families (Stone 600).[4] Hurstfield notes that "There is almost an Old Testament concept of retribution in the way the descendants of Henry VIII inflicted suffering upon the descendants of those who had bought up the confiscated lands of the church" (11).

I Bury a Second Husband

Many a Tudor widow could identify with the opening lines in *All's Well that Ends Well* when the widowed Countess says, "In delivering my son from me, I bury a second husband." Historians Bell and Hurstfield recount the crippling blow to a family if the father died leaving a minor to inherit his estates. But what exactly were the problems with wardship? Who profited from it? Was social injustice inherent in the system?

Wardship was remarkable because it exploited the upper strata of society. It was based on feudalism, and feudalism was based on ownership of property; therefore, wardship affected the propertied classes, not the poor. Upon the death of a father with a minor heir, the Tudor administration sent out agents to determine if the property was held by the tenure of knight service. If the government official suspected that the land, or even a small part of it, had once been part of a royal land grant, he would call for an *inquisition post mortem*. This was a legal examination by which the Court of Wards assessed the kind of tenure and the value of the property that the heir stood to inherit. Significantly, even at this initial stage, the deck was stacked against the heir's family. If only an acre of land could be proven to have originated in knight service tenure, then all the property of the estate, down to the last blade of grass, was pulled into the undertow of wardship (Bell 50). After the verdict of feudal tenure was rendered by the *inquisition* – and this was usually a foregone conclusion – the machinery of the Court of Wards was set in motion. The estate valuations from the *inquisition* were sent to the Court as one of the estimates of value used to determine the all-important price that someone would pay for the wardship (Hurstfield 83-85).[5] From this point forward, the fate of the child and his property would be in the hands of the Master of the Court of Wards.

The power that the Master of the Court held over the landed families of England reached far and wide. Once it was known that a wardship was available, the Master would be besieged with pleas and petitions of suitors (as the prospective buyers were called) wanting to purchase the wardship. It was the Master's job to set the price that the suitor would pay and then select the fortunate individual with the winning offer. This sordid process was made all the more noxious by the fawning petitioners who swore their loyalty to the Master, often broadly hinting at gifts. In a less than ambiguously worded letter, a suitor wrote to Robert Cecil that "If the ward prove well, I would be glad to buy him at the full value of your Honour for one of my daughters" (Hurstfield 264).

Mothers and relatives who likely had the welfare of the child at heart were rarely successful and could get in the queue, beseeching the Master with a bid for the custody of their own child. Curiously, a wardship could be resold at a price higher than the original one set by the Master, and at this juncture mothers or relatives often succeeded in buying back their own children, though at a much higher price than was initially paid (Hurstfield 124). Hurstfield notes that "In essence, a considerable body of the landed classes of England was each year held to ransom" (192).

It became common practice for families to attempt to hide potential wardships from the watchful eye of the government (Bell 52). Landowners countered with efforts to conceal how they owned their property, hiring battalions of lawyers to devise bogus transactions to mask possible feudal tenures left over from earlier centuries (Hurstfield 5-7).[6] The discovery of concealed wardships developed into "one of the great outdoor sports of Elizabethan England" (Hurstfield 34),[7] as the prospect of discovering one gave rise to a multitude of government employees, professional informants, and even neighbors who could look to a monetary reward for revealing a wardship illegally concealed from the Queen (Bell, 50-53).

In the scramble for wardships, participants came from all walks of life from the grandest of the royal court down to the humblest servants in the monarch's stables. Officials of all stripes pursued wardships, including many who are well known to us: Attorney General Edward Coke, Lord Chief Justice John Popham, Sir Walter Raleigh, Sir Nicolas Bacon and his famous son Sir Francis, Lord Chancellor Thomas More, Sir John Fortesque of the Queen's Exchequer, and Dr. Bull of the Chapel Royal. The Earls of Leicester, Bedford, Rutland, Essex, and Cumberland were among the nobility who threw their hats into the ring (Hurstfield 66, 123-125, 274-275, 301, 347). According to Hurstfield, "No less a person than Lord Cobham, hearing of a man's death, wrote the same evening to Cecil for the wardship of the heir, adding that his haste was due to his fear of being forestalled" (62). The word *forestalled* meant that he knew there would be competition for the wardship and time was of the essence. Aristocratic ladies had wards as well. Lady Leighton, Lady Paget, Lady Derby and Lady Burgh are on lists of successful purchasers (Hurstfield 123-125). To explain why the redoubtable Bess of Hardwick had wards, biographer Mary Lovell writes that "These were much sought after, being a perfectly legitimate manner of earning extra money" (484).[8] Unsurprisingly, the richest suitors scooped up the richest wardships, while the heirs with more modest estates went to junior court officials, clerks, under-clerks, messengers and ushers (Bell 35; Hurstfield 222). One historian remarks, "Wardship was a good thing for everyone except the wards."[9]

Wardship was a major source of finance for the Elizabethan administration. But there was one caveat: for each pound that went into the Queen's royal coffers, an estimated twelve pounds went into private pockets (Hurstfield 344). The ever expanding bureaucracy mulcted official fees from hopeful suitors for an unimaginable litany of services. Sir Julius Caesar, an eminent lawyer and administrator of the time, kept records of the expenditures he incurred while purchasing for his wife the wardship of her two daughters from her prior marriage. He made payments to those he called "solicitors and friends," to auditors and attorneys, feodaries (financial agents of the Court of Wards), the Pettibag Office of Chancery, and the Scheduler of Lands. He was charged for privy seals and the engrossing of leases, and he hosted several dinners for the commissioners and the jury, paying the sheriff's bailiff's servant for making the arrangements. He concluded that his expenses came to £1,739 in addition to the £1,000 purchase price for the young ladies (Hurstfield 81-82). This would be well over two million US dollars today.

Oblivious to conflicts of interest, the chief officials of the Court of Wards sought wardships for themselves and benefitted from the lands of the wards as well as the fees that came with their offices (Bell 35). The big money was in the unofficial fees. The giving and taking of "gifts" was standard practice in Tudor government, and modern historians accept the rationale that the parsimonious Queen allowed this mischief because she did not adequately remunerate her court officials for the jobs they did. As Hurstfield explains, "The salaries of the Elizabethan administrators were small and notoriously out of line with their responsibilities, their importance and their standard of living," and the "unofficial fees bridged the gap" (211, 238, 346, 348). Bell states laconically that "the fees mentioned in the accounts are relatively small and in no way represent the real value of the positions" (34). This may clarify why the Queen overlooked the flood of riches that went into private hands rather than her Royal Exchequer.

Lord Burghley facilitated the practice by keeping initial valuations low enough to allow room for the pay-offs to Tudor officials throughout the administrative hierarchy (Hurstfield 276). Upon questioning what his office was worth, the last clerk of the Court of Wards replied "It might be worth some thousands of pounds to him who, after his death, would instantly go to heaven; twice as much to him who would go to purgatory; and nobody knows what to him who would adventure to go to hell" (Bell 35; Hurstfield 344).[10] It would not have been lost on Burghley that feudal wardship would continue to flourish – to the betterment of his own purse – as long as it was widely profitable.

The Extraction of Wealth

When Sir William Cecil became Master of the Court of Wards in 1561, wardship was well entrenched in Tudor society.

A View of the Court of Wards and Liveries. Original engraving from the Society of Antiquaries, London, 1747. From the original caption: *"The person who sits at the head of the table with his hat on, appears by his countenance to represent the Lord Burghley, who was Master of this court from the beginning of Queen Elizabeth's reign until his death in 1598. And the mace at his right hand is the symbol of his office in this court."* Though the court's officers included judges, a Surveyor, an Attorney of the court, a Receiver General, and various administrators, the allocation of wardships was entirely at the discretion of the Master. (Reproduced by permission of the National Portrait Gallery Picture Library).

Cecil would be elevated to Baron Burghley in 1571 by the Queen. He held the Mastership for thirty-seven years until his death in 1598. After a nine-month vacancy, the Queen appointed his son Robert Cecil to the office and Robert retained it until his death thirteen years later (Barnett 51).[11] Thus father and son presided over one of the most powerful and lucrative offices in England for half a century. Although the records that have survived are not complete, it is estimated that over three thousand young people were processed through the Court of Wards during the Masterships of the Cecils (Bell 34). Hurstfield notes that by the end of Elizabeth's reign, "Burghley and his officials had broken through the barriers of silence, concealment and fraud ... to uncover more than ninety wardships in a year" (262).

The prospects for fees, both official and unofficial, were further augmented by the fact that the lease of the lands of the heir was allocated by the Master in another, separate transaction (Hurstfield 84). If calculated at two transactions per ward – one for the custody of the ward and right to bestow him in marriage and the other for the leases of his lands – this looks like six thousand opportunities for money to be made during the fifty years the Cecils controlled this office.

Pauline Croft, an influential editor of a book on the early Cecils, recognizes that "the sheer scale of the Cecils' extraction of wealth must give pause" (xviii). As we might expect, Burghley covered his tracks well. Only two scraps survive to shed some light on how much money might have come his way. A note preserved at Hatfield reveals a quarrel between two perspective guardians over the wardship of a Mr. Cholmeley. The unknown writer says he had paid "my Lord" £350 (estimated equivalent of $350,000 today). Though unnamed, this lord can be none other than Burghley (Hurstfield 82-82, 266).

Another remarkable fragment has survived in the Public Record Office. Appearing at the bottom of the page of this document are the words "This note to be burnt." It is fortunate for posterity that this was not done, for eleven suitor/guardians are named with the payments they made to an unidentified person. As the account ends on August 4, 1598, the date of Lord Burghley's death, it is hard to deny that this individual was Burghley (Hurstfield 266-288;

Bell 31, 35). These payments totaled £3103 (over $3,000,000).[12] An examination of the records shows that the Queen received £906 for nine of these wards, so from these particular wardships, Burghley took in more than three times as much as the Queen (Hurstfield 268). These two documents reveal that Burghley received over £3,400 for thirteen wardships in the last three years of his life, nicely augmenting his official salary of £133 per annum (Stone 403). Hurstfield extrapolates that the ninety wardships handled each year toward the end of Elizabeth's reign could have brought Burghley £27,000 annually (approximately $27,000,000), but does not venture to speculate how much three thousand wardships processed over half a century might have brought the Cecils.

In addition to the unofficial fees that Burghley received directly, the Cecil fortune was increased by the profits to his family as a result of their proximity to him. Paper trails with direct evidence rarely survive, but there is one that tells of six people who claimed perquisites for transmitting a suitor's request to Lady Burghley, and she received £250 for interceding with her husband. Amusingly, for this very wardship, the Queen received £233, £16 less than Burghley's wife (Hurstfield 265-266). Lady Burghley is admired for her benefactions, and Pauline Croft acknowledges that the most likely source of the wealth that enabled Lady Burghley's generosity came from her position as an intermediary between the suitors and Burghley (300). Even her chamberlain accepted money to pass letters to her that, in turn, went on to her husband (291).[13] On another occasion, Burghley's son Thomas Cecil had the wardship of Edward, Lord Vaux, and he profited handsomely by selling it back to the boy's mother (Hurstfield 80, 249, 269). The resale market was hot, and wards could be sold more than once. Another wardship purchased by Burghley's elder son was that of Elizabeth Long, bought for £250 and immediately re-sold for £1,350, more than four times the price fixed by the Court of Wards. The young lady's wardship was sold again for £2,450 (Hurstfield 275).

It is not surprising that Lord Burghley allocated wardships, leases and opportunities for profits to his closet servants, but what is shocking is that he did this in lieu of paying them a salary. In his study of the Cecil servants, Richard Barnett reveals that the ordinary household servants were paid wages, but the gentlemen were not salaried. They were paid in gratuities (15-16). Barnett traces fifty-five wardships granted to thirty-three servants and provides details in an appendix to his book (17, 159-169).

Described by Hurstfield as an "astute and cynical trader in wards," Burghley's secretary Michael Hickes fielded requests from all over the social spectrum. The Earl of Huntington wrote to him, "I have been beholding to you for your travail and pains taken in soliciting my causes for me to my good Lord, for which I hold myself in your debt and will come out of it ere it be long" (68). Hickes died a rich man, and yet for all his labor in the Cecil household, there is no record that secretary Hickes ever received a shilling in wages from either Cecil, father or son. At his death, Hickes left instructions to his executors to use a wardship to increase his daughter's marriage portion (Barnett 85-87). Henry Maynard, another of Burghley's secretaries, was among the gentlemen who received no salary but "whose service placed him in the way of considerable reward." Somehow Maynard accumulated vast landed wealth, and like Hickes, the executors of his will had the profits of a wardship to use for the marriage portions of his daughters (Barnett, 100-103). Hickes and Maynard, among others, learned well from their years of service to the Cecils.

The accumulation of family fortunes and political clout were not the only matters to which wardship could be directed. Inherent in the system was the power to transform England from a Catholic country into a Protestant one. When wardship was visited upon landed Catholic families, the sons were sold to Protestant guardians and given Protestant upbringings. This process can be seen in the Wriothesley family. Henry Wriothesley, the second Earl of Southampton married the daughter of Anthony Browne, Viscount Montagu, uniting two staunchly Catholic families (Stone 342-343). The second Earl had his own Catholic chaplain to conduct mass in his private chapel, and even suffered imprisonment for his Catholic faith in 1571 and again in 1581 after anti-recusancy laws were passed.[14] When the second Earl died, his minor son Henry became Burghley's ward and was removed to Cecil's London house where he was subjected to daily Protestant services. Burghley later sent him to St. John's College, Cambridge, his alma mater and a center of the Protestant Reformation. Initially, the third Earl of

Southampton resisted his guardian's efforts to change his religion, but converted to the Church of England during the reign of King James (Akrigg 177-181).

In short, wardship served many purposes. In addition to its primary purpose of providing funds for the Tudor monarchy and rewards to its loyal servants, wardship was a useful way of converting prominent Catholic families to Anglicanism (Bell 124-125). As such, it had the capacity to influence the religious direction of the English nation (de Lisle 41).[15]

It was to the house of Sir William Cecil that the twelve-year-old Edward de Vere was moved upon the death of his father in 1562.

Notes

1. Hurstfield traces the revival of wardship initiated by Henry VII and continued in the reign of Henry VIII, and shows how royal power was used to exploit the landed classes (3-17).

2. Sir Thomas Smith, *De Republica Anglorum*, as quoted by Hurstfield in *The Queen's Wards* (110).

3. In his chapter "Agitation against the Court," Bell describes the political battles to end the wardship system during the reign of King James. Wardship was so deeply engrained that it lumbered along for several more decades before being eliminated by Parliamentary decree in 1646. A condition of the Restoration was that wardship would never be reinstated. See also Hurstfield (329).

4. Stone states that one in three peers was a minor when he inherited the title.

5. Lord Burghley used three estimates of value, and the *Inquisition* was often the lowest. A survey was made subsequently by the feodory (a financial officer), and a "particular" prepared by the suitor. Of the three, the Master placed the greatest reliance on the feodory's land valuations, though many additional variables (such as the age, health, social status and younger brothers as back-up heirs) were taken into consideration.

6. Bell documents payments to private informers "whose aid was enlisted by a species of bribery," and grants of wardships to informers on "easy terms" (50-51).

7. For more information on the practices of concealment and discovery, see Hurstfield's chapter 3 (33-57).

8. As Lovell tells it: "The law on wardship was greatly improved under Queen Elizabeth when in 1561 the Court of Wards came under the benign and efficient influence of William Cecil, who was to be its Master for thirty-seven years."

9. John W. Russell, Review of *The Queen's Wards* in *Shakespeare Authorship Society Review #3*.

10. Bell and Hurstfield quote from *The Way to be Rich, According to the Practice of the Great Audley*, 1662 (14).

11. Upon the death of Robert Cecil (Earl of Salisbury), the office stayed in the hands of the Cecil court faction, first going to Cecil's close friend and confident Sir George Carew and then to Sir Walter Cope, the Cecil stalwart who served both father and son.

12. Bell identifies the letter as the work of Edward Latimer, the clerk to Receiver-General Sir William Fleetwood, and posits that Fleetwood was responding to a request from the Earl of Essex for this information. Hurstfield agrees that the Earl was interested in gauging what his profits might be if he was successful in his bid to become the next Master after Burghley's death.

13. That gifts from suitors "for intervening in Burghley's favour" are a likely source of Lady Burghley's wealth is supported by a letter from a suiter that is archived in the Lansdowne. This letter, passed on by Lady Burghley, is endorsed by Lord Burghley himself.

14. The family chaplain was Alban Langdale, a Catholic priest known for his disputations with Protestant clergy.

15. Writing about 16th century Catholic families, de Lisle and Stanford tell of a Catholic heir removed from his family to be raised in the Protestant religion, and relate that this was "the fate of other Catholic heirs in this period of persecution."

Chapter
6

What's Past is Prologue
Consequences of the 17th Earl of Oxford's Wardship

In her article "The Fall of the House of Oxford," Nina Green examines the financial crisis of John de Vere, the sixteenth Earl of Oxford that resulted from the extortion of his lands by Edward Seymour, the First Duke of Somerset during the reign of Edward VI. She follows the money through the restoration of the sixteenth Earl's properties and, most importantly, through the nine years of the wardship of his son, Edward de Vere, in the London home of his guardian, Sir William Cecil, later Lord Burghley (Green 41-95). It is well known that de Vere married Cecil's daughter Anne upon reaching his majority and that this marriage was deeply troubled (Cecil 84-85).

Less well known is the information revealed in Green's remarkable research. Sifting through the documentary evidence, Green shows how Queen Elizabeth mismanaged de Vere's properties in order to benefit her favorite courtier, Sir Robert Dudley. After the death of de Vere's father, the Queen allowed Dudley to take de facto control of the core lands of the Oxford estates, a move which gave Dudley the underpinning in landed property that was necessary to make him the Earl of Leicester (Green 68-69). The Queen also allowed Cecil to abrogate the contract that the sixteenth Earl of Oxford had made for his son's marriage with the daughter of the Earl of Huntingdon, thus paving the way for de Vere's marriage into the Cecil family. Hurstfield observes that the ascendancy of the Cecils from the yeoman to the aristocratic class – a feat accomplished in a mere two generations – was largely derived from the marriage of Anne Cecil to the ancient de Vere family (252). In addition, Queen Elizabeth sued the young seventeenth Earl of Oxford for revenue from his mother's jointure, and later ignored clauses in the sixteenth Earl's will that provided for the payment of his son's livery when he came of age (Green 67-77).

While a ward in Cecil's London house, Edward de Vere (hereafter called Oxford) accrued large debts in the Court of Wards. It could be supposed that these wardship debts might have been forgiven as part of Oxford's marriage settlement with Master Cecil's daughter; but, in fact, he was charged with a rigid payback schedule during his marriage to Anne. This he could not maintain, and large fines were levied at each forfeiture. Documentation in the Lansdowne collection at the British Library shows that in 1591, three years after Anne Cecil's death, Lord Burghley claimed that his son-in-law and former ward owed the Court of Wards the staggering sum of £14,553 (approximately $14,000,000) of which £11,446 ($11,000,000) were fines (Green 77). From his study of the wardship records, Joel Hurstfield concludes that "some of his [Oxford's] lands were seized and held for payment" to satisfy the debts that "had long hung over him in the Court of Wards" (253). Although Hurstfield joins the historical consensus in laying the blame for these debts on Oxford himself, it seems that his financial downfall was predestined from the moment his father breathed his last.

One might feel for the plight of the youth who entered Cecil's magnificent London house in 1562. Even the brightest of twelve-year-olds would be no match for the wily, experienced Cecil, a man who at that time commanded the Privy Council and the Court of Wards – and would eventually command the Elizabethan Treasury as well. Because of wardship, Oxford accrued backbreaking debts and entered into a disastrous marriage. At the end, he lost everything: his property, his children, and his reputation – all the tangible and intangible things that make up the patrimony so highly valued by the aristocracy. Burghley himself wrote that "The greatest possession that any man can have is honor, good name, and good will of many and of the best sort" – sentiments that Shakespeare ascribes to Iago (Anderson 118). Furthermore, it's hard to see how the bitter frustrations expressed in the *Sonnets* fit the blissful, upwardly mobile life of the Stratford man. Specifically, Sonnet 66 is a litany of griefs, and Sonnet 29 opens with a grim assessment of the writer's disgrace:

> When in disgrace with Fortune and men's eyes
> I all alone beweep my outcast state,
> And trouble deaf heaven with my bootless cries,
> And look upon myself and curse my fate.

Motivation for the Shakespeare canon

Stratfordian authorities understand that their narrative fails to supply motivation for the creation of the literary works. The failure of the Stratford man's biography is twofold: first, the facts of his life do not match the works he supposedly created; second, there is inadequate motivation for the characters and action in the plays, a serious deficiency that is unexplained by the Stratford man's life's trajectory. In his famous essay on *Hamlet*, T.S. Eliot, pointed out that Hamlet's emotions are "in excess of the facts as they appear," and this observation led to his theory of the "objective correlative."[1] Like Eliot, many have sensed that something deeper is underlying the action, yet try as they might, the literary critics find nothing in the life story of the Stratford man to fill this motivational void.

Explanations are close at hand when looking at the biography of Edward de Vere, the 17th Earl of Oxford. The loss of his patrimony stoked a fury in Oxford that drove him to transform the magisterial education of his youth into a weapon of vengeance (Anderson 329-330). What resulted was a contest of wills between the Queen's brilliant, calculating minister and his brilliant literary son-in-law, a family feud made all the worse as it played out on the public stage. Polonius in *Hamlet* is modeled on William Cecil himself, an identification recognized by leading twentieth century historian Lawrence Stone (abridged ed. 265). Hurstfield calls Burghley's *Precepts* "the authentic voice of Polonius" (257). Richard III may well be modeled on Robert Cecil (Akrigg, *Jacobean Pageant* 109-112). In *Shakespeare by Another Name*, Mark Anderson finds plenty of surrogates for Anne Cecil, Oxford's innocent wife, who he falsely accused of infidelity (xxxii, xxxiii). She is Ophelia in *Hamlet*, Desdemona in *Othello*, Imogen in *Cymbeline*, Hermione in *The Winter's Tale*, and Hero in *Much Ado* (47-48, 51, 125, 144, 146-147, 219-221, 342). In *Merry Wives of Windsor*, Anne Cecil is thinly veiled as Anne Page and her father is William Page. But why is the name Page substituted for Cecil? Could it be that the dramatist took the opportunity to point out that the Cecil family began their rise to power when Burghley's grandfather became a page in the court of Henry VIII? (Collins, ix, x).[2]

How infuriating this must have been to the hyper-sensitive Burghley who took pride in a genealogy that he proposed went back to Charlemagne (Hurstfield 251).[3] The dignity of the Cecil family was at stake. The situation called for some kind of cover story.

The Making of a Narrative

It is often asked how the Stratford narrative developed and why it has held sway for so long. Although a comprehensive discussion of the evolution of the Stratford mythology is beyond the scope of this paper, suffice it to say that it took centuries to establish the Stratfordian attribution of authorship. However, the middle of the eighteenth century was a crucial juncture. At this time, a tourist industry was getting underway in Stratford-upon-Avon, and "pushers and peepers" were showing up, hungry for relics (Brown 53). But there was nothing for an eager public to see by way of manuscripts, books or letters belonging to the Bard. Even so, a "Shakespeare industry" had been launched, though the birthplace had not yet been purchased or even identified, and Ann Hathaway's cottage was far in the future. Nevertheless, if bardolatry was to continue its forward march, the world needed something to venerate and admire.

With the fledgling Shakespeare industry gaining traction, people wanted to know what Shakespeare looked like, and thus far, only two images were held to be representative of the author's appearance: the Droeshout engraving in the *First Folio* and the wall monument in the Holy Trinity Church in Stratford-upon-Avon. Both have serious flaws. The Droeshout engraving is a preposterous floating head with two right eyes peering out of the mask-like face, and left sleeves are on both arms of the disproportionately small torso.[4] An engraving by Wenceslas Hollar published in *Antiquities of Warwickshire* shows the figure on the church monument as a dour fellow with a drooping mustache and arms resting on a sack, perhaps a sack of grain or wool (Dugdale 520.) Hollar's engraving, sometimes called the Woolsack Man, was the only published depiction of the effigy for more than half a century (Whalen 151).[5] In the late 1740s, the effigy underwent "repairing and beautifying," but the Reverend Joseph Greene, the curate of the church, was adamant that the beautified bust "answered exactly to our original bust" and has a "thorough resemblance" to the Droeshout engraving in the *First Folio* (Whalen 153-155). Whatever the similarities between the Woolsack Man (beautified or not) and the harlequin-esque Droeshout engraving, none of these images were particularly appealing. The developing Shakespeare narrative was in great need of more satisfying imagery. It also needed to be in the right place. A place like Westminster Abbey.

Visitors today to Poets' Corner will see a life-sized statue of Shakespeare. He is a pleasant looking, well-attired gentleman leaning on a pedestal, his elbow resting, appropriately, on a stack of books. The heads of Queen Elizabeth, Henry V and Richard III are carved around the base of the pedestal, and the Bard points to a scroll floating down the side. Notwithstanding the strangely inaccurate passage from *The Tempest* inscribed on the scroll, it makes a definitely acceptable impression.

Some helpful information about this monument is on the Westminster Abbey website. It was erected in 1741 by Richard Boyle, the third Earl of Burlington, along with Alexander Pope, Dr. Richard Mead and Tom Martin. The monument was designed by William Kent and sculpted by Peter Scheemakers. Two theatrical companies assisted with fund-raising events.[6] This is fine as far as it goes. But questions remain. With no portraits of the Bard from his lifetime, what inspired this statute? Were the men involved in this project connected in some way? What motivated them to put up this cenotaph commemorating Shakespeare?

GVLIELMO SHAKSPEARE
ANNO POST MORTEM CXXIV
AMOR PVBLICVS POSVIT

WILLIAM SHAKESPEARE 1564~1616
BURIED AT STRATFORD-ON-AVON

The Monument of William Shakespeare in Westminster
Abbey. Used with permission.
Copyright: Dean and Chapter of Westminster.

The Monument Men

The patron of the Westminster Abbey Shakespeare monument, the third Earl of Burlington, is credited with almost single-handedly making Italian Palladianism the national style of Georgian England. One of the wealthiest peers in England, the "architect Earl" was influential in areas beyond architecture, including the fields of politics, literature and the arts. His resolve to see the Shakespeare monument through is evident in his financial underpinning of the project when there was a shortfall in fundraising (Prendergast 100).

Of the other participants, Alexander Pope often gets a billing that outshines Lord Burlington. Alexander Pope's literary legacy is well known, and his biography in the *ODNB* details the important people who held him to be the best poet of the age. His celebrated literary friend Jonathan Swift sought to have one of Pope's *Epistles* addressed to him (*ODNB* 44:867). In addition to his literary friends, Pope successfully cultivated relationships with the highest strata of English society, and his correspondence with the Earls of Oxford, Orrery and Bathurst, as well as other notables of the time, has been published.

Pope's association with Lord Burlington began sometime before 1716 when the Pope family moved into a home on Chiswick Lane – just a few steps from Burlington's Chiswick House (Berry 205). It is said that the Popes lived "under the wing of my Lord Burlington" (Erskine-Hill 218; *DNB* 16:114). Controversial throughout his life, Pope was known for "the wretched series of complex quarrels, maneuvers and falsifications in which he was plunged from his youth" (*DNB* 16:122). So continuously was he scheming that one acquaintance reportedly said he "could hardly drink tea without a stratagem" (*DNB* 16:122-123). But in spite of his character flaws and physical deformities from a childhood illness, Pope dominated both the literati and the high society of London.

William Kent, the artist who designed the statue, was an associate of Pope and another of Burlington's protégés (*DNB* 11:25). Burlington met Kent when the artist was working as a painter at a villa in Italy. The Earl brought Kent back to England where he lived in Burlington's apartments for the rest of his life (Mowl 61). Upon his death, Kent was interred in the Burlington family vault at Chiswick. In spite of many prestigious appointments secured for him over the years by Burlington, Kent turned out to be a man of limited artistic talent (Barnard and Clark, xxiv). His portraits of his aristocratic clientele suffered from "feeble composition and bad draughtsmanship." Perhaps his best qualification for the job of creating the image of Shakespeare was his expertise in garden statuary, an important element in architecture and landscape design that he learned in Italy (*DNB* 11:24).

Dr. Richard Mead was a physician, writer and collector of considerable influence. He was elected to the Royal Society in 1703 and gave the Harveian lecture at the Royal College of Physicians in 1723. In 1720 he was named governor of the hospitals of Bridewell, Bethlehem and St. Bartholomew. Among his medical friends and clientele were the greats of London. Dr. Mead is credited with persuading his friend and patient, Thomas Guy, to found the hospital that to this day bears Guy's name (Jones 87-92). He was appointed physician to King George the Second, and attended Sir Issac Newton during his final illness (Mead 39, 49). Mead was as well known for his collection of books, art, antique medals, manuscripts and coins as he was as a physician, and was consulted by Lewis Theobald in his preparation of Shakespeare's works (*DNB* 12:184). Mead's library at his London home, one of the largest of the time, contained among its other treasures the coveted 1632 second folio of Shakespeare – the very book that had been owned by King Charles the First (Jones, 87-92; *ODNB* 37:639-640).

Dr. Mead was Alexander Pope's physician and received several mentions in Pope's *Epistles.* Judging from the many occasions in which Pope tells of his illnesses in his correspondence, he must have required frequent medical advice (Berry 141). Mead's biographer relates that "further evidence of the close relationship existing between Pope and Mead can be inferred from the record of Pope's appointment with Jonathan Richardson to sit for a portrait commissioned by Mead" (48). Although probable, it is not clear if Mead was Lord Burlington's physician, but they knew each other; it is noted that Mead sold to Burlington a valuable consignment of Palladio's drawings (Lees-Milne 125).

The least documented of the four, Tom Martin is likely to be Thomas Martin of Palgrave, a man who held a stellar place among the collectors of the time. He was an attorney by trade, practicing law with his brother, but "his thirst after antiquities was as great as his thirst after liquor." His longstanding membership in the Society of Antiquaries began in 1720 under the mentorship of Peter Le Neve, the Norroy King of Arms, who was President of the Society at that time. Martin is likely to have come in contact with Lord Burlington after the Earl became a fellow Antiquary in 1724. Admired as a "skillful and indefatigable antiquary," Martin was appointed executor of Le Neve's estate and charged, by the terms of Le Neve's will, to organize his massive collection of books and manuscripts for a public repository (*ODNB* 36:984). This he did not do, but instead married Le Neve's widow and moved the collection to his home in Palgrave (*DNB* 12:1182).

There is no mention of participation in the Westminster Shakespeare monument project in the *DNB* biographies of Mead, Martin or the third Earl of Burlington, an absence that is particularly puzzling in the life of the Architect Earl. Editors Toby Barnard and Jane Clark detail Burlington's illustrious, accomplished career in their book *Lord Burlington: Architecture, Art and Life*. The family genealogy takes up two pages, and an entire chapter is devoted to the third Earl's famous ancestor, the second Earl of Cork who became the first Earl of Burlington (167-199).

However, the Burlington family tree has an even more notable ancestor: the grandfather of the first Lord Burlington's wife was Robert Cecil, Earl of Salisbury. It appears that this Cecil was dropped from the publication, as one finds the following in the index: *Salisbury, earl of, see Cecil, Robert*. But there is no entry for Robert Cecil. Nor is any mention of his name to be found anywhere in the book (325). This is odd as the writer underscores the importance of the marriage of the second Earl of Cork to Elizabeth Clifford – a marriage that ultimately brought the Burlington earldom to the Boyle family. The third Earl of Burlington is a direct descendant of Robert Cecil through the marriage of Robert Cecil's daughter Frances to Henry Clifford, the Earl of Cumberland. Elizabeth Clifford, the only surviving child of this marriage, is the third Earl's great-grandmother. Also, the Burlington and Salisbury families were entwined when the Burlingtons had the guardianship of the Salisbury minor children in the seventeenth century (Cecil 178).

That the Burlington family lineage from the Cecil family is absent from what appears to be a comprehensive account of Lord Burlington's ancestors is puzzling. Perhaps equally strange is the omission of any mention of the third Earl of Burlington's patronage of the Shakespeare monument in Westminster Abbey, surprising given the substantial cultural impact that the sculpture of Shakespeare had when it was unveiled in London in 1741. The erection of this monument in Westminster, in fact the first full-length statue in Poets' Corner, "inspired a Shakespeare revival" (Roscoe 72-82). It even increased the popularity of its sculptor Peter Scheemakers, who thereafter was often preferred to the better established Michael Rysbrack.

Connecting the dots: the Shakespeare monument in Poets' Corner in Westminster Abbey was designed and erected under the direction of a descendent of William Cecil, Lord Burghley.

The All-Pervading Presence

Elizabethan and Jacobean historians have, for the most part, eliminated Edward de Vere, the seventeenth Earl of Oxford, from the chronicles of the times. If for some reason he must be mentioned at all, the writers hasten to attach to his memory as many harsh adjectives as possible. Invariably, the explanation for this is that Oxford mistreated his wife, Anne Cecil. One might think that Oxford is the only person in a millennium of English history who maligned his wife and didn't get along well with her family. Clearly, Edward de Vere lives in the doghouse of history.

Edward de Vere might have been somewhat gratified had he known that the negative historical view of him actually puts him in good company. William Cecil, the family patriarch, had two surviving sons. Robert, Lord Salisbury was his younger son from his second marriage, and the Salisbury line has dominated the political and social structure of England to the present day. Thomas Cecil, his elder son from his first marriage, became the Earl of Exeter and left a large family whose descendants had successful careers, many in the church and the military. However, the Exeter line does not receive the admiring commentary that writers of history regularly bestow on their Salisbury cousins. Barnett disparages Cecil's first marriage to Thomas' mother: "It was probably the only major personal strategic mistake Cecil ever made. Mary's early death corrected his error, but a very ordinary son was the reminder of an imprudent love. There were times when the son even appeared to the distraught father as a punishment" (3). This deplorable reportage may stem in part from the Exeter Cecils' connections to the family of the 17th Earl of Oxford. Oxford's son Henry, the 18th Earl of Oxford, married Diana Cecil, Thomas Cecil's granddaughter. Also, Henry de Vere is buried with the family of Thomas Cecil in his chapel in Westminster Abbey.

It might be asked how this baggage could be carried from century to century? And why? The answer may lie in the political longevity of the Salisbury line of the Cecil family. In his *History of the House of Lords*, Frank, Lord Longford, a twentieth-century leader of the House of Lords, provides insight into the House of Cecil:

> When I became a member of the House of Lords in 1945, it was impossible not to feel the *all-pervading presence of the Cecils*. The fifth Marquis, "Bobbity," was still active and much admired in the House. He had been Leader of the House or of the Opposition in the Lords from 1942 to 1957, and had been throughout that time the leading personality there. His father's bust was in the corridor just opposite the entry to the dining room; his grandfather's portrait was in the same corridor, shown destroying the Home Rule Bill of 1893. His great-grandfather's photograph was in the room I later occupied as Leader. *Four generations of Salisburys, successive Leaders of the House of Lords. An awe-inspiring record.*
>
> (Longford, 52) [emphasis added]

Lord Longford continues with a discussion of the early Cecils, father and son, and closes with the comment that "From that day to this, the Cecils have enjoyed a reputation for a certain ruthlessness with their minds are thoroughly made up" (Longford 53). About the 17th Earl of Oxford, the minds of the Salisbury Cecils have been made up for centuries.

Conclusion

Bertram's words in the opening scene of *All's Well That Ends Well* describe Edward de Vere's predicament as well as that of many other wards: "And I in going, madam, weep o'er my father's death anew; but I must attend his Majesty's command, to whom I am now in ward, evermore in subjection." The word *evermore* is prophetic. Who would have thought that a cover story constructed to ameliorate the feelings and safeguard the privacy of the Cecil dynasty would last through the centuries? Yet the name of Edward de Vere has all but disappeared from history while ostensible admirers of Shakespeare pour through the turnstiles at the supposed birthplace of their Bard in Stratford-upon-Avon.

Notes

1. Eliot's "objective correlative" In "Hamlet and His Problems" (*The Sacred Wood*, 1921) has remained controversial, but the proposal that the motivation of Shakespeare's characters frequently stems from something outside the confines of Shakespeare's plays has held sway.

2. In this early biography of Lord Burghley, Collins traces the family genealogy, noting his father's employment in the Court of Henry VIII. Richard Cecil, the Lord Treasurer's father, was one of the Pages of the Crown in the eighth year of the reign of Henry VIII and rose to a Groom of the Robes fourteen years later. After further promotions to Yeoman of the Robes and steward of several of the king's manors, his career culminated in the grant of 299 acres of arable land in Stamford.

3. Hurstfield expounds on this quirk: "He [Burghley] failed, it is true, to erect an authentic aristocratic past for himself, but there can be no doubt about the nobility of his descendants" (251).

4. For a close look at the costume of the figure in the Droeshout engraving, see the YouTube video presented by Debbie Radcliffe in "The 'Impossible Doublet' in the Droeshout engraving of William Shakespeare." This video can be accessed on the Shakespeare Authorship Coalition website:

   https://doubtaboutwill.org

5. The bust would go through many rounds of "beautification" in subsequent generations. See Whalen for details (145-157).

6. The Abbey's website notes that both Kent and Scheemakers signed the monument and dated it 1740, still using the Old Style in which the New Year began at the end of March. The appearance of the monument in the Abbey was announced in the *Gentleman's Magazine* in February, 1741.

Chapter
7

A Sufficient Warrant
Examining Oxford's £1,000 Annuity

A document extant in the public record may shed some light on the paradox of an individual who – as we saw in chapter four – composed highly seditious works but remained invisible to the authorities. On June 26, 1586, Queen Elizabeth executed a Privy Seal Warrant in which she instructed her Exchequer to pay a thousand pounds a year to Edward de Vere, the 17th Earl of Oxford. A Privy Seal Warrant was the Queen's order to her Exchequer to pay the bills of her royal administration (Adams 114-123). Such warrants were usually issued for a single payment for a specific expense or service rendered. However, this particular Privy Seal Warrant was a kind less often utilized; its language makes it a Privy Seal Warrant Dormant. The word *dormant* meant that the payment is a standing order for a sum to be paid for an indefinite length of time until the Queen commands its cessation – something she never did in this case (Ward 257-260, 357-358).[1] This payment continued for the remaining seventeen years of Elizabeth's life and was reinstated by King James on his accession to the throne in 1603. By the time of Oxford's death in 1604, the grant had continued for eighteen years and approximately $18,000,000 in today's currency had been paid to Oxford out of the royal treasury.

The longevity of the annuity is all the more puzzling as it lasted throughout the years when the Exchequer was seriously strapped for cash. Historians of the Tudor era recognize that Elizabeth I was impoverished from the beginning of her reign, and her finances steadily worsened (Lacey 57-58).[2] After years of sparring with

133

Spain on the high seas and in the Low Countries, the war with
Spain began in 1585. The disastrous nineteen year conflict was
brought to an end by King James when, in 1604, a formal peace
treaty was signed by England and Spain (Akrigg 60-63).

In his *Economic History of England*, Frederick Dietz uses contemporaneous sources to summarize the costs of the wars, giving a
total of over £5,000,000 expended on "economically unproductive
military operations" (155). Over £3,000,000 was spent in the decade 1590 to 1600 with the crown frequently calling on Parliament
for subsidies to finance the costly mess (Black 228-230). The conquest of Ireland cost nearly £2,000,000 in the last decade of the
Queen's life (Dietz 155). Paul Hammer details the "sorry shape" of
the war effort in the Low Countries in his chapter "The War Goes
Sour, 1586-1587" (132-137). It is significant that Oxford's annuity
began in 1586 because this is the year when, according to Hammer, the financial shambles of the war in the Low Countries had
become clear. Over the winter of 1586, the Queen's army was left
destitute (124-133).

The people in her realm were not any better off than the
soldiers, and it was said in the Commons that the poor "were
compelled to sell their pots and pans to meet the already heavy
taxation" (Black 228-231).[3] In his study of the Elizabethan Exchequer, Dietz notes that the sale of crown estates was a last resort,
but lands were sold in 1589 because "conditions were so bad that
Burghley himself seemed to despair" (71). Dietz continues that,
after Burghley's death in 1598, "the Irish rebellion was sucking the
treasury dry and new ministers abandoned Burghley's caution and
sold land in quantities unequalled since Edward VI's time . . ." The
Queen's last Parliament of 1601 was acrimonious. Yet in spite of
the expenses of the foreign wars, the bad harvests of the 1590s and
the poverty of the Exchequer, the payments to the 17th Earl of
Oxford continued.[4]

It would seem that a large outlay of cash during these troubled
years – especially a thousand pounds annually to the Queen's "well
beloved Cousin, the earl of Oxford" – should merit close scrutiny
(Ward 257-260).[5] Remarkably, historical scrutiny is precisely what
this document has not had. The only historian to report on it prior
to Bernard Ward's discovery of it in 1928 was Edmund Bohun in

his 1693 biography of Elizabeth I (Ogburn 689).[6]

The Document

> Elizabeth, etc., to the Treasurer and Chamberlains of our
> Exchequer, Greeting. We will and command you of Our
> treasure being and remaining from time to time within the
> receipt of Our Exchequer, to deliver and pay, or cause to be
> delivered and paid, unto Our right trusty and well beloved
> Cousin the earl of Oxford, or to his assigns sufficiently au-
> thorized by him, the sum of One Thousand Pounds good
> and lawful money of England. The same to be yearly de-
> livered and paid unto Our said Cousin at four terms of the
> year by even portions [beginning at the Feast of the Annun-
> ciation last past]: and so to be continued unto him **during
> Our pleasure, or until such time as he shall be by
> Us otherwise provided for to be in some manner
> relieved**; at what time Our pleasure is that this payment
> of One Thousand Pounds yearly to Our said Cousin in
> manner above specified **shall cease**. And for the same or
> any part thereof, **Our further will and commandment
> is that neither the said Earl nor his assigns nor his
> or their executors nor any of them shall by way of
> account, imprest, or any other way whatsoever be
> charged towards Us, Our heirs or successors**. And
> these Our letters shall be your sufficient warrant and dis-
> charge in that behalf. Given under Our Privy Seal at Our
> Manor of Greenwich, the six and twentieth day of June in
> the eight and twentieth year of Our reign.[7] (bold emphases
> added)

First, this grant is given entirely at Her Majesty's discretion; i.e.,
at "her pleasure," and it will cease at her pleasure. This is why it is
a warrant *dormant*. Next, the phrase "by Us otherwise provided for"
has attracted a great deal of attention, and the explanation is prof-
fered that the Queen assumed financial responsibility for Oxford
in order to maintain him in his nobility. Most curious of all is the
non-accountability clause which states that "neither the said Earl .
. . shall by way of account . . . be charged towards us." But before

these statements are examined, the following facts should be kept in mind:

- Oxford did nothing for which he might have *earned* financial remuneration. He held no important state office, no embassy, and no military posts (Ward 256).[8]

- A thousand pounds was more than one per cent of the Queen's annual domestic budget. Simon Adams estimates that the cost of running the various household departments (some supplied directly through the Exchequer and some through other means) came to roughly £90,000 annually by the end of her reign (119).

- Queen Elizabeth I has been known through the centuries for many fine qualities, but charity has never been one of them (Hazard 118, 227).[9] Lawrence Stone describes the Queen as a master at giving that which cost her nothing (191, 194-197, 201-204, 222). According to Stone, "Money [was] the one thing that Elizabeth could not bring herself to give away" (197).

- The money was paid to Oxford in quarterly installments of £250. Oxford's detractors argue that the Queen was doling out the money, but a more likely explanation lies in the large amount of the annuity. It took time for the funds to accrue during the year, especially in a depleted Exchequer.

- The Royal Exchequer was a hard cash concern with payment in gold or silver coin or bullion. Delivery of the money was not a simple matter. It had to be counted out, packed in saddlebags or carts, and accompanied by armed guards to its destination (Stone, unabridged 508-512).[10]

To explain away this annuity, academics have recently picked up on Edmund Bohun's seventeenth century comment that the Queen wished to maintain the Earl of Oxford in the splendor of a courtier (Nelson 300-303, 379-380).[11] It obliges one to believe that Queen Elizabeth gave the earl this financial underpinning simply to keep up appearances, something hardly credible in the context of her parsimony and impoverished treasury. Stone reports in *Crisis of the Aristocracy* that it took an income of approximately £5,000 annually to support an earl in an earldom (unabridged 547-586).[12] If the purpose was to keep the Earl of Oxford in a manner commensurate with his rank, a thousand pounds a year – though a huge sum – was only 20% of what it would take to do the job (Green 60-78).

The more serious flaw in the argument, however, is that this is not how the Queen did business. Had she wanted to do something nice for him, she could have given him a preferment (Stone, abridged 191, 199-207). Queen Elizabeth regularly gave profitable offices, land grants and monopolies to reward her favorite courtiers, turning her court "into the unique market-place for the distribution of an enormous range of offices, favours and titles" (207).[13] Oxford played the game as best he could, petitioning for a license for the imports of oils, fruits and wools, the gauging of beer, the governorship of Jersey and the presidency of Wales. He repeatedly requested the return of his ancestral properties in Waltham Forest and the tin monopoly in Cornwall (Nelson 337-338, 344, 355-358, 380). The Queen denied them all. Any one of these preferments could have restored his fortunes and provided far more effectively for his livelihood, if that had been her intent – and been far less burdensome on her limited resources.[14]

Better yet, the Queen had a veritable silver bullet in her fiscal arsenal that could ameliorate his financial woes. In 1592, she allowed Oxford to marry Elizabeth Trentham, a wealthy maid of honor in her court. It was an accepted practice for English peers to marry wealthy heiresses in order to restore depleted finances. According to Stone, "Around the turn of the century the growing financial embarrassment of the peerage drove them into a far more single-minded pursuit of wealthy marriages than had previously been their custom" (abridged 282).[15] After Oxford's remarriage, he was in comfortable circumstances for the rest of his life, but the thousand pounds continued to be paid in quarterly installments out of the royal Exchequer until his death in 1604. At this time, the annuity ceased, an indicator that it was payment to the man himself and not his house.[16]

The Historical Question

There is no getting around it: this annuity is a conundrum. So what about the recipient? Following the lead of Sir Sidney Lee in the *Dictionary of National Biography*, historians are nearly unanimous in their condemnation of the 17th Earl of Oxford. Lawrence Stone describes him as "feckless" (unabridged 514), a term defined in the OED as "incompetent, useless, hopeless, spineless, feeble, weak, futile, ineffective, and worthless." In *The Cecils of Hatfield House*, family historian David Cecil applies the pejoratives "unreliable, uncontrolled, ill-tempered and wildly extravagant" (84). To this litany, Tresham Lever adds that he was "eccentric, quarrelsome and absurd" (92). If anything, the severity of the historical characterization of Oxford should bring the thousand-pound annuity into sharp focus. What could possibly have motivated the not-at-all feckless Queen to give cold hard cash from her Exchequer to this feckless wastrel of a courtier? If the historical assessments were true, then this grant from the parsimonious Elizabeth, with its peculiar non-accountability clause, is an anomaly that defies rational explanation.[17]

The Answer

In an article published in the University of Pennsylvania Law Review in 1992, then U.S. Supreme Court Justice John Paul Stevens suggested that the Queen was underwriting Oxford's theatrical activities (1383-1384). Many agree with his proposal that she "may have decided to patronize a gifted dramatist, who agreed to remain anonymous while he loyally rewrote much of the early history of Great Britain." Indeed, the Privy Seal Warrant starts to make sense when it is examined in the context of the biographical facts of Oxford's life that point to him as the author of the Shakespeare canon.

Writing about this in his comprehensive biography of Oxford, Mark Anderson quotes the literary scholar Seymour M. Pitcher who suggested these funds were intended for organized propaganda.

Oxford was to produce plays which would educate the English people – most of whom could not read – in their country's history, in appreciation of its greatness, and of their own stake in its welfare. In point of fact and time, a spate of chronicle plays did follow the authorization of the stipend (211).

Anderson says that "under this scenario, the end products of the Queen's £1,000 annuity were Shake-speare's *King John, Richard II, 1 and 2, Henry IV, Henry V, 1,2,and 3 Henry VI, Richard III and Henry VIII*" (211).

But something beyond simple financial underwriting may be tacitly implied within the warrant's provision clause: *and so to be continued unto him during Our pleasure, or until such time as he shall be by Us otherwise provided for to be in some manner relieved.* It does appear that the Queen is accepting financial responsibility for Oxford. This is a puzzling feature. If there had been a romantic involvement between them, as some Oxfordians have suggested, then why did she not give him a lucrative sinecure? Moreover, Queen Elizabeth was a monarch. There was no legal obligation or superior moral authority that could compel her to support him financially, whatever had occurred in the past.

What the Queen may have in mind might be akin to the modern concept of financial responsibility known as indemnification. In today's legal practice, one person or entity indemnifies another by taking fiscal responsibility for the actions of that person or entity, securing them against future loss, damage or liability.

Let's take a closer look at the non-accountability clause: *Our further will and commandment is that neither the said Earl nor his assigns nor his or their executors nor any of them shall by way of account, imprest, or any other way whatsoever be charged towards Us, Our heirs or successors.* The non-accountability clause broadly implies that Oxford is not to be held to account for what he is doing with the money. By extension, does this not also imply that he need not account for what he is doing? It would seem that with this warrant, the Queen is protecting him from scrutiny. It would seem that she is giving him something along the lines of what today we would call immunity. Oxford can do as he sees fit with the money as long as Queen Elizabeth herself is satisfied with whatever it is that he is doing. No questions asked.

The legal concepts of indemnification and immunity, as we

know them today, were in their infancy in early modern England. What was operational at this time was the feudal concept in which a great lord granted maintenance and protection to his followers in return for their service (Brown 28-29, 92). It is well-accepted that the Elizabethan mentality was steeped in feudalistic traditions (Hazard 125). Historians acknowledge the resurgence of feudalism in the reign of Henry VII and furthered in his descendants (Hurstfield 3-17).[18]

The formula playing out here is simple: maintenance (funds) and protection (immunity from government retaliation) in return for service (the plays and poetry known to posterity as the Shakespeare works). It is plain feudalism.

Justice Stevens and others believe that Shakespeare's history plays established the legitimacy of the Tudor dynasty, quite a fine service to provide to the insecure Tudor woman who nervously ruled a vulnerable country in a dangerous time with three ongoing wars. The plays glorified her reign, all the while providing the royal court with the highest quality entertainment, something Queen Elizabeth coveted.

The Warrant's Unique Language

There may be even more to discover within this short document. Let us read the non-accountability sentence again: *the said Earl … nor any of them shall by way of account, imprest, or any other way whatsoever be charged towards Us, Our heirs or successors.* The pronoun *Us* surely does not refer to the Queen herself, but to her royal administration. Also, the word *Us*, rather than the word *Him*, is odd. The clause might make more sense if it read like this: "nor any of them shall by way of account, imprest, or any other way whatsoever be charged towards **Him**, **his** heirs or successors." Taken literally, the Queen is saying that the recipient cannot charge the royal Exchequer, i.e. *Us*, with accounting. This is nonsensical. Normally, the recipient of funds accounts for how the money allocated to him is spent, not the entity providing the funds.

It was noted by Oxford's twentieth century biographer Bernard Ward that the Queen's instructions in this warrant are similar to the non-accountability clause in her warrant of funds to Sir Francis

Walsingham (260). Research recently conducted in the National Archives reveals that non-accountability clauses appear in all of the nineteen warrants issued by the Queen to Walsingham from 1582-1588.[19] But the odd verbiage "charged toward Us" is nowhere to be found. Of special interest is the warrant to Walsingham dated July 2, 1586. This warrant was issued only a week after Oxford's warrant of June 26, 1586. The language of the non-accountability clause is as follows: *"The said sum to be thus delivered unto him without any imprest or other charge to be set upon him for the same and neither he, his heirs, executors or administrators to be any way accountable therefore."* In this, as in the other warrants to Walsingham, the Queen uses the sensible third person singular pronoun *him*, and it is "his heirs" that are included in the non-accountability instruction – not "Our heirs" as stated in Oxford's warrant.

In the appendix to Ward's biography is a list of Privy Seal Warrants dormant, and among these is a sum of £800 issued to Robert Cecil on September 27, 1596 (355-358). This document is another comparable for the Oxford warrant as a similar amount of money is to be "delivered and paid" in quarterly installments.[20] That its purpose is for secret service is evident in the language. It is "for our private and inward services which by our special trust we have made known to him only." Again, the non-accountability clause follows the language in the Walsingham warrants: the funds are to be delivered to Cecil *"without imprest account or other charge to be set on him for the same."*[21]

Further evidence of the stability of this non-accountability language can be found in the study of the Exchequer warrants from the reign of King James. Published in 1836, historian Frederick Devon transcribed over a thousand warrants dating from 1603 to 1626. Of these, about a hundred contain non-accountability clauses. In every one of them, the third person (to whom the money is given) is the party to be held unaccountable, not the royal Exchequer. An example is found in the October 30, 1612 warrant to the merchant Paul Fourre which states that the funds are given *"without account, imprest, or other charge to be set on him for the same"* (151).

The Elizabethan Exchequer

Since the Privy Seal Warrant is an order to the Exchequer, a closer look at this office might shed light on what these unique words – *charged towards Us* – might mean, and to whom this instruction may be addressed. At this point, it would be helpful to have a better understanding of the departmental structure of the Elizabethan Exchequer, and how receipts and disbursements were managed. But a better understanding is not to be had. Unfortunately, no historian or archivist has made a transcription of the accounts of Queen Elizabeth's Exchequer along the lines of Devon's *Issues of the Exchequer* for the reign of King James.[22] The best resource is a short essay by Frederick Dietz, who has been previously mentioned for his acccounts of Elizabeth's war-time expenditures (65-105).

Dietz explains in his 1923 essay that the Elizabethan Exchequer was made up of two departments: the Lower Exchequer of Receipt and the Upper Exchequer of Audit (105). The money was received and dispersed in the Lower Exchequer and audited in the Upper Exchequer. The four tellers in the Lower House communicated with the three audit courts and the Exchequer barons in various ways, including a primitive system of tallies. This communication was linked together by accountants who carried a slip or bill to the Court of Receipt to be handed to the treasurer's clerk for writing the tallies. Another clerk entered the information into the Pells while two clerks, each representing a Chamberlain, wrote the Controllment of the Pells. The Cofferer of the Household was audited by the Upper Exchequer, but the Office of the Imprest, with its own two auditors, was a separate department. However, Lord Burghley, as the crown-in-council, kept "exclusive control and oversight over the prests" and "there was no provision for regular submission of such accounts to the auditors" (108). Along the way was an array of lesser under-clerks, ushers and messengers (109-111).

With so many offices and positions, it is not surprising that, according to Dietz, "Elizabethan exchequer officials were never quite as accurate as a modern adding machine" and "there are nearly always discrepancies between the totals as they give them at the close of their accounts, and the actual additions of the individual items making up the accounts" (77). Although Dietz's overview is helpful, the internal operations of the Queen's Exchequer remain poorly understood.[23]

Through all this complexity and the passing of many centuries, it is not possible to discern with any certainty to whom the instruction "charged toward Us" is intended. What is proposed here is that this unusual phrase carries unusual significance. It suggests that the Queen is covering several bases with this instruction. Ostensibly, the recipient is not to be held accountable for the money. Biographer Ward suggests that "the Earl is not to be called on by the Exchequer to render any account as to its expenditure" (260). That may well be the long and short of it. But taking it one step further, it appears that this may be a command to the Upper Exchequer auditors or the Auditors of the Imprest to suspend business-as-usual in handling this annuity. It supports the proposal that information about the annuity is a state secret, *to be guarded at every step along the way.* If this is the case, then with one single pronoun, the Queen has circumscribed, if not dismantled, the normal channels of communication within the departments of her own administration, putting another layer of secrecy around the person to whom this money is given.

Lord Burghley would have known about the Privy Seal Warrant with its non-accountability clause. He was the Lord Treasurer of England; he knew in minute detail what went in and out of the royal coffers (Loades 142).[24] An example of Burghley's command of the Treasury can be found in an award of £50 by Queen Elizabeth to the poet Edmund Spenser. It is unknown if this grant, made in February of 1591, was only a single payment or if it continued in subsequent years. However, it is reported in Manningham's Diary and later by Fuller that Lord Burghley objected to the Queen's "largesse." It was also suggested that this grant carried with it the formal dignity of poet-laureate. Whether or not this is the case, it is noteworthy that money from the Queen's treasury could be construed as an endorsement of the recipient's work (*DNB* 18:799).

Conclusion

A symbolic, unspoken communication infused every aspect of court life, and the court was led by a moody, miserly Queen who never gave out a shilling when a smile would do, and never a smile if a curt nod would suffice (Lacey 57-58).[25] For those in the know, saddlebags full of gold coin delivered four times a year to the door-step of the 17th Earl of Oxford must have been a happenstance beyond their comprehension (Hazard 109-140, 118).[26] It would be understandable that the royal officials involved in the payment process would keep a wise silence (Handover 156).[27]

Thus, this Privy Seal Warrant Dormant, with its feudal impli-cations of royal protection, gave the recipient a degree of auton-omy that was unheard of at the time, a veritable freedom of the press. No questions were ever asked of this singular odd man to whom this singular odd act of regal generosity was directed.

The works of Shakespeare contained much material that was treasonable by the standards of the era. It surpasses understanding that the Stratford man could write plays that were clearly sedi-tious and not be invited to drop by the Privy Council for a chat. Another anomaly is the large sum of money paid over many years by Queen Elizabeth to the 17th Earl of Oxford and continued by King James. This money was given with no accountability re-quired, quite possibly not even within the Exchequer of two mon-archs. These anomalous circumstances make sense when it is under-stood that Oxford is the author hiding behind the name of William Shakespeare, and this information was a state secret.

In writing *Hamlet*, the 17th Earl of Oxford might have been reflecting on the royal patronage that allowed him to circumvent the political hazards that often ensnared his literary cohorts. He had the effrontery to model Polonius on his duplicitous father-in-law, Lord Burghley; Queen Gertrude is Queen Elizabeth; Oxford is Hamlet himself. And what does Polonius say to Queen Gertrude immediately before he hides behind the arras? It is an important line in an important scene of an important play: "Your Grace hath screen'd and stood between much heat and him."

Notes

1. In his Appendix C, Ward includes a "Table of Annuities" with an overview of all of the Privy Seal Warrants dormant for annuities, grants, and pensions paid by the Exchequer from 1580 through the end of Elizabeth's reign. In addition, he discusses the three kinds of Privy Seal Warrants: Ordinary, Dormant and Gratuity, citing the *Guide to the Records in the Public Record Office* for the definitions (180).

2. Lacey describes queen Elizabeth as "hopelessly, helplessly poor," and writes colorfully that "she had to scrape together a living and put on an appropriately regal display from a ragbag of odd incomes worth – thanks to a century of inflation – half as much as when she ascended the throne" (57).

3. Supporting information is in Conyers Read's biography of William Cecil (473).

4. Private communication with researcher.

5. To understand the magnitude of this annuity, Ward compares it with the salaries paid to the Earl of Huntingdon as Lord President of the North, Sir Thomas Parry as Resident Ambassador to France, Sir John Stanhope as Master of the Posts, and notes various stipends to dependents of noblemen who had been attainted and whose lands had been confiscated by the Crown.

6. Bohun wrote that "The Earl of Oxford was one of the most ancient houses amongst the nobility but by the excessive bounty and splendor of the former Earl was reduced to a very low and mean condition, so that the family was no longer able to maintain its dignity and grandeur: And the Queen allowed that house one thousand pound the year out of her Exchequer that one of the most illustrious houses in her kingdom might not

suffer want." (Edmund Bohun. *The Character of Queen Elizabeth.* London: R. Chiswell, 1693).

7. The transcript is in the Ward, Ogburn, and Fowler books.

8. Ward notes that Oxford had not "been called on to undertake any of those duties that so often impoverished Elizabethan courtiers. He had never held appointments such as Lord Deputy of Ireland, Custodian of the Queen of Scots, or Ambassador at Paris – appointments that had been so disastrous financially to Sir Henry Sidney, Lord Shrewsbury, and Francis Walsingham."

9. It was a standard practice for New Year's gifts to the Queen to be weighed in order for her to reciprocate with gifts of lesser value. The Queen took care to be precise (Frederick Whigham, *Ambition and Privilege*).

10. In the chapter on "Storage and Transfer of Cash," Stone elaborates on the difficulties of payment in coin or bullion and provides an amusing example of the problems of transporting sizable payments in coin. The Earl of Lincoln attempted to economize by using his personal coach to transport coin to pay a debt, and the coach broke down under the weight.

11. Nelson continues the spin by referencing an account written by Thomas Wilson in which he states that "the Queen . . . gives him maintenance for his nobility sake." A quick check in the *Dictionary of National Biography* reveals that Thomas Wilson was a loyal Cecil man, owing much to William Cecil for his educational opportunities at Cambridge (where Cecil was Chancellor). Wilson served as an intelligencer for Sir Robert Cecil during the later years of Elizabeth's reign, and was appointed by Cecil to the office of the Keeper of the Records. His home adjoined Robert Cecil's at Durham Place, and he supervised the construction of Cecil's Hatfield House. Wilson was hardly an objective observer of current events. For the Wilson document, see *State Papers, Dom. Elizabeth*, vol. cclxxx.

12. In the chapter on conspicuous expenditure, Stone discusses

the responsibilities placed on a member of the high peerage, and the huge income that it took for a nobleman to maintain a lifestyle appropriate to his degree.

13. In his *History of England* published in 1914, Edward P. Cheney writes that "Elizabeth's grants rarely took the form of ready money or direct gifts. An appointment to office, a promotion to a more lucrative office, the reversion of an office, an antiquated sinecure, a grant of confiscated lands, a monopoly of the licensing of some article for import…Such made up the treasury from which the Queen rewarded her courtiers and to which they looked with constant eagerness" (50).

14. In *Shakespeare Revealed in Oxford's Letters*, William Plumer Fowler published a letter written by Oxford to his former father-in-law on May 18, 1591 (411-413). In this letter, Oxford puts a remarkable proposal on the table. He makes an offer to the Queen to buy out his "pension" and sets the price at £5,000 in exchange for property. Bear in mind that the Queen owed him nothing and could discontinue the "pension" at will; but apparently, Oxford thinks he has something durable enough to use as a bargaining chip. It is all the more inexplicable in the context of how badly Elizabeth treated her courtiers. As Mary Hazard relates: "One's fortunes were never permanently secure and they were unstable even on a daily basis, responsive to the moods of the queen" (240).

15. Earlier in the sixteenth century, the preservation of class distinctions took precedence over the quest for financial benefit. However, Stone demonstrates that though "wealth was not the most important consideration" in choosing a spouse, "its supremacy was increasing" during the reign of Elizabeth. Stone sets out the dire financial conditions of many noble families, and it becomes clear that Oxford's financial woes were not unique to him. His second marriage to an heiress was a socially acceptable remedy.

16. In his search for an alternative explanation for the thousand-pound annuity paid for eighteen years to the Earl of

Oxford, Alan Nelson prints a letter from Oxford's surviving spouse, Elizabeth Trentham, in which she sates that "the pension of a thousand pounds was not given by the late Queen for his life, and then to determine, but to continue, until she might raise his decay, by some better provision" (427-428). The Countess of Oxford's letter (with this interesting statement) contains many inaccuracies, and much of the language is standard courtly verbiage. The Countess addresses Robert Cecil and Henry Howard, appealing to their "honor, nature and affection" toward her "desolate estate." These two men despised her late husband, and Oxford's "desolate estate" would have greatly pleased them. That the £1,000 annuity stopped at Oxford's death in 1604 is a strong indicator that it was to the man, not to his House.

17. The Queen's constant financial woes can be gauged by the important officials who pleaded for their salaries. As early as 1572, Henry Carey, the First Lord Hunsdon, "prayed Lord Burghley to procure his recall from Berwick on the ground that his salary was unpaid and his private resources could not endure the constant calls which his office made on them." Things had not improved in twelve years, for in 1584, Hunsdon again appealed to Lord Burghley for his salary in arrears, and "that his soldiers and servants were in want of food and clothing" (*DNB* 3:977-978). In similar destitution after returning from service in The Netherlands, Thomas Digges wrote to Lord Burghley in May of 1590 that "I am forced to beseech your favour that I may have my pay so long forborn…" In a contemporaneous observation made by Sir Robert Naunton, "We have not many precedents of her liberality, or of any large donative to particular men . . . Her rewards consisted chiefly in grants of leases of offices, places of judicature" (Hurstfield 348, citing Naunton's *Fragmemta Regalia*, ed. E. Arber, 18).

18. For details of Tudor feudalism and wardship, see Hurstfield's chapter, "Feudalism Resurgent," in *The Queen's Wards*.

19. Documents from research conducted in the National Archives in January 2017.

20. Document from research conducted in the National Archives in March, 2016 and transcribed by Nina Green, for which the author is most grateful.

21. The non-accountability clauses in all of the warrants to Walsingham imply something secretive, usually incorporating the words "for Our special services." However, Ward finds no indication in the court records that Oxford was involved in secret service work, stating that "This quite rules out the possibility that the £1,000 a year was secret service money." It seems that later commentators have conflated the instruction for secrecy implied in Oxford's non-accountability clause with secret service duties indicated by the words "for Our special services" in the Walsingham warrants. It should be clearly understood that no purpose for the money is stated in Oxford's warrant.

22. It has been confirmed though private communication with a researcher in England that no one has transcribed and published the entry books of receipts and expenditures from Elizabeth's reign. Individual documents can be purchased through the National Archives, but the books were kept in secretary hand and require transcription by a paleographer. Thus a substantial cost and effort is involved to access each document.

23. Dietz provides the sources and totals of the Elizabethan Exchequer Receipts (87-89) and Expenditures (96-104) for each year of the Queen's reign. Individual entries are not included.

24. In his duties as Lord Treasurer, Lord Burghley presided over the Exchequer (*DNB* 18:799).

25. Lacey gives examples of the Queen's parsimony, noting that some of her "servants were paid part in money and the rest with grace" (58).

26. In the chapter on "Shape and Substance as Matters of Weight," Mary Hazard expounds on the status attributed to tangibles such as jewelry, medals, coins, architecture and various artifacts.

27. The sensitivity of her courtiers to the Queen's mood is apparent in a letter to the Earl of Essex from his uncle Sir William Knollys. As reported in a letter written in June 1597, "Mr. Secretary [Cecil] remaineth in all show firm to your Lordship, and no doubt will, so long as the Queen is so well pleased with you" (Birch, ii, 351).

Chapter
8

Why is the First Folio
Missing from Lady Anne's Bookshelf?

In northern England, Lady Anne Clifford is still remembered for many acts of benevolence. She constructed castles, restored churches, put up monuments to family and friends, and funded hospitals and almshouses. Her record books, family histories, and genealogies are invaluable to historians of early modern England. Her personal diaries provide a candid look at important people and events during the reigns of four monarchs. However, her most remarkable achievement was her victory in a forty year legal struggle to win the Cumberland estates that her father, George Clifford, the 3rd Earl of Cumberland, willed to his brother.

Anne was fifteen years old when her father died in 1605, and the Clifford properties that she considered her birthright passed to the collateral male line, in effect disinheriting her. For nearly four decades, Anne fought a tenacious battle for these properties. She was fifty-three when her cousin Henry Clifford, the last Earl of Cumberland, died without male heirs, and the decades of legal maneuvering paid off. In 1643, all of the estates of the Cumberland earldom in northern England came to her. But ownership did not necessarily mean that she would be a successful landlord. Taking charge of what she called "the lands of mine inheritance" would present a challenge for a woman in a patriarchal society.

In the mid-1640s, the English civil war was still ongoing, and Anne had to wait until 1649 to travel from London to northern England to claim her lands. She knew that once she entered her northern properties, she would have to administer the vast ancestral

The Great Picture, also called The Appleby Triptych, 1646/7. (Reproduced by courtesy of Abbot Hall Art Gallery, Kendall.)

estates that Clifford men had managed for centuries (Spence 113). She used the time preparing how she would assert her seigneurial authority, and her plan included the creation of two giant triptychs intended to proclaim her legitimacy to the Clifford inheritance.

Of the two triptychs, only the Appleby Triptych has survived to the present; the other, known as the Skipton Triptych, deteriorated and is no longer extant (Spence 181-186).[1] *The Appleby Triptych* is now housed at the Abbot Hall Art Gallery in Kendal, England. Its three panels are nine feet high, and with a ten foot wide center panel plus four feet panels on each side, the entire width is a show-stopping eighteen feet across.

The three panels of the triptychs – also known as "Lady Anne Clifford's Great Picture" – were designed to commemorate landmark events in her life. The center panel depicts Lady Anne's family when her two older brothers were still living in 1589; Anne appears there *in utero*. The panel on the left represents the young Lady Anne. In an inscription on the canvas, she describes herself as "lively depicted" at age fifteen, the crucial year in her life when she became her father Earl George's sole and rightful heir – in her view of things. The right panel shows Anne approximately forty years later when the coveted properties, "wrongfully detained," were finally hers.

Posterity has no information about the artist. Modern opinion favors Jan Van Belchamp, a copyist associated with the studio of Sir Anthony Van Dyck. This is a reasonable assumption as a professional copyist is what Anne needed. All but one of the fourteen portraits displayed in the Great Picture were reproduced from earlier paintings (Foister 40).[2] Though the painting is unsigned, it is dated 1645/6, and the last family event referenced in it occurred in 1647.

Through the ages, the Great Pictures have not received high marks for artistic merit. Critics complain about the "undeniable stiffness" and some of the painting techniques are deemed inadequate (Parry 201-204). Even so, the surviving Appleby Triptych makes an impressive statement. Quoting Graham Parry, "no picture of the age aspires to function as a family chronicle and intellectual history in a way comparable to Lady Anne Clifford's triptych at Appleby Castle" (202). What gives this painting its commanding intellectual stature is the presence of books. Moreover, the books are the vehicle through which Anne Clifford speaks to us centuries later.

What is striking about this bibliographic presentation is that so many books are on view. There are approximately fifty volumes; most located in the right and left side panels. Some appear loosely shelved, some are on the floor, and others are carefully arranged in the background. The books are boldly labeled to be readily identifiable, but just to make sure the viewers are aware of the volumes chosen for display, the titles and authors are also listed in inscriptions accompanying the books (Williamson 489-507). It is abundantly clear which authors have been selected to receive Anne's endorsement. The problem to be examined in this paper is that Shakespeare's *First Folio* – or any of Shakespeare's work – is missing.

This omission is all the more puzzling because Lady Anne Clifford was the wife of Shakespeare's patron. Her second husband, Philip Herbert was the 4th Earl of Pembroke and the 1st Earl of Montgomery – one of the "Incomparable Paire of

Brethren" to whom the *First Folio* was dedicated. This makes her a historical person of interest, especially when her excellent education and life-long interest in literature and literary people are taken into consideration. She is in the right place, at the right time, and with the right resume to know who Shakespeare was – or was not. She is in a position to know "who loses and who wins, who's in, who's out" (*King Lear*, 5.3). Shakespeare is out. His *First Folio* is not among the chosen volumes for her shelves, and this case of conspicuous absence is not in keeping with the orthodox story of the beloved Bard from Stratford-upon-Avon.

In a law review article published in 1992 in the University of Pennsylvania Law Review (discussed in chapter 7), United States Supreme Court Justice John Paul Stevens wrote about the Shakespeare authorship question. Emphasizing the importance of "significant silence" in cases brought before the United States Supreme Court, Justice Stevens shows that silence is indeed a form of testimony. He discusses the 4th canon of statutory construction which directs the judiciary to look at the legislative history of an issue, and provides examples of cases in which legislative silence was a pertinent factor in judicial decisions.

Justice Stevens relates this canon to what he calls the "Sherlock Holmes principle that sometimes the fact that a watchdog did not bark in the night may provide a significant clue about the identity of a murderous intruder." Then he compares the dog-that-did-not-bark to a number of absences in the orthodox accounts of "Shakespeare's" life, most notably, the absence of "Shakespeare's" library, the absence of mention of books in his will, and the absence of eulogies on his passing. To quote Justice Stevens, "Perhaps the greatest literary genius in the country's history . . . did not merit a crypt in Westminster Abbey or a eulogy penned by King James, but it does seem odd that not even a cocker spaniel or a dachshund made any noise at all when he [Shakespeare] passed from the scene" (1381-1382). Stevens' comment can be applied to Lady Anne's Great Picture; here is another instance of the dog's "deafening silence."

The Shakespeare First Folio

It is important to keep the Shakespeare *First Folio* in historical perspective. In the introduction to the Norton facsimile of the *First Folio*, Charlton Hinman makes several observations concerning the pragmatic issues involved in such a massive project:

> The mere presence of Shakespeare's name on the title page of such an edition, as the publisher of one of them [the quartos] tells us, was enough to ensure rapid sale. But a folio edition of thirty-six plays was another matter entirely. It would call for a considerable outlay of capital, would take a long time to produce (the *First Folio* was "in press" for almost two years) and would hardly, when finished, be in great popular demand. It would be too expensive.
>
> (*Introduction to the First Edition, x*)

Hinman goes on to say that "quick returns could not be expected on a large folio priced at one pound a copy – the sum, we are told, at which the *First Folio* was originally marketed – forty times as much as the single-play quarto." The *Folio* was a "decidedly chancy venture and one not likely to appeal to many publishers of the time unless some kind of guarantee against disastrous loss could be secured." Although Hinman states that "we know nothing of any such guarantee," it is inescapable that the brothers who bore the dedication were the only parties involved in the *Folio* production who were in a financial position to bear the cost (x, xi). Moreover, the 3rd Earl of Pembroke – William Herbert, the elder brother – was King James's Lord Chamberlain, and his responsibilities included all matters relating to the theater and court entertainments. Not many years later, Philip Herbert, the younger brother – who would inherit the Pembroke title at his brother's death in 1630 – would also hold this same influential position of Lord Chamberlain in the court of King Charles I. It seems an unavoidable conclusion that the Pembroke family's political connections and probable financial underpinning were essential in making the collected works of William Shakespeare available to the public (Ogburn 218-219).

Lady Anne Clifford's Background

When the *First Folio* was underway in 1622/3, Anne was married to her first husband, the Earl of Dorset. Her future husband, Philip Herbert, Earl of Montgomery, was married to his first wife Susan Vere. Susan was the daughter of Edward de Vere, the 17th Earl of Oxford from his first marriage to Anne Cecil. Susan Vere and Philip Herbert had ten children – six survived infancy, becoming Anne Clifford's step-children upon their father's remarriage to her. It is unknown if Susan Vere and Anne Clifford were close friends, but they knew each other. As young noblewomen in the royal court of King James, they both acted in 1608 in Ben Jonson's *Masque of Beauty*, and then again the next year in his *Masque of Queens* (Spence 20). The following year they danced once again in Samuel Daniel's masque *Tethys' Festival* (Holmes 23).

The Earl of Dorset died in 1624. Susan Vere died five years later in 1629, and soon after Philip's older brother William died, leaving Philip the Pembroke title and estates. Now a wealthy and available widower, Philip moved quickly to propose marriage to Anne Clifford, the widowed Countess of Dorset.

With her marriage to Philip Herbert, holder of both the Pembroke and Montgomery titles, Anne Clifford was attached to an astonishing collection of earldoms. As previously noted, her father George Clifford was the flamboyant 3rd Earl of Cumberland. Her mother, Margaret Russell, was the daughter of the Earl of Bedford, a stalwart member of the royal administration of Queen Elizabeth I. Totaled, the number of earldoms that Anne held sway over came to seven after her two daughters from her first marriage both married earls. By the end of her life, her extended family included her Bedford cousins, her Clifford cousins, the Pembroke children, the Dorsets, the Thanets, the Northamptons, and the Burlingtons. She was on surprisingly affectionate terms with many of them, and, as might be expected, a thorn in the side of others (Acheson 133-183).

Anne's social standing contributes to her credibility as a historical witness. She was in a position at the top of the social register to be steeped in the cultural values and mindset of England's upper class in the seventeenth century. But this is only part of the reason why she is called as a witness in this literary question. Central to this study is Anne's education which led to her literary interests and later, her public display of erudition in her triptychs.

According to her biographer Richard Spence, her mother, the Countess of Cumberland (hereafter called Countess Margaret) hired the poet-historian Samuel Daniel to provide her daughter and heir with an education "not just equaling but superior to that [which] her male contemporaries received at the university." The beloved teacher of Anne's youth developed in her "a familiarity with the most widely studied works of her time" (12-14). For these reasons alone, there should not be the slightest possibility that Lady Anne was simply unaware of Shakespeare's work or unable to comprehend its literary significance.[3]

Anne's literary patronage is evident in her memorialization of Edmund Spenser. At his death in 1599, Spenser was buried in the Abbey, but exactly where in the South Transept was unknown (Prendergast 166).[4] In 1620, Lady Anne, then Countess of Dorset, paid the noted mason Nicholas Stone forty pounds for a monument so elaborate that it was considered to be above Spenser's station in life. The inscription on it linked Spenser to Chaucer, and was taken from a Latin treatise by William Camden (Spence 68). Decades later in 1654, Anne commissioned a wall monument for Samuel Daniel in the church in Beckington, Somerset. Again, the monument with its epitaph was "superior to that which his social position merited." Its classical style was enhanced with volutes, garlands and an open segmental pediment, and the bust of Daniel is attired in a Roman toga and a wreath (Spence 151, 154).

It is tempting to compare the two monuments with the sorrowful woolsack figure in the church in Stratford-upon-Avon, and propose that the Stratford monument would have been greatly improved had Anne Clifford taken charge of it. But in a more serious vein, Anne had the intellect and education to understand Shakespeare's literary merit, and the financial means to do for him what she did for Spenser and Daniel. That she did not is a signal that for some reason, "Shakespeare" simply did not resonate with the aristocracy in quite the same way that Spenser and Daniel did.

The Battle for the Clifford Properties

The events that led Anne to commission the two great paintings are the next piece of the puzzle. Historians give Anne credit for the legal victory that brought her the Clifford estates, and it is likely that her indomitable strength of will made the difference. Yet a closer look reveals that Anne's mother, Countess Margaret Russell, did the heavy lifting, especially in the early stages of the litigation. Countess Margaret took it badly when her estranged husband, Earl George, did not make Anne his heir, directing the Clifford properties to his brother rather than Anne, his only surviving child. In order to do this, Earl George broke the original entail from earlier centuries. "Breaking the entail" was a significant legal point of controversy: when King Edward II awarded the property to the Cliffords, the entail directed the inheritance to heirs general rather than to heirs male, so that the property would stay in the direct line whether the heir was male or female (Holmes 5-6).[5] When Earl George died in 1605, Countess Margaret moved quickly to file the lawsuits for her daughter's claim to the property. The Countess hired the best lawyers London had to offer, and saw to it that her daughter's case was argued with evidence from inquisitions, exemplifications of grants, charters, abstracts from wills, pedigrees and analogous cases.

Anne Clifford's mother did much of the laborious research herself. She frequented the chambers at Westminster where the records of the Exchequer were kept, and sought out vital documents in the Quo Warrento records which were in the custody of the Treasurer and the Chamberlain (Spence 40-58). Amazingly, the Countess's diligent efforts resulted in her discovery of a serious flaw in the arguments of the opposing counsel. This weakness became one of the mainstays of Anne's case and a major factor in the litigation (Spence 42).

An amusing story illustrates just how proactive Anne's mother was in the fight. In 1614, Countess Margaret came to London to be with her daughter as the birth of Anne's baby neared, and took the opportunity to visit the Tower of London to conduct research into the immense repository of the Chancery records. The Tower officials were closing early that day, and either the Countess did not know that, or they did not realize she was still there. She was accidentally locked inside the Tower of London overnight. By the time she was released the next day and made her way to Dorset House, the baby was born, and both Anne and the baby were doing well (Williamson 86; Spence 8).

Two years after Countess Margaret's unexpected sojourn in the Tower, King James took it upon himself to stop the legal battles. Called the King's Award, James intervened in 1616 to arbitrate a settlement. The terms of it were a disaster for Anne, and had she signed it, her biographers think that the Clifford properties would have been lost to her forever.

The King, the Archbishop of Canterbury, her husband the Earl of Dorset, and many other notable personages demanded her signature. Anne resisted, writing to her mother that she would not sign the King's Award "no matter what misery it costs me." And misery is what she got. Under the laws of coverture, Dorset, not Anne, would pocket the cash. Deeply in debt from his extravagant life style, Dorset was merciless. He needed the £20,000 settlement to cover his gambling losses. In an act intended to humiliate Anne, he dismissed her household staff, leaving her stranded at her mother's estate in northern England. He cancelled the jointure estates that he had settled on her when they married, taking away the income that would be her safety net if he died. Then ratcheting up the pressure even further, he took custody of their only child, her not yet two-year-old daughter, and hustled the little girl away to his brother's house. Still, Anne refused to relinquish her claim to the Clifford lands (Holmes 4, 49, 79, 87). The terms of the King's Award were finally put into effect by compulsion, and Dorset received the money.

A quarter of a century would pass before the last of the Clifford earls died in 1643 without a male heir, and, as previously noted, all of the properties of the Cumberland earldom went to Lady Anne. Although her longevity was the primary factor in winning back her father's properties, her perseverance in the litigation put her in a better legal position than she might otherwise have had to retrieve the lost estates. Anne Clifford had endured decades of disgraceful, vicious treatment, and had finally emerged victorious in the struggle for dominance. It made sense that she wanted the world to know of her triumph. But her personal victory could not have come at a worse time: England was in a civil war.

By 1643, Anne had been married to her second husband the Earl of Pembroke for thirteen years, but they had been separated for most of that time. Pembroke had been furious with Anne when he booted her out of his lodgings at the court in 1634, but in a strange twist, he must have felt her safe-keeping to be his duty with war in the offing. At his behest, Anne and her younger daughter Isabella Sackville took refuge at Baynard's Castle, his magnificent London property. Pembroke apparently thought Baynard's was his most defensible stronghold, moving his household goods from Wilton House to Baynard's early in the conflict. It was a mutually beneficial arrangement: Anne had a safe, comfortable refuge, and Pembroke had a house-sitter (or rather a castle-sitter) to watch over the Pembroke furnishings, silver, gold plate, tapestries and art collection.

Anne remained at Baynard's, the "House of Riches" as she called it, for seven years from 1642 until 1649. She was not idle during this time. From her mother, Anne Clifford had learned that collecting rents from the Westmorland tenants presented substantial challenges. These properties, among others, were now Anne's, and the eight hundred tenants on the Westmorland properties alone, not to mention her other estates, could be unruly. There were likely to be hundreds of law suits. Anne's mother had taught her the importance of "holding herself up as a model to be admired and followed" (Spence 138-145). This is where the triptychs come in.[6]

By the summer of 1649 the war had ended, and the small, aging woman departed from London with her two giant triptychs in tow, never to return.

The Great Pictures

A lot of information and imagery can be conveyed in a painting covering 162 square feet of wall space. A brief survey reveals fourteen figures, related inscriptions, coats of arms, memorabilia, jewels, armor, and furnishings. The center panel is bordered by several dozen shields and biographies going back six centuries.

The fifty books are the most striking feature of the triptychs, and have evoked much commentary over the centuries. In *Women, Reading and Cultural Politics in Early Modern England,* Edith Snook states that the books were there to "confirm her [Anne's] class position and substantiate her identity as a landowner" (1-3). These were power books, deliberately chosen to showcase her exceptional erudition when she received visiting nobility, gentry, officials, clergy, and even her tenants. Spence concurs that she expected her literary choices to be "appraised approvingly" (182, 195).

That the books were meant to impress the viewer makes the absence of Shakespeare all the more puzzling. But before discussing the possible reasons why Shakespeare is missing, an overview of the books worthy of inclusion is in order. (See **Appendix B** for a compilation of books and titles provided by Anne's biographers George Williamson and Richard Spence).

Called an "inventory of the furniture of the mind" by Graham Parry in his essay on the triptychs in *Art and Patronage in the Caroline Court* (202-219), the books shown in the triptychs represent the foremost authorities on important cultural subjects.

Along with three obligatory Holy Bibles, the heavy hitters appear on Anne's shelves: Plutarch and Seneca among the ancients and Chaucer and Castiglione among the more recent great writers. It is, however, the contemporary English writers that deserve the most attention. Starting with Edmund Spenser, there is a solid line up from the Elizabethan Romantic school of writers, some of them the hangers-on of the Sidney crowd. Beginning with Spenser and going down the line, one finds Philip Sidney's *Arcadia,* George Herbert's *Poems,* and Sir Fulke Greville's *Works.* One might note that Greville's most memorable literary effort was his hagiography of Sir Philip Sidney in which he perpetuated a variation of the infamous tennis court quarrel between the worthy Philip Sidney and the notorious Edward de Vere, the 17th Earl of Oxford (Looney 300).[7]

Anne Clifford's childhood teacher Samuel Daniel is commemorated with two books, his *Chronicles of England* and *All the Works in Verse;* plus he is singled out for an additional tribute with a background portrait and a laudatory inscription. Ben Jonson shows up with his *Works,* and his literary circle is represented with his mentor

162

William Camden's well received *Britannia*. John Donne, a member of Jonson's Mermaid Tavern group, is represented twice, both with his *Poems* and his *Sermons* (Riggs 192). Donne's close friend Sir Henry Wotton is present with his book on architecture. Pausing to reflect on these authors, it is the inclusion of Ben Jonson, the editor of Shakespeare's *First Folio*, that makes the absence of Shakespeare all the more imponderable. If Lady Anne thought stage plays undeserving of recognition, it is odd that she included Jonson's 1616 *Works*, the first large volume collection of plays published in England.

Samuel Daniel with books from left panel of Lady Anne's Triptych.
(Reproduced by courtesty of Abbot Hall Art Gallery, Kendall.)

It would seem that Shakespeare's work would go well alongside Ovid's *Metamorphosis*, as the Golding translation of Ovid had been one of the building blocks for his own canon. Or maybe Shakespeare might fit between John Florio's translation of Montaigne's *Essays* and John Gerard's *Herbal*, both utilized as Shakespearean sources.

In all, it appears that the books chosen for the triptych were from writers for whom Anne felt a warm personal inclination or those who were politically appropriate. Biographer Spence sums it up: here was a woman who "recognized the dues of friendship" while she "kept abreast of current political and religious issues" (193).

Ever-mindful of the academic imperatives, orthodox partisans tip-toe around Shakespearean irregularities – of which this is one. Martin Holmes does not comment on the absence of Shakespeare's *First Folio*, but infuses his book with Shakespearean quotations, a handy device to give Shakespeare a presence which in fact he does not have. Historian Spence is more forthright. Noting the "lacunae," as he calls it, he cleverly puts additional names on the table:

> The towering giants by today's criteria, Shakespeare and Milton, are absent, likewise Raleigh, Sir Francis Bacon and James I. In view of the Pembrokes' patronage, Shakespeare's absence is a little surprising… She may have had political and personal reservations about the rest (194).

Political and Personal Reservations

What might the political reservations have been? The absence of King James I is understandable: had Anne yielded to James' bullying arbitration, she would never have succeeded in her litigation. Both Bacon and Raleigh were disgraced: Bacon was charged with criminal conduct and had resigned his high offices; Raleigh had been executed for treason. In the mid-1640s, Milton was establishing himself as a Parliamentarian polemicist, and Anne was loyal to the Royalist cause. It would be two more decades before *Paradise Lost*,

Milton's most famous work, was published.

It is hard to see what problems Anne Clifford might have had with Shakespeare if the traditional story were true. Writing the account of Shakespeare's life for *The Dictionary of National Biography*, Sir Sidney Lee states: "The highest estimate was formed of Shakespeare's work by his contemporaries, by critics as well as playgoers." Noting the popularity of *Hamlet*, he goes on to stress Shakespeare's "literary power and sociability." Lee states that "Elizabeth quickly showed him special favor" and insists that "until the end of her reign, his plays were repeatedly acted in her presence" (1301, 1313). Moreover, it is well accepted that "Shakespeare" enjoyed the patronage of the Earl of Southampton (as per the dedications of *Venus and Adonis* and *Lucrece*); and if Ben Jonson's introduction to the *First Folio* can be believed, Anne's second husband and his brother "prosecuted both [the plays], and their Authour living, with so much favour."[8]

It is a different picture when the author of the Shakespeare works is thought to be Edward de Vere, the 17th Earl of Oxford. Now it gets personal. Anne Clifford was the step-mother of Oxford's grandchildren, and a possible cause of friction could have been the fact that Pembroke gave to Anne the property that King James had given as a wedding present to Pembroke's first Countess, Oxford's daughter Susan Vere. Parting with his first wife's property – lands that Susan's children could expect to inherit – might cause some serious rancor between his children and their step-mother. Also, Anne may not have wanted to commemorate in her own family memorial the publication of a work written by the father of Pembroke's first wife.

More to the point is the political perspective of the aristocracy. As "Shakespeare," Edward de Vere wrote about the people he knew. In an article published in *The Washington Post*, Roger Stritmatter states that "The author aired the power elites' dirty laundry through literary indirection, and used stage symbolism to conduct his own fiercely partisan feuds." Stritmatter describes the "audacious liberties" taken by the author of *Hamlet*, and many English historians have agreed that Polonius in *Hamlet* is a characterization of William Cecil, Lord Burghley (Bevington 321).[9] No doubt, Anne Clifford (and the upper strata of Tudor, Jacobean and Carolinian society) would have known of the deep-seated bitterness between the Cecils and the Veres, and Anne's natural inclination went with the Cecils.

This inclination, as it were, is supported by a long-standing political alliance between the Cecils and the Russells. As part of the Protestant Reformation, William Cecil and the Earl of Bedford had been new men in Henry VIII's court. The political influence of both families grew with their prosperity during the reign of Edward VI. By the early days of Queen Elizabeth I, they were neighbors with adjacent London estates at Covent Garden. In 1561, Cecil sent "trusty Bedford" to France to deal with ramifications of the recently widowed Queen of Scots (Smith 80, 85). It would be no surprise to Elizabethan insiders that when the rich Cumberland wardship came into his hands, William Cecil, then Master of the Royal Wards, allocated the guardianship of young George, Earl of Cumberland, to the Earl of Bedford.[10] In the next century, Earl George Clifford's brother married his son to Robert Cecil's daughter Frances Cecil, and it was proposed that he did this to gain Robert Cecil's support for his side of the litigation over the Clifford estates (Spence 21-22).

Anne's alignment with the Russell and the Cecil families should be clearly recognized. When Anne was a child, her father, the Earl of Cumberland, deserted her mother, and Countess Margaret went to live in the homes of her Russell sisters. In addition to her mother's tutelage, Anne is said to have had her "chief breeding" under the direction of her aunt, Lady Warwick, who prepared her for the instruction she would later receive from Samuel Daniel. The Russell aunts also provided Anne with her training in music, dancing and drama. Anne understood her mother's bitterness toward her father, and when this is combined with her upbringing in Russell houses, it stands to reason that Anne Clifford grew up to be a Russell at heart. She would later model herself on her mother's successful proprietorship of her Westmoreland jointure lands, seeking to be "tough, resolute and lordly until she had full command of her lands and rights" (Spence 3, 14-15, 27).

The backing from her Russell relatives continued throughout Anne's life. Her faithful cousin Francis Russell, the 4th Earl of Bedford, was indispensable in promoting her welfare. His presence is seen at crucial junctures: countering the influence of her late husband Dorset's brother at King Charles' court; negotiating the marriage arrangements for Anne's daughter Margaret and giving her away at her wedding; later negotiating the terms of Anne's formal settlement at her separation from the Earl of Pembroke (Holmes 95; Spence 88-89, 91, 101).

Thus the protracted fight for the Cumberland properties was not entirely a contest between two lines of the Clifford family, but a battle between the Cliffords and the Russells. In Richard Spence' assessment, Anne's father recognized these dynamics, and "George had worried that if his inheritance came to Anne, it would be to a Russell in mentality who would take it out of the family" (17).

The Meaning of the Triptychs

At the outset, the triptychs would be perceived as the physical embodiment of Anne Clifford's great patrimony. The shields and inscriptions bordering the center panel supported her chain of title to the Clifford properties, proclaiming the legitimacy of her claim to the lands that made her rich. The books were there to signal wealth and authority. Books were costly and "ordinary men, even professional men, would not be able to afford so many" (Snook 9).[11] The sheer size and grandeur of the paintings would leave those who looked upon them gasping in open-mouthed awe.

Yet the presence of the books opens the door to something more significant than mere admiration. The triptych destined for Appleby manor would be bequeathed to her older daughter along with the Westmoreland estates; the Skipton Castle triptych would ultimately be part of her younger daughter's inheritance along with the Craven lands. The triptychs were a bridge to future generations, serving as literal, tangible icons of the new dynasty that Anne envisioned for her two daughters. Moreover, the books were freighted to carry a cultural message. Along with the wealth that future generations would inherit, these books on a broad spectrum of important subjects would instruct them on the best in intellectual thought throughout the ages. In short, the books are a vital part of the cultural heritage that Anne Clifford wanted her posterity to understand, appreciate, and uphold.

If the orthodox story of Shakespeare's life is true, an observer may ponder why Shakespeare's works are missing. Far from being left out, Shakespeare should have been given a prominent place on the canvas, especially when considering the Pembrokes' patronage of Shakespeare's *First Folio* plus its cost of production which made it one of the most expensive books printed at the time.

It has been suggested that Anne might have had a bit of pique with Shakespeare for the "vengeful" characterization of a Clifford ancestor in *2 Henry VI* and *3 Henry VI*. This explanation might hold some water had the story originated with Shakespeare, but it had long been in the public domain, published in 1548 in *Hall's Chronicles,* in 1559 in William Baldwin's popular *Mirror for Magistrates,* and in the 1587 edition of *Holinshed's Chronicles* (Bullough 160-161, 178, 181-182, 209).[12] Also, more options were available had Anne wanted to display something other than the *First Folio* itself. She could have placed a favorite quarto, say, *Romeo and Juliet,* next to *Don Quixote,* or showcased one of Shakespeare's great lyric poems if her taste ran to verse rather than drama. After all, his *Venus and Adonis* and his *Lucrece* enjoyed public acceptance and critical acclaim. According to the *Riverside Shakespeare, Venus and Adonis* was Shakespeare's most popular work during his lifetime, and *Lucrece,* along with *Hamlet, Prince of Denmark,* were remarked by Cambridge University don Gabriel Harvey to "have it in them to please the wiser sort" (1704, 1720).

When the triptychs were underway in the 1640's, the Civil War was going strong. It was a time of violent social upheaval; both the monarchy and the aristocracy were fighting for their very survival. Princeton University historian Lawrence Stone states that during this time of Revolution, "the stock of the aristocracy was lower than it had ever been before or was to be again for centuries" (350). It was possible that the works of Shakespeare could impact the outcome in this struggle.

Mark Anderson points out in *Shakespeare By Another Name* that the "Shakespeare ruse" was "a subterfuge that distanced the scandalous works from its primary subjects: the queen and her powerful inner circle of advisors" (xxxiii). If "Shakespeare's" identity was revealed, the identities of the people in the plays would be publicly unveiled, possibly fueling even greater public animosity toward the aristocracy. Many a reputation might be tarnished, perhaps beyond redemption. For a noblewoman like Lady Anne who sided with the Royalists during the war years, the plays of Shakespeare held dangerous implications. It is easy to understand that a spirit of co-operation could exist among the aristocracy to maintain a dignified silence regarding Shakespeare and his works (Whalen 115-117).[13]

Like the dog that did not bark, Anne Clifford knew who Shakespeare was. She also knew why his work was not acceptable to her peers. So Anne followed the smartest course of action; she left him out. Perhaps along with the better informed members of the other ruling families, she hoped that the Shakespeare problem would just fade away. It could be that the Shakespeare canon would become no more than an esoteric offering to posterity, a quaint oddity along the lines of the Elizabethan neck ruff. Something succeeding generations could well do without.

Taken at face value, these two paintings were advertisements of Anne's authority and the legitimacy of her patrimony. Next, they would serve to inculcate her children and her children's children with their illustrious place in the social order. Lady Anne Clifford had every reason to believe that her Great Pictures would continue to carry her message long into perpetuity. Ironically, she left out the one whose legacy would prove to be the most enduring.

Notes

1. The Skipton Triptych was more accessible than the Appleby
    Triptych, and was reproduced in a fine water color (still extant)
    by George Perfect Harding. Spence concludes that both trip-
    tychs were substantively alike, though minor differences did
    exist.

2. Foister notes that while he was a member of London's Paint-
    ers-Stainers Company, Jan von Belchamp was sent to France
    to paint portraits of the King and Queen, and while there was
    responsible for imaginary portraits of royal ancestors.

3. As Samuel Daniel was the primary influence in Lady Anne's
    education, his own familiarity with Shakespeare's writings
    should be noted. *The Riverside Shakespeare* credits Daniel's *Civ-
    il Wars* as a source for *Richard II*, stating that Shakespeare is
    "probably indebted" to Samuel Daniel. Daniel's *DNB* biogra-
    pher (5:480) goes more deeply into the matter of Daniel's in-
    debtedness to Shakespeare with this critique of Daniel's work:
    "His epic on the civil wars fails as a poem. It is merely histori-
    cal narrative, very rarely relieved by imaginative episode. Some
    alterations made in the 1609 edition were obviously suggested
    by a perusal of Shakespeare's *Richard II*." An alert reader will
    also find that Geoffrey Bullough concurs with the *DNB* in Vol-
    ume III of his *Narrative and Dramatic Sources of Shakespeare* (375).
    The questioned is: Who was "indebted" to whom?

4. In his book *Poetical Dust*, Prendergast provides much detail
    about Spenser's burial in the Abbey. He also credits Lady Anne
    Clifford with erecting the monument to the poet Michael Dray-
    ton in 1631 (64). It is more likely that the subsequent Countess
    of Dorset, the wife of Edward Sackville, was responsible for
    Drayton's monument, for by this time Anne had remarried
    and was the Countess of Pembroke. Nevertheless, it could still
    be argued that Earl Edward's Countess was influenced by her
    predecessor.

5. In chapters one and two, Holmes gives a sympathetic account of Anne's youth, the death of her father, and the disputed inheritance.

6. It has been suggested that Anne was inspired by or wanted to outdo the Van Dyke portrait of her second husband and his family (Howarth 226-226, 304).

7. The Oxford/Sidney rivalry existed ostensibly on literary grounds between competing court poets of the Euphuist and Romantic schools respectively. Looney recognized the "social tendencies" inherent in this dichotomy, noting the "glamour that has gathered round one name and the shadow that has remained over the other." Anne's inclusion of Philip Sidney's *Arcadia* and exclusion of the Euphuist school (of which Shakespeare's *Love's Labours' Lost* is an example) indicates that this trend was taking hold by the mid-1600s.

8. This statement appears in the Epsitle Dedicatory to the *First Folio* that is signed by the two actors, John Heminge and Henry Condell: "but since your L.L. [Lordships] have been pleas'd to think the trifles something, heretofore; and have prosecuted both them, and the Author living, with so much favor: we hope that (they out-living him, and he not having the fate, common with some, to be executor to his own writings) you will use the like indulgence toward them…" (spelling modernized).

9. The Polonius identification was first put forth by John Russell French in the nineteenth century. Among the twentieth century historians who concur are Lawrence Stone, Joel Hurstfield, Alan Gordon Smith, and Susan James.

10. Hurstfield remarks that everyone in Tudor England knew that guardianship "was a means to an end: marriage;" and a guardian often bestowed his ward in marriage with his own daughter, sometimes bringing the ward's property into his own family holdings (129).

11. Snook footnotes information on book ownership in past centuries from Richard Altick's *The English Common Reader*, Ohio State University Press, 2002.

12. In *Narrative and Dramatic Sources of Shakespeare*, Geoffrey Bullough published the material from these three sources for the scenes in *2Henry VI* and *3 Henry VI*.

13. Whalen proposes that Oxford's authorship of the Shakespeare canon was an "open secret" at the time, and recalls the secrets of twentieth century Presidents: Roosevelt (crippling polio), Kennedy (womanizing) and Wilson (disabling stroke). These secrets were successfully kept from the public even in the "intense scrutiny" of modern journalism.

Chapter
9

A Countess Transformed
How Lady Susan Vere Became Lady Anne Clifford

Since the sixteenth century, Wilton House has been the country manor home of the Earls of Pembroke, and among its treasures is a large painting centered on the wall of the majestic Double Cubed Room. This room was specifically designed by the seventeenth century architect Inigo Jones to display this painting which spans seventeen feet across and is eleven feet high. Considered the greatest painting of an English family ever made, it is "a perfect school unto itself"[1] in the oeuvre of the Flemish artist Anthony Van Dyck. Ten life-size figures, costumed in shimmering satins, are elegantly arranged across the canvas. At the viewer's left is a pastoral landscape, and it might seem that the three cherubs coming through the top of the opening bring with them a breeze, gently stirring the drapery swag on the right side of the painting. Behind the Earl and Countess of Pembroke is a large shield with the coats-of-arms from past generations of Herbert marriages; the columns symbolize the durability of the family dynasty into the future.

However, it is not the brilliance of the painting or its importance in art history that is of interest, but the identity of the woman in black with her arms folded, sitting beside Philip Herbert, the 4th Earl of Pembroke (hereafter called "Pembroke"). In the 1968 catalogue *Paintings and Drawings at Wilton House*, she is identified as Pembroke's second wife, Lady Anne Clifford. The official reason for this identification is that Pembroke was married to her when the portrait was painted. We will determine if this attribution can stand up to scrutiny when the portrait is considered in its historical context.

We should also note that during Pembroke's long marriage to his first wife, Susan Vere, the *First Folio* of William Shakespeare was published (in 1623). Philip Herbert was, during this marriage, the 1st Earl of Montgomery. His older brother William Herbert was the 3rd Earl of Pembroke. They are the "incomparable paire of brethren" to whom the *Folio* was dedicated.[2] The familial relationship between the Herbert brothers and Edward de Vere, the 17th Earl of Oxford, was cemented by the marriage of Philip Herbert and Susan Vere in 1604.[3] Also, we should remember that Susan's father, Edward de Vere, is a leading candidate for the authorship of the works of Shakespeare canon.

In my view the woman seated at Pembroke's side is not his second wife, Anne Clifford – per the Wilton House catalogue – but his first wife, Susan Vere. If so, then let us suggest that the substitution of Anne Clifford for Susan Vere in the Van Dyck painting may have something to do with the authorship issue.[4] The presence of Susan Vere opens the door to issues which have been largely unexplored. First of all, there is the question of the Herbert brothers' motivation for lending their names and political clout to the publication of the *First Folio*. It may be that their motivation was the preservation of the masterpieces of a family patriarch, an interest not shown by the descendants of the Stratfordian Shakespeare. Another problem with the publication of the *First Folio* is the expense of the project; any publisher would need a funding source for what Charlton Hinman describes as a "decidedly chancy venture." The wealthy Herbert brothers were the likely source of the "considerable outlay of capital" needed to finance it (x, xi).

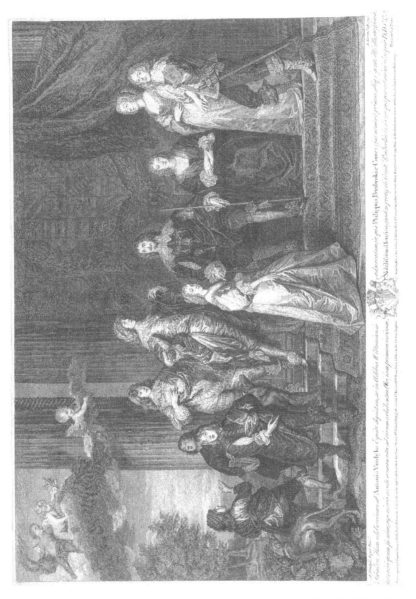

The Pembroke Family, engraving by Bernard Baron (1740) of Van Dyck's painting of the Pembroke Family, courtesy of the National Portrait Gallery, London. The orginal by Van Dyck is available in color at various websites such as wikipedia.org, if one searches for Philip_Herbert,_4th_Earl_of_Pembroke,_with_his_Family.jpg

With much at stake, the identity of the Countess in Van Dyck's painting takes on special import, and the circumstances of Pembroke's two marriages must be examined. In 1604, the court of King James was bustling with the news of the marriage of the handsome young Philip Herbert and Susan Vere, the third daughter of the 17th Earl of Oxford (Chamberlain 198; Aiken 205).[5]

It was considered a love match, a surprising occurrence in a time when marriages were arranged for dynastic aggrandizement. Even more remarkable is the largesse that King James bestowed on the union. He was, in effect, the wedding planner, financing the celebration which went on for days at enormous cost, and supplying the new couple with gifts of money and property, even fulfilling the patriarchal duty of providing Susan Vere with her marriage portion. The King walked the bride down the aisle at Whitehall Palace, accompanied by his royal family. In a statement not often reiterated by historians, King James is reported to have said that had he not already been a married man, he would have married Susan Vere himself, rather than give her to his favorite Philip Herbert (Carleton 66-67). The next morning, the King showed up bright and early for a firsthand account of their wedding night. Susan and Phillip managed to have ten children, presumably without the King's supervision, and their marriage of approximately twenty-five years ended when Susan died from smallpox in 1629.

Not long after Susan's death, Philip Herbert's older brother William died and Philip inherited the Pembroke title and properties. He remarried in 1630. His choice, Lady Anne Clifford, was unexpected for, in the words of a Herbert family biographer, her "attractions could not have been conspicuous" (Lever 98).[6] It is odd that the eligible bachelor took on the widow of the Earl of Dorset, a stubborn woman whose negotiating skills had been well honed in decades of legal battles with her Clifford cousins. She had put up a fight of such magnitude to reclaim the Clifford properties that she considered rightfully hers that King James stepped in to referee the legal bloodbath. When his royal judgment went against her, she refused to accept it, withstanding enormous pressure from her first husband, the Earl of Dorset, and just about everybody attached to the royal court. We can gauge Anne's strength of character in one of her letters, in which she wrote that she would not accept the

King's Award "no matter what misery it cost me." The King's decision, put in place without her consent, allowed the Clifford men to keep the Clifford estates, and the money intended as a settlement for Anne was snapped up by her husband Dorset for his own use (Spence 40-58).

Unsurprisingly, Anne brought a steely determination to her marriage with Philip, and it is even less surprising that the marriage was a disaster, certainly from Philip's point of view. The marriage ended after four years when Philip cast her out of his lodgings in Whitehall Palace in December of 1634, leaving himself "virtually widowed a second time" (Spence 99-101).

When Did Van Dyck Paint the Pembroke Family?

Some historians suggest that Van Dyck began the painting of Pembroke and his family in 1634. This would have been impossible as Van Dyck was out of the country from October of 1633 until March of 1635 (Barnes et al. 8-9, 573).[7] Van Dyck could not have begun work on this painting until the summer of 1635, when the negotiations for the final separation between Pembroke and Lady Anne were completed. The formal separation was signed on June 5, 1635, and given Pembroke's temper and Anne's obstinacy, it is a safe bet that the discussions had not been pleasant.

As bad as it was to be turned out of Pembroke's palace lodgings, the greater problem for Anne Clifford was that she was effectively banished from the court of King Charles as well. According to her biographer Richard Spence, "it was a catastrophic collapse of her status and her cause" (99, 101). Moreover, even Anne's own biographers agree that this enormous breach was her fault.

What Pembroke sought in marrying Anne was a marriage between her younger daughter, Isabella Sackville, and one of his younger sons (Wilkinson 209; Nicholson 222; Holmes 132; Spence 101). A union of their families in the next generation would give Pembroke a claim to the properties of the Cumberland earldom, provided Anne was successful in her lawsuits to claim her father's land. By 1634, it was time to formalize the betrothal of his son and her daughter – something that Pembroke considered part of their agreement when they married four years earlier.

On December 18, 1634, Pembroke had apparently called her hand and found that his wife could not be prevailed upon to finalize an engagement between Isabella and his son. Pure and simple, Anne wanted Isabella to marry an Earl. A younger son, even a scion of the prestigious Pembroke family, just was not good enough. Pembroke's fury toward his second wife is understandable in light of the fact that she reneged on their deal. Not only was it a breach of good faith, but a humiliating rejection of his family (Wilkinson 290; Spence 111). It should be out of the question that Pembroke would choose to immortalize Anne Clifford in his family celebration portrait.

Lady Mary Villiers

The beautiful young woman in the luminous silver dress can hardly be overlooked. She is Lady Mary Villiers, and it is fitting that she is the central figure in the portrait, for it is her place in the Pembroke family group that Van Dyck's remarkable work of art was intended to commemorate. .

Mary Villiers was the daughter of George Villiers, the Duke of Buckingham, whose rise to the top ranks of the English nobility is well known. Mary was his first born child, and after his assassination in 1628, she was taken into the royal household where she was raised as the "spoilt pet of the court" (Wilkinson 297).[8] Her marriage contract had been signed in 1626 when she was four years old and Charles Herbert was seven. Her dowry, a staggering £25,000, would go into the coffers of the Pembroke family once the marriage was solemnized (Nicolson 222).[9]

Another element in the story is the munificence that King Charles I bestowed on the Flemish master painter Anthony Van Dyck. Van Dyck was knighted in 1632, and, upon his return to England in March of 1635, the King himself paid the rent on Van Dyck's resplendent waterfront studio at Blackfriars, even building a causeway for his more convenient access to it by boat. Replete with musicians and sumptuous banquets, Van Dyck's studio rapidly became the principal gathering place for the Caroline Court. An observer wrote that the Van Dyck workshop "was frequented by the highest nobles, for example the King, who came daily to see him and took great delight in watching him paint and lingering with him" (Gordenker 10).

It is easy to connect the dots: King Charles visited Van Dyck's studio regularly, and he could hardly have missed the massive painting of the Pembroke Family taking shape before his eyes – even more compelling as Mary Villiers, the favorite of the royal court, occupied center stage in the family group. After the banishment of Lady Anne, it is bizarre to suggest that Pembroke would rehabilitate her before the King and his court in the Pembroke family dynastic portrait. By contrast, Pembroke's first wife, Susan Vere, had been well thought of in court circles. In his book *The Earls of Paradise*, Adam Nicolson acknowledges that Philip's first marriage was "a love-match with a beautiful and universally admired woman" (180-181).

There is a sad postscript regarding the young couple who are celebrated in the painting. Following the custom of separating newlyweds due to the youth of the bride, Charles, the young Lord Herbert, was sent to Italy where he died of smallpox soon after his arrival in Florence (Lever 105; Nicolson 230-231). Philip "took the news most grievously," and, eventually, the lucrative Villiers dowry was returned (Nicolson 221-223, 230-231).[10]

Historical Notice of Van Dyck's Pembroke Family Portrait

In assessing the context of the painting, David Howarth, an art historian at the University of Edinburgh, has this to say in his book *Images of Rule*:

> To Pembroke's left a woman sits huddled in black. It has come to be assumed that her tense, sullen isolation indicates Pembroke's second wife, Lady Anne Clifford, with whom Pembroke had contracted a loveless marriage. However, this woman is shrouded in black, hands folded on stomach as was conventional in recumbent effigies of the dead, and it was presumably these features which made [Freeman] O'Donoghue in his catalogue of the British portrait prints in the British Museum, suggest that this disconsolate creature is in fact a posthumous likeness of Pembroke's first

wife, Lady Susan Vere. This is surely right (226-227).

It is significant that an expert of Howarth's stature disputes the attribution of Lady Anne Clifford. In addition to the sitter's somber appearance, Howarth might have mentioned that it is written at the base of the 1740 engravings by Bernard Baron that the principal sitters are "Philip Herbert… with his wife Susan Vere." When Freeman O'Donoghue published his catalogue in 1922, he was simply following the historical information (49).[11]

The Earliest Records

Along with the Baron engravings of 1740, four eighteenth century catalogues contain inventories of the paintings and art at Wilton House. The first, published in 1731 by Gambarini of Lucca, refers to the Earl's "Lady, Daughter to the Earl of Oxford" (8-9). In later catalogues authored by Richard Cowdry and James Kennedy, the name of the "lady's" father is eliminated, but the description implies that the Earl's lady is Susan Vere:

> This consists of ten whole Lengths, the two principal Figures (and they are sitting) are Philip Earl of Pembroke and his Lady; on the Right-Hand stand their five sons Charles Lord Herbert, Philip, (afterwards Lord Herbert) William, James, and John; on the Left their Daughter Anna Sophia , and her Husband Robert Earl of Carnarvon; before them Lady Mary, Daughter of George Duke of Buckingham, and wife to Charles, Lord Herbert; and above in the Clouds are two Sons and a Daughter who died young (Cowdry 58; Kennedy 53).

There is no question that the children in the portrait, referred to as "their five sons" and "their Daughter," are Susan Vere's children. There were no children from Pembroke's marriage to Anne Clifford. However, Susan's name is only implied because the children are hers. This does seem to be a bit of an oversight. After all, Susan Vere was the daughter of an Earl and the granddaughter of Lord Burghley, whose position in Elizabethan government needs no elaboration here. There is no difficulty identifying Lady Mary

Villiers, referenced in these very catalogues as the "Daughter of George Duke of Buckingham." It should not be too much to ask that "his Lady" be recognized both by her name and aristocratic lineage. In the fourth and last of these catalogues, Richardson's *Aedes Pembrochianae*, her identity is revived; she is again "Susan, daughter of Edward, Earl of Oxford" (74).

In addition to the catalogues, posterity also has an eyewitness account from a traveler to Wilton House in 1738:

> And now I am gone so far I am come to the grand point, the account of the great picture, my heart begins to fail me . . . and a bold undertaking it is for me, to give you any account of the noble picture . . . On my Lord's left hand sits my Lady in a great chair, all in black, with her hands before her in a great tranquility: she was Susan, daughter to Edward, Earl of Oxford (Wilkinson 302-303).

In 1801, the antiquarian John Brittan wrote an extended account of the Van Dyck portrait in his *Beauties of Wiltshire*, mostly describing the unfortunate cleaning processes to which the painting had been subjected. At this time, Philip is still sitting next to "Susan his wife" (180). The last time that her name appears in print as the Earl's Countess is in an 1823 guidebook. The authors J. P. Neale and T. Moule identify the sitters as "Philip, Earl of Pembroke, and Susan his countess, daughter of Edward, Earl of Oxford."[12]

These sources demonstrate that it was understood for nearly two centuries the Earl's "Lady" was Susan Vere. The change of the sitter's identity from his first wife to the second is a subsequent phenomenon. But when was this change made?

The Nineteenth Century

Notices of the painting are few and far between in the nineteenth century. Writing in 1824 in his *Picture Galleries of England*, William Hazlitt notes that "there are the old Lord and Lady Pembroke" (106-107). "Old Lady Pembroke," as he calls her, has no name at all, but she is not quite yet Lady Anne Clifford. Continuing in his customary gruff tone, Hazlitt describes the Earl's Countess as "his help-mate looking a little fat and sulky by his side..." On behalf of the Royal Gallery in Berlin, in 1838 Director Gustav Waagen published a multi-volume tome: *Art and Artists in England*. Van Dyck's painting is now of "The Earl and His Countess." Again, the name of the Countess is omitted, but in a tiny slip twixt cup and lip, Waagen notes that "her daughter," Anna Sophia, is to "her left" (153).[13]

After Waagen, there are only occasional references to the portrait, and these recall Horace Walpole's *Anecdotes of Painting in England*. Published in the late eighteenth century, Walpole's book is the source of the oft quoted (and previously mentioned) praise that the Van Dyck portrait of the Pembroke family "would serve alone as a school of this master." However, Walpole avoided mentioning any of the sitters by name; later commentaries, based on his observations, are also silent on this point.

Twentieth Century Commentary

Now we turn our attention to the distinguished authority and art connoisseur, Sir Lionel Cust. He was the curator of the National Portrait Gallery, editor of the *Burlington Magazine*, and a member of The Shakespeare Birthplace Trust (xix). In 1900 he published a supposedly definitive volume on the work of Anthony Van Dyck in which he has this to say about what he calls this "work of great importance."

> The principal painting there [at Wilton House] is the immense composition representing the fourth Earl of Pembroke with his second wife, Anne Clifford, and his family, including his son Philip, Lord Herbert, afterwards fifth Earl of Pembroke, his son's wife Penelope Naunton, and also his daughter Anne Sophia, with her husband Robert Dormer, Earl of Carnarvon (119).

Cust's identification seems to be the line of demarcation for the official attribution of Anne Clifford as the Earl's lady in black, and this identification has been adhered to throughout the twentieth century (with the exception of O'Donoghue's catalogue and Howarth's book). Aside from the introduction of Anne Clifford onto the canvas, Cust made an obvious mistake when he substituted

Penelope Naunton for Mary Villiers. Where did Penelope Naunton come from? A quick check in any book about the peerage will reveal that Penelope, the wealthy heiress of Ralph Naunton, married Paul, Viscount Bayning in 1634 and was widowed in 1638, thereby freeing up her person and her pocketbook for the Pembroke earldom. When she married Philip, Lord Herbert in 1639, the paint on Van Dyck's canvas was quite dry (Lever 106).

In 1907, a new catalogue of the Wilton House treasures was published. The author, Nevile R. Wilkinson, had been a Captain of Her Majesty's Coldstream Regiment of Foot Guards, but perhaps his qualifications for the task of an art historian were enhanced by his marriage to a daughter of the 16th Earl of Pembroke. In his grand two-volume folio – later referred to as the *Great Catalogue* – Captain Wilkinson repeats the Anne Clifford attribution. His chapter about the 4th Earl of Pembroke and his family contains four pages extolling the virtues of Lady Anne, while Susan Vere's name appears only once, specifically as the mother of one of Pembroke's children. For all practical purposes, Susan Vere disappears, as the nearly anonymous first wife.

In 1922, Dr. George C. Williamson contributed to the proliferation of the Anne Clifford identification in the Van Dyck portrait. Williamson was the author of an impressive array of books on literary, historical and cultural subjects, and it was surely his endorsement that sealed the deal, so to speak (40).[14] In his limited edition biography of Anne Clifford, he went to great lengths to describe her "grave countenance" in Van Dyck's painting (349).

Portraits of Two Countesses

At this point it would be helpful to have a portrait to work from that is a likeness of Susan Vere. In a catalogue from 1842 titled *A Hand-Book to Public Galleries of Art In and Near London*, there is a listing of a "Portrait of a Lady in Rich Dress" at the Dulwich Picture Gallery. Here, it is identified as a portrait of "Susan Vere, first wife of Philip Earl of Pembroke."[15] Better yet, it is listed as a painting by Van Dyck. It would be just what the doctor ordered for comparison, even though the compiler of the catalogue observed that the painting was in poor condition, noting that it "has suffered terribly" (Jameson 464). Since the 1842 attribution, the identity of the painter has been changed from Van Dyck to Cornelius Johnson the Elder, and the identity of the sitter is officially classified as unknown. Now called *A Lady in Blue*, it remains in the collection of the Dulwich Picture Gallery, London.

Since the *Lady in Blue* is not an established portrait of Susan Vere, we cannot be sure what she looked like. However, there are many paintings of Anne Clifford, and quite a different face is apparent in them all. Anne Clifford was painted often and consistently over the entirety of her life, and the lack of resemblance between her portraits and Van Dyck's sitter are compelling evidence that she is not Earl Philip's Countess in his family painting. At approximately age twenty-eight, Anne sat for William Larkin

Detail from Lady in Blue.
Reproduced by permission of the Dulwich Picture Gallery.

and the next year for Paul van Somer, both distinguished artists of
the era (Strong 26-27, 313). A likeness of Anne in a private collection dates from 1629, a year before her marriage to Earl Philip.
Attributed to Gerard Honthorst, this portrait is the closest in time to
Van Dyck's family portrait. There are two representations of her by
Peter Lely in the mid to late 1640s; they correspond almost exactly
to her portrait in the right panel of her great triptych painted in
the mid-1640s, about a decade after Van Dyck painted the Pembroke family (Spence 74-77, 93, 112-113).

Noticing the ten year lapse between the Lely paintings and Van
Dyck's portrait of the Pembroke family, Anne's biographer Spence
remarked how much she had aged in "the intervening years," perhaps hoping to explain why Lely's paintings bear no resemblance
to Van Dyck's Countess (111). It should not be even a remote possibility that Van Dyck could fail to capture such elementary elements
as Anne's dark hair and her distinctive features with the dimple in

Portrait of Lady Anne Clifford by William Larkin, c. 1618/19.
Reproduced by permission of the National Portrait Gallery Picture Library.

her chin.[16]

Despite the lack of similitude between the portraits of Anne Clifford and the sitter in the Van Dyck, her identification continues to be perpetuated by her twentieth century biographers, who put their imaginations to work to account for the sitter's remote, withdrawn appearance, disengaged from the family group. Martin Holmes describes her "detachment" (128); Spence calls her look an "oblivious gaze" (102). Neither biographer can explain why the Countess is clothed in basic, somber black, a stark contrast to her husband with his rich Garter regalia and the colorfully attired young people around her.

Clues to the Paradox

The costuming itself is an indication that the presence of Susan Vere in the painting is a fiction, an example of what one authority calls "the typical Jacobean taste for ingenuity in paradox" (Lightbrown 148). Emilie Gordenker discusses how Van Dyck used clothing to fictionalize his subjects, placing them "between the actual world and the realm of mythology" (52, 62). That the lady in black is not in the opulent dress of a countess, while all the other figures are elaborately attired, sends a signal that her status is different. In addition, Countess Susan is the only one of the ten figures who is not even in contemporaneous court dress. She is fictionalized through her costume, and the three cherubs floating at the top left corner are obvious allegorical iconography that further enhances the fictionalization of the family group (53).

The folded, overlapped arms of the sitter in black are another clue that the she is Pembroke's deceased wife, not his living, estranged one. Van Dyck uses this pose in only one other portrait: that of Cecilia Crofts. According to Malcolm Rogers, "Her arms are folded in a cradling gesture over her womb, perhaps indicating that she was pregnant when the portrait was painted" (222-223). It seems that the folded hands and cradled arms are associated with motherhood, an appropriate motif for the matriarch of a dynasty (Millar 240).[17] A closer look at Cecilia Crofts reveals that her arms are more rounded, her fingers more delicate and loose than Pembroke's Countess. Though the pose is essentially the same, Cecilia

Crofts appears graceful and natural. Again, the skill of the master painter is apparent in these subtle effects. Cecilia Crofts' arms are curved and gentle; the arms of Pembroke's Lady are squared and rigid.

If you were standing before this painting in the Double Cube Room at Wilton House – and could see it clearly without being blinded by the magnificence of the room and its treasures – you might notice that the Countess is "noticeably thinly painted" in comparison to the rest of the figures (Barnes 573). The austere Countess is a foremost example of Van Dyck's "miraculous rendering of surface textures" (Ollard 197). She is ethereal. A gossamer figure captured in the thin paint. She is not quite there, even on the canvas, in the same way that the other family members are.

The contrast between this stationary figure and the rest of the family, in motion about her, could not be more striking. It could be a scene from a well-choreographed ballet. Reaching for her husband's hand, daughter Anna Sophia has just found her place next to her mother. Her husband, the Earl of Carnarvon, is moving up to the next step, as is Mary Villiers, who turns to glance back at the viewer. Pembroke is turning and gesturing to his right, as if he was introducing his heir to his bride (Moir 114). The two older boys are turning towards him, flaunting their attire, and one of the three younger boys is looking upwards, as if the cherubs floating above were a distraction. Amidst the moving figures, the thinly painted woman gazes vacantly away, and her stillness is palpable.

Clearly, the purpose of the painting was to celebrate the Pembroke family dynasty. It is reasonable that Countess Susan Vere would be given the respect she is due at her husband's side, as the dynastic survival of the Pembroke family was assured by the children of their marriage. David Howarth comments that "It was entirely appropriate that Van Dyck should have included the mother of Pembroke's children. The spirit of the Earl's first wife thus compliments the presence of Lady Mary Villiers, by whom Pembroke expected to be provided with grandchildren" (227).

In summary, there are five reasons for the Susan Vere identification: (1) the breakup of the marriage between Pembroke and his second wife; (2) the eighteenth century historical identifications; (3) the sitter's lack of resemblance to Lady Anne's established portraits;

(4) the rigid, funereal pose of the sitter with the fictionalized attire and symbolism of matriarchy, all rendered in thin paint by Van Dyck; and (5) the logical expectation that the matriarch of a dynasty would be represented in the family dynastic portrait.

Twentieth century scholars use the marriage of Pembroke and Anne Clifford to justify their identification of her in the painting, in spite of the circumstances of their *de facto* divorce.[18] Granted, it would have been a departure from real time for Pembroke to put his deceased wife at his side in this family group: doing so is called "chronological incongruity" by art historians. Therefore, one question is still on the table: were posthumous likenesses used in other paintings of the era?

Chronological Incongruity in Art

Another example of chronological irregularity, as well as an example of the custom of commemorating lifetime landmarks in works of art, can be found in the charming family gathering of Henry VIII. In this painting, the King celebrates his decision to put his two daughters back in the line of succession in 1544 (Starkey 30-31). Henry's son and heir Prince Edward is dutifully standing at his father's right knee. The Queen chosen for the place of honor at the King's left is his third wife, Jane Seymour, who died giving birth to the Prince six years earlier. Of course, in real time, Henry was happily married (more or less) to his sixth wife, Queen Katherine Parr.

It is thought that this painting, The Family of Henry VIII, was a precedent for Van Dyck's portrait, so it must be asked if art historians are sure – absolutely certain – that it is the deceased Jane at Henry's side and not the contemporaneous Queen Katherine? (Moir 114).[19] The identification is iron clad. The image of Jane Seymour was copied, almost exactly, from an earlier painting by Hans Holbein dating from 1537. The queen's gabled hood and whelk-shell headdress are an unmistakable mark of Queen Jane. In *Tudor Costume and Fashion*, Herbert Norris explains that Henry's later queens chose the more fashionable French hood and headdress (287-288). There is no doubt whatsoever that the queen at King Henry's side is Jane Seymour.

Van Dyck himself painted a posthumous portrait of William,

Family of Henry VIII, c. 1544. (By permission of the Royal Collection Trust / © Her Majesty Queen Elizabeth II, 2018)

3rd Earl of Pembroke, presumably for his brother Philip (Barnes 569). As noted in the Wilton House catalogue: "that it is a post-humous portrait there is little doubt, as he [Earl William] died in April1630, two years before Van Dyck came to England" (Sidney 60). At about the same time that Van Dyck painted the Pembroke family portrait of Philip and his brood, another artist painted an-other notable group portrait titled A Charles I Conversation Piece. Dated approximately 1635, the two "incomparable brethren" of Shakespeare's *First Folio*, William and Philip Herbert, are appar-ently enjoying a visit with King Charles I and his Queen Henri-etta Maria (Sidney 52). Set either at Whitehall Palace or Durham House, this is a fine example of architectural painting. But what makes it applicable to the matter at hand is that, by this time, the older of the two "incomparable brethren" had been dead for about five years (Toynbee 244-247).[20] The posthumous appearance of the 3rd Earl of Pembroke is copied from an earlier painting by Daniel Mytens or Abraham van Blijenberch (Hearn 204-206).

The Pembrokes were not the only family to memorialize de-ceased relatives in oil. In 1594, Thomas More II commissioned a multi-generational family composite painting called "Sir Thomas More and his Family." Here More's elderly appearance indicates that he was painted from life. Oddly, he looks about the same age as his great-grandfather at the other side of the painting. His own father is a young man, and his famous grandfather, who was executed by Henry VIII in 1535, appears as he did when painted by Holbein (Hearn 128-129). Obviously, the figures in this painting were patched together from existing portraits.

The tomb of George Villiers, the Duke of Buckingham, af-fords another example of chronological incongruity. Located in the Henry VII Chapel in Westminster Abbey, the dress and appear-ance of the Duke's children have been used to determine when the monument was constructed (Lightbrown 150-152).[21] Mary Villiers appears in effigy as a child on the tomb, alongside her brothers. In a few years, she will be a young woman on Van Dyck's canvas. Included in this funerary scene is a boy, reclining with his right arm supported on a skull. This is Charles, the Duke's deceased son. His presence along with the three surviving children is another example of the convention of including deceased family members in the living family group.

Conclusion

In his later years, things did not go well for Philip Herbert, the 4th Earl of Pembroke. His marriage to Anne Clifford cost him dearly. He never saw a shilling from her estates, and did not even manage to reel in her younger daughter as a match for his younger son – which would have been a coup for the Pembroke family (Spence 111). When the issues of his marriage to Anne are considered, it is startling that her memory is extolled by Pembroke family historians. The misidentification of Anne in the Van Dyck painting seems to have had the approval of generations of Pembroke heirs.

It brings up the question of motivation. Has this exchange of identity been merely an inadvertent error? A small historical glitch? Or could this erroneous attribution be motivated by something more profound? Might the suppression of Susan Vere's identity be connected, somehow, to the Shakespeare Authorship Question? Researchers Bernice and Alan Cohen, among others, think that there is a connection, and provide additional information about the Van Dyck portrait in an article published in the *De Vere Society Newsletter* (24-28). The Cohens propose that it was Susan's influence that motivated the "incomparable brethren" to support the Shakespeare *First Folio* project. Furthermore, it would explain how the editors and printers of the *Folio* had access to Shakespeare's unpublished plays; Susan Vere would have inherited the manuscripts from her father and passed them along. (Anderson 371-372).

Commenting on the poetry of Susan Vere's father, Edward de Vere, the nineteenth century editor Alexander B. Grosart wrote that "An unlifted shadow lies across his memory" (11).[22] The suppression of Susan's identity in the Van Dyck portrait suggests that this shadow has fallen on her as well. If the Wilton House catalogues and the family biographies are any indication, the Pembroke family descendants – her own descendants – have systematically removed her from her rightful place in the family chronicles. Only one problem remains after centuries of mysterious effort to erase her memory: Countess Susan Vere's face cannot be erased from the Van Dyck masterpiece on the wall at Wilton House.

Notes

1. For this quote in full, see Richardson, *Aedes Pembrochianae A New Account and Description of the Antiquities and Curiosities in Wilton-House (London: R. Baldwin, 1774), p. 74.*

2. Philip Herbert inherited the title Earl of Pembroke at the death of his older brother in 1630.

3. In *Phillip's Phoenix,* Margaret P. Hannay provides a detailed account of the efforts of Lord and Lady Pembroke to arrange the marriage of their older son William to Oxford's second daughter, Lady Bridget Vere (159-162). Oxford gave his consent to the match, writing that it "do greatly content me, for Bridget's sake, whom always I have wished a good husband . . . " These marriage negotiations fell apart in 1597 due to political reasons, but the next attempt at a Herbert/Vere marriage worked out between the younger siblings.

4. Another question explained by the Herbert/Vere marriage is the extent of Ben Jonson's participation in the *First Folio.* Although some orthodox authorities would like to overlook him as the editor and give this credit to the actors Heminge and Condell, a closer examination of the long-standing relationship between Ben Jonson and the Pembroke family (including Susan Vere) diminishes the supposed role that has been attributed to Heminge and Condell.

5. Details of the wedding celebration and information about the King's gift of 500 pounds land for Susan Vere's jointure can be found in the contemporaneous correspondence of Dudley Carleton to John Chamberlain (66-68).

6. Anne Clifford had also contracted smallpox; she wrote "which disease did so martyr my face."

7. In spite of more recent research, confusion still surrounds the dating of the painting. The 1968 Wilton House catalogue states

that it was painted in London in 1634-35, an understandable error as the fact that Van Dyck was out of the country through-out 1634 was not known. To compensate for the newer infor-mation, it has been suggested that the painting dates to a time prior to Van Dyck's departure for Brussels in the fall of 1633, and the dates of Van Dyck's sojourn in Brussels vary (59-60). A date preceding October of 1633 does not fit the age of Mary Villiers (born in 1622) who, at the center of the painting, would have been only eleven years old if this were true. Moreover, Robert Dormer, the Earl's son-in-law, had been out of the country on an extended trip, returning in June of 1635 (Barnes 573).

8. After remarrying, Lady Mary Villiers became the Duchess of Richmond.

9. Differences of opinion on dates and facts of the Herbert/Vil-liers marriage vex the researcher every step of the way. Even the exact amount of the dowry is in question. Nicolson seems uncertain and gives the amount as £20,000 and £25,000 in different places in his book. Lever agrees with the £25,000 (105). Howarth comes in on the low side with £10,000 (227). Writing in 1907, Wilkinson puts the figure at £20,000 (297).

10. Marriages between the children of aristocratic families were solemnized as soon as possible after the financial arrangements were made, sometimes when the betrothed were still young-sters. Certainly this is the case with Mary Villiers and Charles Herbert. According to Nicolson, the ceremony was conduct-ed at Whitehall by the Archbishop of Canterbury during the Christmas season of 1634. It was done privately with few invit-ed, and "sooner than was intended." If this date is correct, then the bride was only twelve or barely thirteen years old. In such marriages, it was customary that cohabitation should not occur until the bride was older, and this could be up to four more years. Also, following the custom, the young groom was sent off to travel in Europe. Extrapolating the time line from Nicolson's account, Charles, Lord Herbert and his younger brother Philip departed for Italy in the summer of 1635. Both brothers took

ill with smallpox shortly after their arrival in Florence in December. Charles died there in late December of 1635 or early January 1636.

11. The two Baron engravings are in the permanent collection of the National Galleries of Scotland.

12. Alan and Bernice Cohen, "The Riddle of the Countess of Pembroke," in *The De Vere Society Newsletter, June, 2009 (26)*.

13. Several editions of this book are available through Google Digitized Books, but the pages describing the paintings at Wilton House appear in only one of the online books.

14. Dr. Williamson was one of the general editors of Bryan's *Dictionary of Painters and Engravers*, still an important reference on library shelves. His *Curious Survivals: Habits and Customs of the Past That Still Live in the Present* as well as books on Pietro Vannucci, George Morland, and *The Anonimo: Notes on Pictures and Works of Art in Italy* are among his recently republished work. His versatility is apparent in the wide range of subjects on which he wrote, to name a few: *The Book of Amber, The Money of the Bible, Everybody's Book on Collecting, Guildford in Olden Times, The Imperial Russian Dinner Service,* and *A Reader's Guide to T.S. Eliot*.

15. Mrs. Jameson lists this portrait as Item #134. It is now catalogued as Item #DPG89 (Personal correspondence with the Dulwich Picture Gallery).

16. In the *Complete Catalogue* edited by Barnes, et al, there is no listing of a Van Dyck portrait of Lady Anne Clifford alone. If this book is as comprehensive as it appears, then Van Dyck did not paint Lady Anne (assuming that the identification of her in the Pembroke Family group is erroneous). As Van Dyck's subjects were courtiers, families and friends in the inner circle of the Royal Court, it is unsurprising that she was not granted the privilege of "sitting" for Van Dyck after her estrangement from Pembroke. Also, since many portraits of Anne survive, it is odd that a Van Dyck would have "gone missing," if indeed one was painted by this master.

17. Martha von Monmouth is painted by Van Dyck with similarly folded hands, considered symbolic of her pregnancy (Barnes 558-559). Millar notes that Van Dyck painted Queen Henrietta Maria with similarly folded hands when she was pregnant, though the arms were not overlapped as they are in the Crofts and Pembroke paintings.

18. David Lindley discusses the difficulties that the aristocracy faced in obtaining a divorce in his book about the infamous divorce trial of Lady Frances Howard and the Earl of Essex (86). Roderick Phillips observes: "England was unique in the sixteenth century as the only country where an established or dominant reformed church did not break with the Roman Catholic doctrine of marital indissolubility."

19. In writing about the influence of Holbein as a model for Van Dyck's Pembroke Family, Moir notes that "Holbein's mural of Henry VIII and Jane Seymour was destroyed by fire in 1698, but in the 1630s, it was at Whitehall where Pembroke had his London accommodations."

20. In looking at the four figures, Toynbee says "I feel pretty sure that these paintings are composite pieces. Pembroke's figure is almost certainly posthumous, for the style of the Queen's dress suggests the Van Dyck fashion of 1632 onwards, whereas the Earl, as has been said, died in 1630, and the Montgomery, as has been noted, may actually be based upon a Van Dyck original."

21. Lightbrown writes that the appearance of the younger son, born in April of 1629, is an important factor in dating the monument, as is that of Lady Mary, the oldest child (150-152).

22. It was remarkable that J. Thomas Looney found Dr. Grosart's *Miscellanies* when he was researching *Shakespeare Identified*. Only 106 copies of Grosart's book were printed and these were intended only for private circulation. In his introduction to Oxford's poems, Grosart writes that "there is an atmosphere of graciousness and a culture about them that is grateful."

Chapter
10

She Will Not Be a Mother
Historical Evidence for the Seymour PT Theory

Two theories, called the Prince Tudor hypotheses, have generated much debate in discussions of the authorship of Shakespeare's works. The release of the film *Anonymous* in the fall of 2011 brought more attention to these theories. Of the two, the one most often put forth holds that Queen Elizabeth had a son with the 17th Earl of Oxford. The child of this liaison was placed as a changeling with the Southampton family to be raised as an Earl's son and educated in a privileged environment suitable to one who might ultimately become heir to the throne of England (Ogburn 812-938).[1] In the other theory, it is posited that Queen Elizabeth in her youth had a child with Thomas Seymour, the Lord Admiral of England. According to this hypothesis, the child was placed in the household of the 16th Earl of Oxford where he was raised as an Earl's son, receiving an upbringing befitting a royal prince.

In an article published in 2006 in the *Shakespeare Oxford Newsletter*, Richard Whalen summarized the pros and cons of these two theories. (Prince Tudor is hereafter abbreviated to PT.) Whalen noted that both theories contain the seductive elements of a good story, including "a possible love affair, potential adultery and bastardy, political intrigue, royal succession, clandestine surrogate parents, changeling children." Looking at these themes from the perspective of the Shakespeare authorship mystery brings new depth to the interpretation of Shakespeare's literary work, most especially the *Sonnets*, making this inquiry worth pursuing in spite of the dismay that it sometimes engenders.

Though both the Southampton PT and Seymour PT hypotheses reflect curious circumstances that defy traditional explanations, the major weakness of both theories is that there is no direct biographical evidence to support either one. This paper will be limited to a historical investigation of the Seymour PT theory. The objective is to examine two questions:

1. Did Princess Elizabeth have a child as a result of the Seymour incident – and – if so

2. What is the likelihood that this child might have been raised as the son of the 16th Earl of Oxford?

In the Seymour PT Theory, these two questions seem to be woven together, but I suggest that these two issues can be disentangled by a close study of primary documents and well-informed biographies.

The Historical Context

Soon after the death of Henry VIII in January of 1547, Princess Elizabeth moved into Chelsea Manor, the country home that the King provided for Katherine Parr, his sixth queen (James 91-94). Now the Queen dowager, Katherine occupied Chelsea with her fourth husband Thomas Seymour, the attractive, swash-buckling Lothario whom she married within months of the King's death.[2] Thomas was the brother of Jane Seymour, Henry's third queen, and this made him uncle to King Edward VI, who at this time was only nine years old. King Edward facilitated his uncle's ascendency into the peerage as Baron Seymour of Sudeley along with his promotion to the rank of Lord High Admiral, the most powerful military position in England (Starkey 65-66, 335).

Known for his boundless ambition, Seymour had wanted to marry either Princess Mary or Princess Elizabeth but had settled for Henry's last queen because she had been in love with him prior to her marriage to Henry (Fraser 397-403). As noted by Katherine Parr's biographer Susan James: "For Seymour, the queen-dowager would be a valuable asset in his quest for greater influence on the council. She was still in love with him and to his experienced eye, ripe for seduction" (298).

To her credit, Katherine had made a concerted effort to bring Henry's three estranged children together as a family during the final years of his reign, and she established what appeared to be an especially warm and nurturing relationship with the young Princess Elizabeth (Starkey 42-46). The editors of *Elizabeth I Collected Works* published two dedicatory letters that accompanied the translations that the young Princess made for her stepmother as New Years' gifts, an indication of their shared literary interests (6-7, 10-13). It was understandable that Katherine wanted to keep the adolescent Princess under her wing after she remarried. However, once Elizabeth and the newly wedded Seymours were together at Chelsea, this arrangement would prove problematic. In the Samuel Haynes' edition of the *Collection of State Papers Left by William Cecil, Lord Burghley*, we have reports that the Admiral made advances to the attractive teenage girl who lived in his house (95-97, 99-100).[3]

Seymour's character is a significant component of this narrative. James describes him as "an omnivorous lover whose taste in women seems to have been thoroughly eclectic," and his reputation for licentious behavior is not in dispute (298). John Strype reports in his *Ecclesiastical Memoirs* that in 1543, a "lewd woman" accused him of debauchery. No action was taken against Seymour, but the woman was executed.

Historians accept the reports that Seymour frequented Elizabeth's bedchamber in his bed clothes. This was easy for him to do as he had pocketed a key to her quarters. He is reported to have "struck" or "patted" the young Princess "on the back or buttocks familiarly," snatching kisses and embraces under the very nose of the Queen (Starkey 69). Even on the surface, it doesn't look good, and appearances were important in the royal family. Elizabeth's older sister Mary had been so carefully reared as to be kept away from the "company of men, lest she become attached to the male sex" (Erickson 42-43).[4]

But was an inappropriate flirtation as far as it went? Generations of historians stoutly perpetuate the story that Elizabeth fended off Seymour's advances (Creighton 5-11).[5] Writing in 1900,

Jacob Abbott notes that Elizabeth and Seymour "got into frolics" (55). Frederick Chamberlin insists that "the girl was never alone with Seymour upon any of these occasions, and that her attendants saw to it that there was no real danger for her." As Chamberlin tells it, Queen Katherine "saw no harm in the proceedings," and later "accompanied her spouse upon these pleasant visits, except upon one occasion where she appears to have been too tardy, for by the time she reached Elizabeth's apartment, Katherine found her husband having her [Elizabeth] in his arms." It is Chamberlin's opinion that "there was, however, no greater guilt than these words exactly state" (3). One may turn to Thomas Parry's confession, recorded in Haynes, for a more contemporaneous account of these events (97-99).

Elizabeth's governess Katherine "Kat" Ashley was responsible for protecting her virtue, and historians accept her story that she gave Seymour a stern dressing down for his behavior (Mumby 34-35; Strickland 14).[6] However, Ashley is criticized for failing to deal effectively with the developing situation (Creighton 7).[7]

An occurrence, often described as the incident in the garden, sheds some light on the ménage a trois. As this story is received by historians, Queen Katherine is supposed to have held the Princess while Seymour cut off her clothes, taking a knife and ripping her dress into a hundred pieces. Then they "tickled" Elizabeth. The event is accepted as a prank (Weir, *Elizabeth* 14-15). Historian Antonia Fraser called it "sexy horseplay" (404). Elizabeth's biographers also accept the report that earlier in the spring, the Queen went with her husband to the Princess's bedchamber and participated in other "tickling" sessions (Haynes 99).

Perhaps the story of Seymour's morning visits to Elizabeth's bedroom is true and it was an innocent though indecorous amusement. Maybe the nascent relationship between Elizabeth and the Admiral was not consummated. It could be that Elizabeth was just lucky and did not get pregnant. But the dress-cutting event in the garden lends itself to another interpretation.

Although historians gloss over exact dates, we have information from which to develop a timeline. One helpful detail is the record of the visit of Queen Katherine and her entourage to Seymour's London house during the Christmas season of 1547/8. Here

Seymour reportedly entered Elizabeth's bedchamber without his pants on (Haynes 99-100; Starkey 335). If Elizabeth had been seduced sometime in late December or early January of 1548 – quite possibly during the London visit – by the spring, a pregnancy would be becoming evident.

Perhaps Katherine didn't hear the gossip or was reluctant to believe it, but there had to be a point when she realized that there might be something to the rumors that her husband was involved with the young Princess. In an attempt to explain Katherine's collusion in the garden scene and the tickling sessions, David Starkey suggests that the effects of Katherine's first pregnancy had "unbalanced her judgement" (70). This scant notice from Starkey is hardly an adequate explanation for Katherine's bizarre behavior. Described as a "shrewd, tactful, patient" woman with "wisdom and discretion," Queen Katherine had kept her cool during the turbulent years of her marriage to King Henry VIII (Starkey, *Wives* 710, 729).

Posterity knows about the dress cutting incident because it was reported in 1549 in a deposition given by Elizabeth's governess, Kat Ashley. (Haynes 99-100). But could Ashley's story, reported the following year, have a touch of spin? Looking at it from a different perspective, it wasn't Seymour who was cutting off Elizabeth's clothes, aided and abetted by the Queen, but far more likely that an enraged Queen Katherine was slicing off Elizabeth's clothes in an effort to examine her body and see her condition for herself. It is hard to see how there could have been anything playful about it. Bear in mind that a knife was used to shred Elizabeth's clothes. Where did a knife come from? And the dress was cut in a hundred pieces. These elements indicate a serious altercation. It sounds more like an attack than a prank. Moreover, the Queen had motivation for this outlandish deed: she wanted to know if Elizabeth was pregnant. In another reading of the event, it could be proposed that Katherine's ladies were holding Elizabeth while Katherine was slashing away at her clothes. Seymour arrived on the scene and was running interference, wrestling the knife from the Queen's hands.

Returning to the rest of the story, by May of 1548, the

slow-learning Queen "decided that things had gone too far" and sent the Princess away (Starkey 70). Elizabeth's removal, long overdue, was to the safe haven of Cheshunt, the country estate of Sir Anthony Denny. This brings up the next line of questioning: Who was Sir Anthony Denny? With all the palaces and properties in the Tudor portfolio, why was Princess Elizabeth moved to his manor home? Did he have a pregnant Tudor princess on his hands?

Before these questions can be answered, let's take a moment to discuss the dynastic imperatives that drove the life of a Tudor princess, or any Renaissance princess for that matter. From the vantage point of history, we know that Elizabeth became Queen of England, and was a great monarch as well. But in 1548, this prospect was not on the Tudor horizon.

The first Tudor king, Henry VII, ruled from 1485 to 1509, and proved to be a master of international diplomacy-through-marriage with the unions of three of his offspring with royal dynasties outside of England (Crowson 64-66, 78, 89-91). With marriages into the royal houses of Spain, Scotland and France, he neutralized long standing enemies of England, at least for a time. His son and successor, Henry VIII, continued this practice, negotiating the marriage of his daughter Mary while she was still in the cradle. In 1518, Henry VIII solemnized a proxy wedding between the two-year-old Mary and the son of the King of France (Erickson 30-33).[8] Abrogating this agreement, he betrothed Mary, at age six, to the Emperor Charles V as the two rulers made plans for the invasion of France (Erickson 52-55, 67-72). The Emperor eventually tired of waiting for his child bride to grow up and broke off the engagement.

By the time Mary reached her mid-teens and the proper age to marry, Henry was at the end of his patience with his first Queen, Katherine of Aragon. After the divorce, Mary's status as a Royal Princess was thrown into doubt, lessening her attraction to potential suitors (Erickson 193-194).[9] Later, in his still greater fury with Anne Boleyn, he bastardized daughter Elizabeth as well.

Six years after Jane Seymour, his third queen, gave birth to his longed-for son and heir, Henry VIII brought his daughters back into the line of succession, though he never reinstated them as legitimate issue (Starkey 30-33). Once upgraded back to a Princess of sorts, Mary resumed her accustomed role as a bargaining chip, but by this time she was twenty-eight years old. Mary had remained unmarried despite the many suitors for her hand that had come and gone and two celebrated betrothals – a circumstance that needs an explanation (Erickson 224-232; Ives 83).

King Henry was a master at playing the double game in court intrigues, and in the waning years of his reign, it was not readily apparent whether Henry favored the "conservative" Catholics or the Protestant "Reformists" in his court (Starkey, *Six Wives* 728). It was, however, understood that the faction in power when the king died would control not only the young Prince Edward but also the religious direction of England. But which group would prevail? Mary's elusive marriage arrangements may indicate the course that Henry wanted his dynasty to take. If Mary remained unmarried, there would be no Catholic Tudor heirs.[10] Young King Edward VI was brought up in the Reformed religion, and if his sister Elizabeth married into a European Protestant House, the Tudors would become an influential Protestant royal family on the world stage.

It is with marriage in mind that Elizabeth Tudor's destiny was mapped out for her by the Protestant faction surrounding her brother. With her fairly good looks, excellent Renaissance education and, best of all, linguistic accomplishments, what a fine consort she would make for a top-tier continental Prince. In fact, the founding of a European branch of English royals was a dynastic niche that was filled two generations later by Elizabeth Stuart, the daughter of King James the First, and the current royal family is descended from her marriage to Frederick V of the Palatinate.

Now back to Princess Elizabeth's savvy handler, Sir Anthony Denny. He was educated at St. John's College, Cambridge, a center of Protestant Reformation scholarship and intrigue.[11] After entering King Henry's service in 1536, he became the King's most trusted Gentleman of the Bedchamber and an influential member of his Privy Council.[12] Stating that the full import of Denny's role in the King's administration has only recently been "identified by historians," Robert Hutchinson characterizes Denny as "Henry's real fixer, his man about court, trusted messenger and true confident" (96-97, 151-159). As was customary with the King's closest circle, Denny profited handsomely from the dissolution of the monasteries.

Historian Starkey describes Denny as the "smoothest opera-tor of the era," and everything that is known about him confirms this assessment (78). This being said, accurate information about Denny's personal life is hard to come by; details are conflicting or missing. He is remembered for a rich endowment that he gave a school in Yorkshire that had formerly belonged to St John's Col-lege, Cambridge, but even the date of his death and place of burial are uncertain. In a document dated August 8, 1549, William Cecil wrote that "Sir Anthony Denny is dead, whereof none have greater loss than very honest [and virtuous] men" (Hutchinson 152, 297). Cecil's announcement may have been premature. An addition to Denny's will was dated a month later on September 7, 1549, and his death is thought to have occurred on September 10, 1549.[13]

There is no doubt that the discreet Sir Anthony was indispens-able to his King. Along with his place on the Privy Council, he was the Keeper of the Palace and the Keeper of the Privy Purse. His duties with this latter office included the control of the dry stamp, the facsimile of King Henry's signature used often in the last years of his life; and he facilitated the King's personal expenditures (Hutchinson 154-156; Weir *Henry VIII* 467).

Was Sir Anthony Denny involved in the upbringing of Prin-cess Elizabeth? It is likely that he had been overseeing Elizabeth's care for a long time. Denny's high favor with Henry was apparent by 1537 when the king gave him the priory of Hertford and other lands (*DNB* 5:823-824). In the years following the birth of Prince Edward in the fall of that year, Anthony Denny married Joan Champernon, the accomplished daughter of Sir Philip Champer-non. In this timeframe, Joan's sister, Katherine Champernon, was taken into Princess Elizabeth's service. She would later become Elizabeth's governess, a coveted position likely facilitated by Denny. When the time came for Katherine to marry, Denny found a suit-able match for her in his friend John Ashley whom he knew from St. John's College, Cambridge. It is this very Katherine Champer-non who entered the history books as Princess Elizabeth's beloved Kat Ashley, the woman whose devotion to Elizabeth would be sorely tested.

Once removed to Denny's country manor of Cheshunt, Elizabeth was in a safe haven from which she could deal with the ramifications of her time in the Seymour/Parr household. She was sequestered at Denny's estate from May until December of 1548, and during these months made no public appearances. Elizabeth did not return to attend Katherine at the birth of her baby in late August (*DNB:* 3:1220-1221). Besides missing an opportunity to show herself to the people in the Queen's service – which would *immediately* have dispelled rumors about her own possible pregnancy – attendance on Katherine at this important time was a duty owed by a loving daughter to the woman who had been the only mother she had ever known (*DNB:* 3:1218).[14] It was a conspicuous absence.

Another indication of the breach between Elizabeth and Katherine was the fact that Katherine appointed the eleven-year-old Lady Jane Grey to be her baby's godmother. To stand godparent, especially to a royal child, was a high honor in court circles; and, as Princess Elizabeth was the older and higher ranking royal, she would have been the more appropriate choice. This is a snub that figures hard in the equation.[15] Furthermore, historians concur that the Queen named her baby Mary in honor of Elizabeth's older sister, the Catholic Tudor Princess (Borman 121; Frazer 406; James 330). Although Queen Katherine and Princess Mary (later Queen Mary) had been on good terms during Katherine's marriage to King Henry, Mary did not endorse her marriage to Seymour, a refusal that hurt the Dowager Queen (Porter 291-292; 301; James 309-312).[16] That the Protestant Katherine and Catholic Mary were firm in their opposing religious convictions made Katherine's choice of Mary's name for her baby over the Protestant Elizabeth all the more puzzling.[17]

The next public opportunity that Elizabeth missed was Queen Katherine's funeral in September of 1548 (James 332). Katherine died of puerperal fever on September 5, and, as she lay dying, she accused Seymour of betrayal. The inference can be drawn that her misery was worsened by the prospect that her husband had his eye on another marriage after her passing, though historians generally give this interpretation short shift, attributing her accusations to delirium resulting from her fever (James 331; Frazer 407; Haynes 103-104).[18] It would have behooved Elizabeth mightily to attend the funeral, and better yet, she might have taken on the ceremonial duties of chief mourner – another prestigious appointment that went to the Lady Jane Grey (Erickson 79, James 332, Ives 45).[19]

In a society where a woman's honor "rested solely with her sexual chastity," had Elizabeth succumbed to the advances of the Admiral, it was a dishonor to the House of Tudor and everyone associated with it (Foyster 32-33, 77). Mary Hazard writes in her book *Elizabethan Silent Language* that the physical presence or absence from important royal occasions was scrutinized in the 16th century (231-235). Absence indicated disgrace. Hazard goes on to say that by the time Elizabeth became a Queen herself, she "had suffered first-hand some of the psychological and political manipulations of presence."[20]

Clearly, the May to December time frame away from public view provided an adequate window for Elizabeth herself to bear a child (Paul 51; Starkey 82).[21] If she were four months pregnant in May, she would have had the child in late September or early October. Even factoring in a margin of error of a month or so, there is still enough time for her recovery and for arrangements to set her up with her own household at Hatfield House in December (Beauclerk 39).[22]

Are there historical accounts to support the proposal that Elizabeth bore a child? In his book *Shakespeare's Lost Kingdom*, Charles Beauclerk quotes from the *Memoires* of Jane Dormer.[23] In this gossipy story written decades later and published in 1887, a newborn baby of an important young woman (thought to be Elizabeth) is put to death. Jane Dormer married a prominent Spanish nobleman, and her *Memoires*, coming from a time when England was at war with Spain, do not have much credibility.

A more contemporaneous source is a letter written by Roger Ascham. It is dated July 8, but no year is given. The nineteenth century editor of Ascham's correspondence dates it to 1549. Ascham writes this letter from Cheshunt, but he refers to an unspecified time when Elizabeth was still at Chelsea. Ascham notes that a young woman came to Chelsea when he was not there, stating that "I was at court that day." Had he been there, he writes that he would have introduced this person to the "illustrious Lady" – certainly he means Princess Elizabeth. It has been suggested that Ascham's letter indicates that Elizabeth could not have been pregnant when she was at Chelsea, as no visitors would have been allowed around her then. But since Ascham himself was not at Chelsea and no meeting took place, why does he bother with such a curious comment? Ascham was a loyal member of Anthony Denny's Protestant faction from St. John's College, Cambridge, and it appears that Ascham was visiting Denny at Cheshunt when this letter was composed. By the summer of 1549, the rehabilitation of Elizabeth's reputation was underway, and it is possible that Ascham was attempting to create a cover story, fabricating a narrative to give an impression of a normal flow of people coming and going around Elizabeth while she resided at Chelsea.

Was A Child Born to Elizabeth?

Whether Elizabeth was pregnant of not, it is evident in the official biography of Elizabeth in the *DNB* that the rumor mill had done its job. It is admitted that this time of Elizabeth's life was caught up in "hearsay stories, backstairs gossip, and all the vulgar tattle of waiting maids and lackeys" (6:623). The Dowager Queen's household had numbered approximately two hundred servants, and this, presumably, is where the rumors originated (*DNB*: 3:1221). But aside from the stories of maids and lackeys, the most compelling – and damaging – testimony comes from Elizabeth herself. In her own correspondence, she acknowledges *her awareness* of the scandal as it gathered around her.

Although a mere public appearance would have quickly squelched the rumors, the clever fourteen-year-old Princess chose (from the safe confines of Cheshunt) to deal with the matter in writing. Three of Elizabeth's letters from the summer of 1548 are extant: two to Queen Katherine and an extraordinary letter to Thomas Seymour.

It appears that Elizabeth initiated the correspondence to Katherine, though the date of the first letter is conjectural. Writing possibly at the end of June, 1548: "I weighed it more deeper when you said you would warn me of *all evils that you should hear of me ….,*" and Elizabeth goes on to say that the Queen has "offered friendship to me that way, *that all men judge the contrary*" (Marcus, et al. 17-18).[24] The phrase "all evils" indicates misconduct, and "all men" means that the knowledge of Elizabeth's conduct is widespread. In saying that the Queen has offered her "friendship" when "all men judge the contrary," Elizabeth implies that Queen Katherine is taking her side in this contretemps, an interpretation that does not square with the Queen's actions in sending her away. This letter can be read in its entirety in the Marcus et al. edition of *Elizabeth I Collected Works*. Elizabeth's next letter is to the Admiral (Marcus 19).

> My Lord,
> You needed not to send an excuse to me, for I could not mistrust the not fulfilling of your promise to proceed for want of goodwill, but only the opportunity serveth not, wherefore I shall desire you to think that a greater matter than this could not make me impute any unkindness in you. For I am a friend not won with trifles, nor lost with the like. This I commit you and all your affairs in God's hand, who keep you from all evil. I pray you make my humble commendations to the queen's highness.

Apparently, this letter is a reply to communication from the Admiral. Strong emotion runs through these few lines. The negative tone is evident: the word "not" is used six times along with other negative words, such as "not mistrust," "not fulfilling your promise." What could this "promise" be? What is "want of goodwill" and "unkindness in you" all about? Most striking is the line "I am a friend not won with trifles nor lost with the like." Why does Elizabeth need or expect to be "won" or "lost" by her stepmother's husband? These words contain a familiarity that is out of place when compared to the effusive, complimentary language of courtly communication.[25] Lastly, why should they be corresponding at all? The reader can judge for himself, but it is hard to see in this letter the lighthearted banter of an infatuated teenager.[26]

Historians often quote from Elizabeth's third letter because it would appear that all is forgiven and she is communicating graciously with Queen Katherine (Fraser 404-408; Chamberlin 3).[27] It begins well enough: "Although your highness letters be most joyful to me in absence," but there is no joyfulness in this stiff, laconic, repetitive letter (Marcus 5-7, 10-11).[28] It would be nice if the Queen's side of the correspondence had been preserved, and nicer still if the rapprochement proposed by historians was supported by Katherine's appointments. As we have seen, Queen Katherine honored Princess Mary and Lady Jane Grey with recognition at her baby's birth.

By December of 1548, Elizabeth and her household were settled at Hatfield House. They may have thought the storm had passed. Now a widower, Seymour interrupted his mourning long enough to start the process for the hand of Elizabeth in marriage (Maclean 72-76). Using Elizabeth's cofferer Thomas Parry as a go between, Seymour gathered information about Elizabeth's landholdings, inquiring about their location, value and condition. According to Parry's testimony in Haynes' *State Papers*, he wanted to know "if it were good lands or no," "what state she had in the lands, for terme of life, or how," and "whether she had out her letters patentes or no" (97-99).

But Seymour's plans came to a halt with his sudden arrest on January 17, 1549. Kat Ashley, Thomas Parry and others who were connected to either Elizabeth or Seymour were arrested the next day. Ashley and Parry were questioned and as their depositions are the basis of the historical account of the Elizabeth/Seymour relationship, the circumstances of these depositions deserve some consideration. While Elizabeth was grilled at Hatfield House by Robert Tyrwhit in early 1549, Ashley and Parry were questioned in London.

Interestingly, it appears that their depositions were taken by Sir Thomas Smith, the accomplished Cambridge University academic who, at this time, was serving as the clerk of the Privy Council (Marcus 28-30; Haynes 95, 99). Elizabeth's servants were in friendly hands with Smith. The capable Sir Thomas was another Cambridge associate of Sir Anthony Denny's and an adherent to the Protestant Reformation. Smith's presence suggests that the prisoners would be spared the full force of the brutality that might have been used against them. Moreover, Sir Anthony Denny had come to Hatfield House to tell Ashley and Parry of their impending arrest, and accompanied them to London (Starkey 79). His presence suggests that he continued to oversee the situation.

We turn again to Elizabeth's own words. In a letter written to

Edward Seymour, now the Duke of Somerset and Lord Protector of the young King Edward, "Master Tyrwhit and others have told me that there goeth *rumors abroad* which be *greatly both against mine honor and honesty...*"[29] Elizabeth knows about the "shameful slanders," writing *"that I am in the Tower and with child by my Lord Admiral,"* and she "heartily" desires *"that I may come to the court* after your first determination, that *I may show myself there as I am"* (emphasis mine). How interesting. Elizabeth had spent six months in confinement at Cheshunt the previous year with no public appearances. Had she turned up somewhere, *anywhere,* she could have ended the "shameful slanders" then and there, and restored her reputation. It would have gone a long way to mitigate the indignity that her behavior had caused the House of Tudor. Now, somewhat belatedly, "showing myself there as I am" has finally occurred to her. The fifteen-year-old Princess Elizabeth has the nerve to float a straw man argument. Tyrwhit was with her at Hatfield, reporting regularly to the Lord Protector Somerset. Of course Somerset knew that she was not in the Tower. Elizabeth is well on her way to becoming what Alan Gordon Smith describes as "imperious of mood and with a mind already formed and hardened. Also she happened to be devoid of principles" (47).

Next, let's look at the depositions of Elizabeth's two most trusted servants. Both Kat Ashley and Thomas Parry were examined on the relationship between the Princess and Seymour. Both conceded that inappropriate sexual advances were made by the Admiral the previous year, though neither provided dates for these various notorious occurrences. Parry's deposition, a jumble of statements and quotes, attests that Elizabeth was discovered by the Queen in the arms of the Admiral and was thereupon sent away (Haynes 95-9; Mumby 45-49). He was not pressed for details and made no comment about the dress cutting in the garden.[30] Kat Ashley described the dress cutting as a joke, and this is the genesis of the prank explanation (Haynes 99-100). It does not seem plausible that such an extraordinary episode in Elizabeth's life could be ignored by Parry or explained away so blithely by Ashley, yet their stories related in these depositions have been taken at face value by later generations of historians.

In the early months of 1549 when Seymour was in the Tower

awaiting his fate and Elizabeth was concurrently questioned at Hatfield House, Robert Tyrwhit tried to use the depositions of Ashley and Parry to entrap Elizabeth. His report to the Lord Protector is often quoted: They "all sing one song, and so I think they would not do unless they had set the note before, for surely they would confess or else they could not so well agree" (Mumby 50-51).

It might be thought that the purpose of these interrogations was to get Elizabeth to confess that she had a child with Seymour. But this is to misconstrue the nature of the situation. What Tyrwhit was after from the Princess was an admission that she had entered into *an agreement to marry* Thomas Seymour after he became a widower. Elizabeth's troubles at this juncture stemmed from the fact that she was forbidden to marry without the consent of the Privy Council (Ives 48). The objective was to build the case against Seymour in order to execute him through an Act of Attainder. The possibility that Elizabeth might have borne a child out of wedlock made a secret marriage agreement between them more likely as a marriage would legitimatize a previous, illicit relationship. However, to establish the guilt of the Admiral without pulling Elizabeth into the undertow was a fine line to walk.

Returning to Seymour, he was in grave trouble. Thirty-three counts of treason were drawn up against him and passed unanimously by the Privy Council (*DNB* 17:1270). Some of the charges dealt with profiteering on the high seas and negotiating agreements with pirates – something that he might have thought was in his job description as Lord Admiral. Other charges related to his take-over of the mint at Bristol to coin money, though he could argue that the money went to pay his men and supply his ships (*DNB* 17:1337-1338).[31] But it all added up to high treason if it passed the Parliament, and under the Act of Attainder, the penalty for treason was death (Porter 336).

Straightaway, the House of Lords passed a guilty verdict, but the unruly Commons asked questions. Seems there were some members who thought that the charges were not commensurate with the Attainder that would result in Seymour's execution without a trial. The Commons were right to balk. Eric Ives writes that "the charges were the usual farrago of half-truths and imaginative construction which characterize so many Tudor treason cases." Even the royal lawyers were not "wholly persuaded that the charges amounted to treason" and thought that the evidence supported the lesser charge of misprision of treason (47). In the end, enough votes were mustered in the Commons to pass the Attainder, though there were still hold-outs (*DNB* 17:1270). Thomas Seymour was executed on March 19, 1549 without a trial, which in turn denied him the opportunity to speak in his own defense.

By early March Seymour's attainder was a *fait accompli*, and, happily for Elizabeth, it appears that the Council had lost interest in interrogating her further.[32] It would seem that the Protestant hegemony did not want to destroy Elizabeth too. This interpretation of events is supported by two things. In a letter dated March 7, 1549, Elizabeth gave the Privy Council her "most humble thanks" for a proclamation against rumor-mongering (Marcus 33).[33] She was surely thanking them for the effort to suppress gossip directed toward her. Then in May, she sent her picture to her brother the King as a gift. That she was allowed to approach her brother with a gift is another signal that the rehabilitation process was underway. It is possible, though not certain, that this gift is the portrait in which Elizabeth is depicted as the quintessence of maidenly virtue.[34] Accompanying the portrait was a letter dated May 15, 1549, ending with a quote from Horace: "feras non culpes quod vitari." One might wonder what the Princess was thinking when she wrote this; it translates "what cannot be cured must be endured" (Marcus 35-36).

All things considered, it was a disastrous chapter in Elizabeth's life. Her mentor Sir Anthony Denny dropped out of sight sometime in 1549, and his departure coincides with the entrance of a new advisor. His name was William Cecil.

What Might Have Happened to Elizabeth's Child?

After the historical circumstances are examined, the question remains: what happened to this child if there was one? In exploring this query in the cultural context of the 16th century, an examination of the structure of Tudor society is in order. If the idea was to salvage Elizabeth's future as a marriageable Tudor princess, how wise would it have been to place this child in a highly visible position as the heir of an earl? Elizabeth herself had indicated in her letter of January 1549 to Edward Seymour, Protector Somerset, that the word was out she was with child, and up and down the social ladder, people would have had their eyes open for anomalies surrounding newborns in high places (Stone 568).[35]

In the 16th century, the nobility as well as royalty did not have the same expectations of privacy that we do today. In *Crisis of the Aristocracy*, Lawrence Stone states that "a nobleman was obligated to live in a style commensurate with his dignity." Put quite simply, the peerage "lived in a crowd" (253). Stone details the life of the great magnate who was "expected to have one principal and two subsidiary country seats, a house in London and a staff of 60 to 100 to run them. Additionally, he had to keep a generous table freely open to visitors and a plentiful supply of horses for transport and communications" (249). In keeping with her status as Queen Dowager, Katherine Parr's household numbered over two hundred servants (*DNB* 3:1221), and this multitude of people had been the cauldron for the rumors over the Seymour incidents to develop and spread. But another great household was hardly a safe harbor for a princess in a matter that required careful, discrete handling.[36]

An even greater difficulty came with the obligation put on the propertied class by the Court of Wards to show proof of age. This meant that an heir was required to prove that he had reached twenty-one years of age in order to sue for his livery and obtain the release of his lands. According to Joel Hurstfield, "…in the case of a feudal ward, his age might raise serious questions: his land, his right of marriage, the sale of his wardship might all turn on the exact month and year of his birth…" (157). If a land-owning father died before his son and heir was twenty-one, the heir would be called by a jury to provide testimony or documentation to substantiate his date of birth. This burden of proof was serious business: godparents, household servants and wet-nurses could be summoned as witnesses to give their recollections of the heir's birth and baptism (157-170).[37]

A letter calendared in the State Papers Foreign supports the proposal that a nobleman's death and the age of his heir were newsworthy.[38] Dated August 18, 1562, this informational, gossipy correspondence is from John Somers in London to Sir Nicholas

Throckmorton, Elizabeth's ambassador to France.[39] After a lengthy paragraph relating recent court events, Somers reports that "The Earl of Oxford has departed to God, leaving a son about twelve years old." John de Vere died on August 3, 1562, so by August 18th – the date of this letter – the word is getting around. It is the spontaneous chatter that the death of a grandee should generate. An opposing position might hold that the official story of the future 17th Earl's age was adhered to on general principles, but at a minimum, this letter supports the view that an earl's death was a noteworthy event.[40]

With large numbers of people in the loop and the possibility that someday the family and witnesses could be pressed to confirm the child's birthday, a changeling scenario where a royal child is placed with an aristocratic family does not make for a sound strategic policy. It would be dangerous even if the dates were somewhat in synch – but they are not. The marriage of John de Vere and Margery Golding was recorded in the Parish Register on August 1, 1548. Edward, their first child, was born on April 12, 1550, a date corroborated by the recognition of the Privy Council with a gift of a baptismal cup (SP 13. 142.)[41]

The idea of a changeling carries romantic mystique generations later, but exchanging a child born in the fall of 1548 for a child reportedly born to the 16th Earl of Oxford in April of 1550 has some practical considerations. Are the 16th Earl and his Countess going to explain to their friends, neighbors and household that they simply forgot to inform them of the birth of their son and heir eighteen months earlier? Or did they just expect that servants and others would not be able to tell the difference between a newly born infant and an eighteen-month-old toddler? Not a smart move if the idea was to calm the waters and curtail the gossip surrounding Princess Elizabeth.

The circumstances of the 16th Earl of Oxford's home life are another matter that should be taken into account (Ward 7-9). His personal life had been chaotic, and in 1548, he was in the midst of a bizarre extortion involving much of his property (Green 49-58). Besides the possible loss of his estates, the litany of issues surrounding the 16th Earl included an unhappy first marriage that put him in an adversarial position with his first wife's influential relatives, a scandalous love affair that ended violently, and accusations of bigamy that followed in the wake of his remarriage (Golding 2, 6, 23, 32, 37-46).[42] Though the details are beyond the scope of this paper, he was hardly running a tight ship. If Elizabeth's advisors wanted a secure place to foster off the child, it's hard to see how the 16th Earl of Oxford's household could even make the short list.

Other historical circumstances serve as an indicator that Edward de Vere was not a royal changeling. After Elizabeth's ascendency, she never took him into the Royal Order of the Garter. Then as now, membership in the Garter was highly coveted. A candidate would be voted upon by the members, but the final selection was made by the monarch. Peter Moore examined the Garter records to ascertain where the 17th Earl of Oxford fits into this picture (263-274). He found that Elizabeth was partial to her favorites over the years, taking in the Earl of Leicester, the Earl of Essex and Sir Christopher Hatton for membership. In the Garter voting of 1572, the 17th Earl of Oxford had adequate votes for admission, and this was the timeframe in which he was considered a court favorite (Ward 56-50, 61, 78).[43] It is puzzling that the Queen passed over Oxford, choosing two peers of lower rank, Lord Grey and Viscount Hereford.[44] Had he been her son, or if she had been romantically involved with him, it would seem that she would have selected him for membership.

Most telling of all is Edward de Vere's financial position after the death of his father. In her paper "The Fall of the House of Oxford," Nina Green gives a detailed account of the destruction of Oxford's inheritance, facilitated by the Queen herself after young Edward became her royal ward in 1562 (67-71). Green relates that "the cavalier manner in which the Queen abrogated her responsibilities, and even prevented de Vere's own mother and friends from at least partially protecting him from financial disaster, is shocking" (73).

Once twelve-year-old Edward became her ward, Queen Elizabeth began a series of legal maneuvers that gave Robert Dudley de facto control the core Oxford lands now held for the boy by the Court of Wards. In addition to the income from Oxford's lands that went to Dudley, other issues included the seizure of more than the legal one-third interest in his lands, lawsuits against Oxford for the remainder of the revenue from the lands which were his mother's jointure, a £2,000 fine against Oxford in the Court of Wards, plus failure to adhere to the clause in the 16th Earl's will which would have provided sufficient funds for young Oxford to pay the fine for livery. By her actions, the Queen laid the foundation for de Vere's eventual financial downfall while the income from the Oxford earldom advanced Dudley's rise to the Leicester earldom. The Queen's actions, as documented by Green, are nonsensical if the young 17th Earl was her own changeling son, placed in the Oxford family to ensure a successful future for him.

If the Queen's mismanagement of Oxford's patrimony was not hindrance enough, Elizabeth consistently denied Oxford's suits for preferment in his later years. She refused his requests the governorship of the Isle of Jersey, the Presidency of Wales, the monopoly on oils, fruits, and wools, and monopoly on the tin in Cornwall. She ignored his pleas to return to him the keepership of the de Vere lands of Waltham Forest, property that had belonged to the Oxford earldom since the time of William the Conqueror (Nelson 337, 355-358, 394, 397, 420).

In closing, there are statistical issues with the scenario that Edward de Vere was the Queen's son. For one thing, a child born to Princess Elizabeth could just as well have been a girl. Highly significant too are the infant and childhood mortality rates in the 16th century which show that the very survival of a child was problematic (Wrigley and Schofield 2-4, 248-250). In *The Population History of England*, the authors rely on parish registers to provide information on fertility and mortality rates, stating that "England is exceptionally fortunate in having several thousand parish registers that begin before 1600." Using reconstruction data from registers that are regarded as sufficiently complete, it appears that childhood mortality (defined as death before age nine) was approximately 40% from 1550 to 1599.

If there was a child – if the child was male – if the child survived – if the child was placed in a nobleman's house: all are obstacles for a changeling scenario to overcome, most especially the theory that Edward de Vere was that child.

Conclusion

Aficionados of television crime shows are aware that there are three components of a circumstantial case: motive, means and opportunity. With respect to the question of Princess Elizabeth's alleged pregnancy, these three elements are found in abundance here. They add up to a compelling circumstantial case that Elizabeth had a child with the Admiral. Elizabeth lived in Seymour's house for approximately a year, providing him with ample opportunity for the seduction. Seymour's sexual interest in her is historically documented in letters, depositions and state papers.

The explanations for Queen Katherine's bizarre behavior support the proposal that something was amiss in her household. How credible is it that the Queen and the Admiral visited Elizabeth's bedroom for tickling sessions and that the dress-cutting scene in the garden was a prank? At the birth of her daughter, Queen Katherine chose the eleven-year-old Lady Jane Grey to be the godmother and named the baby for Princess Mary. Both are honors that should have gone to Elizabeth if all was well.

Most significantly, Queen Katherine sent Princess Elizabeth to live elsewhere. After her dismissal from her step-mother's household, she was cloistered at Cheshunt where she remained out of public view from May through December, providing ample time for a pregnancy, birth and recovery. Had she made a public appearance *anywhere* during the summer or early fall of 1548, the rumors of her own possible pregnancy would have vanished. During this time, she was sheltered by Sir Anthony Denny, one of the most loyal and capable of the Tudor counselors. These circumstances provide the means with which the pregnancy was contained within the Protestant inner circle. The matter was further contained by the beheading of Thomas Seymour in accordance with the Act of Attainder, an act that could be seen as retribution for what was a treasonable offense against the House of Tudor. If Elizabeth did not have a child, then there is inadequate motive for her six month confinement at Cheshunt and the Admiral's execution (Bernard 134-160).

However, a scenario in which this child might have been placed as a changeling into the Oxford household presents insuperable obstacles. Although substituting a royal child for a noble one may seem plausible centuries later, it was problematic in the 16th century when the birth of an heir in a grandee family would be examined by the Inquisition Post Mortem at the time of the nobleman's death. Moreover, it defies common sense to expect an eighteen month old toddler to pass muster for a newborn, as put forth in the Seymour Prince Tudor Theory.

In and of itself, the household of the 16th Earl would have been a poor choice for a changeling. His person life was in shambles and his estates were caught up in a bizarre extortion, leaving the earldom itself unstable. Last of all, Queen Elizabeth's deliberate and systematic destruction of de Vere's patrimony during his wardship is hardly consistent with the idea that he was set up as her changeling son to prosper in a nobleman's house.

Historical events can be easily conflated when viewed retrospectively, but when the facts are taken together, there is a compelling circumstantial case supporting the likelihood that Elizabeth had a child as a result of the Seymour affair. Yet there are equally convincing reasons to conclude that this child was *not* the 17th Earl of Oxford.

Sir Anthony Denny is the lynchpin of the story. He played a crucial role in rescuing Elizabeth from the Seymour debacle. His death the following year opened the door to the rise of a new man in the Tudor court. The new man, William Cecil, proved to be every bit as discreet and capable as Sir Anthony. After Elizabeth became Queen, he wielded great power as her Principal Secretary, Lord Treasurer, and Master of the Court of Wards and Liveries. Had there been a changeling somewhere, he would know. It is instructive to look at one of his last letters to his son, Robert Cecil. Written in his own hand, he describes a recent visit from the Queen (Conyers 545): "Though *she will not be a mother*, yet she showed herself by feeding me with her own princely hand, as a careful nurse."

The comment is curious for an aging Queen whose childbearing years were long past. However the events of 1548 are interpreted – and whether or not she was a mother – one thing is certain: the "careful nurse" was not Queen Elizabeth. The careful nurse was William Cecil, Lord Burghley.

Notes

1. Dorothy and Charlton Ogburn were among the earliest proponents of the Southampton Prince Tudor hypothesis in their book *This Star of England* (New York: Coward-McCann, Inc., 1952). Hank Whittemore builds a case in *The Monument* (Massachusetts: Meadow Geese Press, 2005) that Shakespeare's Sonnets support the PT Theory of Southampton's birth. Helen Heightsman Gordon concurs in *The Secret Love Story in Shakespeare's Sonnets*. Paul Streitz proposes that Oxford is the Queen's son in *Oxford, Son of Queen Elizabeth I* (USA: Oxford Institute Press, 2001). In *Shakespeare Lost Kingdom* (New York: Grove Press, 2010), Charles Beauclerk incorporates both hypotheses, calling them "double PT theories."

2. As per Rymer's *Foedera XV*, p. 116, Queen Katherine Parr was well provided for under Henry's will with money and property. Of her two principal country seats Hanworth and Chelsea, the latter was her favorite.

3. It is remarkable that the confessions of Thomas Parry and Katherine Ashley survive in the Cecil papers with accounts of such serious sexual misbehavior on the part of Thomas Seymour, the Lord Admiral. It is possible that these records were sanitized during Queen Elizabeth's forty-five year reign. Also, it is unknown if any editing was done by Haynes two hundred years later.

4. Queen Katherine of Aragon consulted the Spanish humanist Juan Luis Vives to design a plan of study for Mary, and it was severe. Vives regarded women as inherently sinful and in dire need of protection. As Erickson states, this protection was to guard "more securely and safely Mary's virginity." Erasmus concurred that the preservation of modesty was paramount, and that the primary value of education for girls was to impart the understanding that their chastity was "an inestimable treasure."

5. Although Creighton's 1899 account of the Queen Elizabeth's life supposedly ushered in a more objective outlook on her reign, he glosses over the scandalous events at Chelsea. He mentions briefly the familiarity that led to Elizabeth's dismissal from her step mother's home. He further notes that after she moved to Cheshunt, "everything was done to repair past indiscretion and let it sink into oblivion." He doesn't give details of what "everything" might have been. In his biography *Queen Elizabeth* (New York: Harper & Brothers Publishers, 1900), Jacob Abbott writes that "mysterious circumstances produced a somewhat unfavorable impression in regard to Elizabeth, and there were some instances, it was said, of light and trifling behavior between Elizabeth and Seymour, while she was in his house during the lifetime of his wife."

6. The source of this story is the deposition of Kat Ashley herself, and her statement is not corroborated by accounts of other witnesses. Frank Mumby reiterates the relevant parts of Ashley's deposition without comment in his *Girlhood of Elizabeth*. In her 1904 book, Agnes Strickland posits that Ashley "remonstrated with the Admiral."

7. Creighton accused Kat Ashley of being an accomplice, noting that the governess "discussed with Elizabeth the attentions of her admirer, and connived at water-parties by night on the Thames." This might be seen as an attempt to transfer blame from Elizabeth for her actions, to Ashley for dereliction of duty.

8. Called "an alternative to war" with France, this proxy marriage was accompanied by a treaty between the two countries. The plan was to consummate the marriage when the Dauphin turned fourteen.

9. Even though he bastardized her, Henry VIII continued to use Mary as a tool in his foreign policy. "From Henry's point of view, the diplomatic rivalries generated by Mary's availability were far more important than any betrothal that might be concluded." According to the *DNB*, after Mary became Queen, she legitimized herself in her first Parliament, in which it was

declared that she had been born "in a most just and lawful matrimony."

10. In spite of the loss of her legitimate status, Mary retained a more desirable position as an available princess than Elizabeth did, as in the eyes of the Catholic Church, the marriage between Henry VIII and Catherine of Aragon passed the test of good faith.

11. Many of the men who surrounded Princess Elizabeth had matriculated to St. John's College, Cambridge, where, as reported in the *DNB*, "many of the fellows in Cardinal Wolsey's time privately studied the scriptures and the works of Luther." (4:178). In addition to Sir Anthony Denny, Cambridge fellows included the influential educators Roger Asham, William Grindal, and Sir John Cheke, and the latter counted among his students Sir William Cecil and William Bill (whose brother Dr. Thomas Bill was a physician to King Edward VI).

12. Though Denny officially entered the King's service in 1536, he had Henry's endorsement for election to Parliament the year before. By 1538, Denny had replaced his own mentor, Sir Francis Bryan, and was "privy to Henry's innermost thoughts and changing moods."

13. When the Denny biography as reported in the 19th century *Dictionary of National Biography* is compared with the 2004 *Oxford Dictionary of National Biography*, it appears that some of the gaps have been filled in, yet the sources for the later version are not impressive. These sources include several PhD dissertations and articles in esoteric journals. The *ODNB* biography notes that Denny provided for nine children in his will. The earlier *DNB* states that he and his wife Joan had six children. Robert Hutchinson reports twelve children in his book *The Last Days of Henry VIII*. If this report were true, then Mrs. Denny would have borne twelve children in their eleven year marriage, quite an accomplishment for a woman who was also busy at court, participating in Queen Katherine Parr's religious studies and befriending the Protestant martyr Anne Askew. In the *ODNB*,

the Dennys' marriage is dated February 9, 1539 (probably New Style date) and Denny's death is September 10, 1549. Bearing nine surviving children in little more than a decade would have been remarkable considering the terrible child mortality of the times. The earlier *DNB* relates that Denny's death has been variously reported as occurring in 1551, 1550 and 1549, though the last date is supported by documentation. It states that "it appears that he was buried at Cheshunt." The *ODNB* provides more details on Denny's accumulation of wealth and his ascendency in King Henry's court, yet no mention is made of his sister-in-law Katherine Champernon Ashley, a connection that is difficult to overlook.

14. In the *DNB* biography, Queen Katherine is credited with facilitating the restoration of both Henry's daughters Mary and Elizabeth from the bastardy into which they had been put by the King. The Queen obtained a pardon for Elizabeth for which the she composed "a very grateful epistle" to her step mother.

15. Failing in his accustomed thoroughness, Starkey does not mention the fact that Lady Jane Grey stood godmother to the Queen's child in either his account of Elizabeth's early life or in his *Six Wives*. Wier and Erickson also take no note of it, but Frazer mentions it on page 406.

16. Both the Dowager Queen and Seymour conducted a letter-writing campaign to obtain the approval of the royal court for their union. Mary resisted the pressure, responding to the Admiral's solicitation (at Katherine's behest) that "my letters shall do you but small pleasure..." and that she was "not to be a meddler in this matter." Mary's endorsement would have been helpful as the marriage was publicly greeted with "surprise, disgust and anger."

17 Queen Katherine Parr could have given her daughter her own name, and it might have been thought a tribute to her close friend, Katherine Willoughby, the Duchess of Suffolk, who was the standard bearer for the Protestant cause. It is this Katherine

who took the Queen's baby into her home to raise after Queen Katherine died.

18. In addition to betrayal, the Queen accused her husband of poisoning her. In Lady Tyrwhit's Confession, reported somewhat vaguely by Haynes, Lady Tyrwhit implied that the Queen realized that her death would leave Seymour free to pursue Elizabeth.

19. Of Elizabeth's biographers, only Erickson reports that Lady Jane Grey was the chief mourner at Queen Katherine's funeral held at Sudeley. James acknowledges the conscientiousness of the eleven-year-old Jane as she watched "hour after hour beside the candlelit bier" and made "the traditional offerings of money to the alms box at the funeral."

20. In Hazard's intriguing chapter on Absent/Present, Present/Absence, she examines the rules and conventions that governed public appearances. "From the earliest moments of her reign, Elizabeth dramatized her appearances so as to render them both politically useful and historically memorable." Elizabeth was well versed in silent and symbolic communication.

21. Christopher Paul provides perspective on these issues in his article, "The 'Prince Tudor' Dilemma: Hip Thesis, Hypothesis, or Old Wives Tale?" According to the *DNB*, Asham became Elizabeth's tutor upon the death of William Grindal, but Grindal died from the plague in the summer of 1548 (8:708). There is nothing to indicate that Grindal went with Elizabeth to Cheshunt in May. Perhaps he took a hiatus from her service. The record does not say if Asham was at Chelsea or Cheshunt. Moreover, Asham cannot be looked upon as a disinterested observer. There should be no doubt of his loyalty to the Protestant cause, the House of Tudor, and most of all, to the Princess whom he served.

22. In support of both Prince Tudor theories, Beauclerk believes that "if Elizabeth did give birth, it most likely was in September of the previous year, [1548] just before she left her seclusion at

Cheshunt to go to Hatfield, and could easily have been hushed up among her inner circle."

23. *The Memoires of Jane Dormer, the Duchess of Feria (1538-1612)* can be accessed on the internet. The Duchess was the wife of Count de Feria and spent her adult life in Spain. As a partisan of Queen Mary, her objectivity with regards to Queen Elizabeth's reign is questionable.

24. The editors date this letter to June, 1548, though the PRO Calendar has it incorrectly dated December, 1547. Mumby is even earlier with a date of June, 1547 (35-36). Both of the earlier dates are impossible as the letter is clearly written after Elizabeth's departure from Chelsea in May of 1548. Also, Elizabeth's expression of concern for Queen Katherine's condition, as noted in her use of the phrase "undoubtful of health," is a reference to Katherine's pregnancy.

25. See Mumby for examples of courtly correspondence between Prince Edward and Elizabeth written in December of 1546; and Roger Asham's undated letter to Kat Ashley (26-28). In Appendix I of her biography, Susan James has published all of the love letters between Queen Katherine and Seymour.

26. See Marcus for two additional letters from the aftermath of this timeframe (21-22). Both are undated but are clearly from the fall of 1548. Elizabeth claims illness when writing at this time to her brother the King: "For an affliction of my head and eyes has come upon me, which has so sorely troubled me since my coming to this house that, although I have often tried to write to your majesty, I have until this day ever been restrained from my intention and undertaking. The which condition, having somewhat abated..." Now really! She had been at Cheshunt for at least four months from May to September. One would think that sufficient time to get a paragraph or two off to her brother. The second letter is to Edward Seymour, Lord Protector Somerset. She thanks him for being "careful for my health, and sending unto me not only your comfortable letters but also physicians as Doctor Bill, whose diligence and pain has been a

great part of my recovery." It can be readily extrapolated that Elizabeth's condition was known at court, and a trusted court doctor (or doctors as Elizabeth uses the plural) were sent to ascertain the state of her health and speed her "recovery" from her headaches. The Dr. Bill to whom Elizabeth refers is Dr. Thomas Bill, physician to both King Henry VIII and Edward VI. His brother was Dr. William Bill, dean of Westminster and graduate of St. John's College, Cambridge.

27. In her account of Queen Katherine, Fraser insists that these letters are a show of affection, and that the Queen sent Elizabeth away merely to preserve decorum. Chamberlin notes that "she and her former hostess remained upon the best of terms until the death of the latter three months later."

28. Compare this to the three letters to her step mother written when Elizabeth was about 10 years old, at which time the Princess could affect a fluid style with lengthy praise.

29. Elizabeth knew that her sexual behavior was in question. Recalling Foyster's explanation, a woman's "honour" depended exclusively on her sexual chastity.

30. In Parry's words: "I do remember also she told me that the Admiral loved her but too well, and had done so a good while: and that the Queen was jealous of her and him in so much that one time the Queen, suspecting the often access of the Admiral to the Lady Elizabeth Grace, came suddenly upon them, where they were all alone (he having her in his arms): wherefore the Queen fell out, both with the Lord Admiral, and with her Grace also."

31. Seymour's partner in the alleged crime was Sir William Sharington, vice-treasurer of the mint at Bristol, who was attainted along with the Admiral. Although Sharington used his position at the mint to perpetrate extensive frauds as well as support the Admiral's misdeeds, he was pardoned within a year and re-purchased his forfeited estates. The restoration of Sharington's status and fortune further suggests that something more serious

was behind the charges against Seymour.

32. Beginning on January 23, 1548/9, Robert Tyrwhit had been reporting regularly from Hatfield House to Lord Protector Somerset (Haynes 71, 88-90, 94, 107-108). His last report was on February 19, 1548/9 when he described Princess Elizabeth's crying fit over the replacement of Katherine Ashley with his own wife, Lady Trywhit. On February 25, the Admiral's Attainder was introduced into parliament and immediately passed the Lords. On March 5 it passed the Commons. Seymour was executed two weeks later on March 19, 1548/9 (Bernard 230).

33. There is no record of a proclamation from early March, but a local order may have gone out to this effect. On October 30, 1549, the Council did issue a declaration against rumors.

34. In his book *The Elizabethan Icon: Elizabethan & Jacobean Portraiture*, (Great Britain: Paul Mellon Foundation for British Art, 1969), Roy Strong suggests on p. 74 that the iconic portrait of Elizabeth richly dressed in red and holding a book may date to Elizabeth's girlhood in 1546. It is thought to have been painted by William Scrots, the successor to Hans Holbein, but other versions of it were done.

35. The upper strata of society were subjected to scrutiny from within its ranks as well as from the outside. Even the birth of noble children could be the object of a bet. "There seemed to have been no form of human activity which the nobility did not contrive to turn into the subject of financial speculation."

36. Sir Anthony Denny's Cheshunt seems to be an exception. Such a silence surrounds the discreet Sir Anthony that, as previously mentioned, even the date of his death is unknown.

37 For more details on feudal wardship and the kinds of land ownership that triggered an *inquisition post mortem* for which proof of the heir's age was required, see Hurstfield's *The Queens Wards* and H.E Bell's *The Court of Wards & Liveries*.

38. I am indebted to Dr. Martin Hyatt for calling my attention to

this entry.

39. From the internet: Calendar of State Papers Foreign, Elizabeth, Volume 5: 1562 (1867), pp. 240-258.

http://www.british-history.ac.uk/report.aspx?compid=71925

The abstract as it appears in the CSP: "Has forwarded his letters to Randolph M. De Vielleville has been thrice at the Court and very well received, and the second time dined there, the same being purposely prepared for him, accompanied with divers Lords and counselors. Lord Robert, Lord Hunsdon, and Mr. Secretary accompanied him one day into St. James park, where they hunted, and he killed a fat buck with a crossbow from a standing, but it was at two shots. Lord Chandos accompanied him to Gravesend. Sir Thomas Smith is willed to be ready. All the members appointed are ready and in good order, Master Woodhouse has gone to the sea with five great ships attending the Queen's pleasure. Mr. Henry Knolles has gone to Almain to know the intents of the Princes Protestants. The Queen and all the Lords of the Council are in good health. The Earl of Oxford has departed to God, leaving a son about twelve years old. Greenwich, 18 Aug. 1562."

40. Arthur Golding's son, Percival Golding, wrote an encomium about his noble relative in which he gives Oxford's date of birth as April 12, 1550. He also notes that Oxford's death is in June of 1604, oddly leaving out the day. Archived in the Harleian, Golding's notice is helpful, but neither contemporaneous nor spontaneous.

41. Christopher Paul discovered this entry in the State Papers. For more information, his article, "The 'Prince Tudor' Dilemma: Hip Thesis, Hypothesis, or Old Wives' Tale?" in *The Oxfordian, Volume 5*, October 2002 can be accessed on the Shakespeare Oxford Fellowship's website.

42. Golding documents the "bitter family quarrel" between the

descendants of the sixteenth Earl's two marriages.

43. In his *Book of Honour*, Sir William Segar provides an account of Oxford's tournament success. Contemporaneous correspondence from Georges Delves to the Earl of Rutland, dated May 14 and June 24, 1571, reports that "Lord Oxford has performed his challenge at tilt, tourney, and barriers, far above expectation of the world...;" and "There is no man of life and agility in every respect in the Court but the Earl of Oxford." Next, the oft quoted letter from Lord St. John that "the Earl of Oxford hath gotten him a wife — or at least a wife has caught him...." and his description of the "great weeping, wailing, and sorrowful cheer of those that had hoped to have that golden day." Gilbert Talbot wrote to his father in May of 1572 that "the Queen's Majesty delighteth more in his personage and his dancing and his valiantness than any other." Talbot comments on Oxford's "fickle head," but this minor drawback did not deter William Cecil from matching Oxford with his daughter Anne Cecil.

44 Moore relates that after the votes were cast, the final selection for membership in the Order rested with Queen Elizabeth, and she could be capricious in her choice. She was influenced by family, status, and service to the crown. "Mere rank was not enough," and "family connections helped." In 1572, both the Earl of Oxford and Lord Grey of Wilton received seven votes. The Queen chose Lord Grey and Viscount Hereford (who only had four votes) to fill two of the three vacancies, and the third went to Lord Burghley. It could be argued that Viscount Hereford and Lord Grey had provided the crown with more "service," but the Queen controlled the opportunities for royal service as well. Oxford had family history of Garter memberships on his side: both the 15th and 13th Earls of Oxford were Knights of the Garter.

Appendix A

William Shakspere's Last Will and Testament

The will is presented line by line, displaying interlineations between the lines. Cancelled passages are in italics and have been crossed out. No punctuation is added. Spelling is modernized for easier reading, but proper names and places, as well as capitalizations, are as they appear in the original document.

Martii
Vicesimo Quinto die *Januerii* ^ **Anno Regni Domini nostri Jacobi nunc Regis Anglie**
&c decimo quarto & Scotie xlix° Annoque domini 1616

T W ᵐʲ Shackspeare

In the name of god amen I William Shackspeare of Stratford upon Avon in the county
of Warr gent in perfect health & memory god be praised do make & Ordain this
my last will & testament in manner & form following That is to say first I Commend
my Soul into the hands of god my Creator hoping & assuredly believing through
the only merits of Jesus Christ my Savior to be made partaker of life everlasting
And my body to the Earth whereof it is made   Item I Give & bequeath
unto my ~~son in L~~ daughter Judith One Hundred & fifty pounds of lawful
English money to be paid unto her in manner & form following that is to
          in discharge of her marriage portion
say One Hundred Pounds ^ within one year after my decease with consideration
after the Rate of two shillings in the pound for so long time as the same
shall be unpaid unto her after my decease & the fifty pounds Residue thereof
          of
upon her Surrendering ^ or giving of such sufficient security as the overseers of
this my will shall like of to Surrender or grant All her estate & Right that
          that she
shall descend or come unto her after my decease or ^ now hath of in or to one
Copyhold tenement with the appurtenances lying & being in Stratford upon Avon
aforesaid in the said county of Warr being parcel or holden of the manor of
Rowington unto my daughter Susanna Hall & her heirs for ever
Item I Give & bequeath unto my said daughter Judith One
Hundred & fifty Pounds more if she or Any issue of her body be
Living at the end of three Years next ensuing the day of the date
of this my will during which time my executors to pay her consideration from
my decease according to the Rate aforesaid And if she die within the said
term without issue of her body then my will is & I do give & bequeath
One Hundred Pounds thereof to my Niece Elizabeth Hall & the fifty
Pounds to be set forth by my executors during the life of my Sister
Johane Harte & the use & profit thereof Coming shall be paid to my said
Sister Jone & after her decease the said lⁱ shall Remain Amongst the
children of my said Sister Equally to be divided Amongst them But
if my said daughter Judith be Living at the end of the said three Years or

Appendix A

any issue of her body then my will is & so I devise & bequeath the

by my executors & overseers

said Hundred and fifty pounds to be set out ^ for the best benefit of her & her

the stock   to be

issue & ^ not ^ paid unto her so long as she shall be married & covert Baron

~~by my executors & overseers~~ but my will is that she shall have the consideration
yearly paid unto her during her life & after her decease the said stock and
consideration to be paid to her children if she have Any & if not to her
executors or assigns she living the said term after my decease provided that if
such husband as she shall at the end of the said three Years be married unto or attaine
after do sufficiently Assure unto her & the issue of her body lands Answerable to
the portion by this my will given unto her & to be adjudged so by my executors
& overseers then my will is that the said cl^{li} shall be paid to such husband as
shall make such assurance to his own use Item I give and bequeath unto my said
sister Jone xx^{li} and all my wearing Apparel to be paid & delivered within one year

the house

after my decease And I do will & devise unto her ^ with the appurtenances in Stratford wherein
she dwelleth for her natural life under the yearly Rent of xij^{d} Item I give and bequeath
unto her three sons William Harte   Hart & Michaell Harte
five pounds A piece to be paid within one Year after my decease

~~to be set out for her within one Year after my decease by my executors~~
~~with the advice and directions of my overseers for her best profit until her~~
~~Marriage and then the same with the increase thereof to be paid unto~~

the said Elizabeth Hall   except my broad silver & gilt bowl

~~her~~ Item I give & bequeath unto ^ ~~her~~ All my Plate ^ that I now
have at the date of this my will   Item I give & bequeath unto
the Poor of Stratford aforesaid ten pounds to mr Thomas
Combe my Sword to Thomas Russell esquire five pounds &
to ffrauncis Collins of the Borough of Warr in the county of Warr
gent thirteen pounds Six shillings & eight pence to be paid within

Hamlett Sadler

one Year after my decease Item I give & bequeath to ~~mr Richard~~ ^

to Wiliam Raynoldes gent xxvj^{s} viij^{d} to buy him A Ring

~~Tyler the elder~~ xxvj^{s} viij^{d} to buy him A Ring ^ to my godson William
Walker xx^{s} in gold to Anthonye Nashe gent xxvj^{s} viij^{d} & to Mr

& to my fellows John Hemynge Richard Burbage & Henry Cundell xxvj^{s} viij^{d}

viij^{d}   *A piece to buy them Rings*

John Nashe xxvjs ^ in gold   Item I Give Will bequeath & Devise unto

for better enabling of her to perform this my will & toward the performance thereof

my daughter Susanna Hall ^ All that Capital Messuage or tenement

in Stratford aforesaid

with the appurtenances ^ Called the new place wherein I now dwell
& two messuages or tenements with appurtenances scituat lying and being
in Henley street within the borough of Stratford aforesaid And all
my barns stables Orchards gardens land tenements & hereditaments whatsoever
scituat lying & being or to be had Received perceived or taken
within the towns Hamlets villages fields & grounds of Stratford
upon Avon Oldstratford Bushopton & Welcombe or in any of them
in the said county of Warr and also All that Messuage or
tenement with the appurtenances wherein John Robinson dwelleth scituat

lying & being in the blackfriers in London near the Wardrobe & all
other my lands tenements & hereditaments whatsoever To Have & to hold All &
singular the said premises with their Appurtenances unto the said Susanna
Hall for & during the term of her natural life & after her
Decease to the first son of her body lawfully issuing & to the
heirs Males of the body of the said first Son lawfully
issuing & for default of such issue to the second Son of her
body lawfully issuing & to the heirs Males of the body of the
said Second Son lawfully issuing & for default of such
heirs to the third Son of the body of the said Susanna
Lawfully issuing & of the heirs Males of the body of the said third
son lawfully issuing And for default of such issue the same so
to be & Remain to the fourth son fifth sixth & seventh
sons of her body lawfully issuing one after Another & to the heirs
Males of the bodies of the said fourth fifth Sixth & Seventh sons
lawfully issuing in such manner as it is before Limited to be & Remain
to the first second & third sons of her body & to their heirs Males
And for default of such issue the said premises to be & Remain to my
said Niece Hall & the heirs males of her body Lawfully
issuing & for default of such issue to my daughter Judith
& the heirs Males of her body lawfully issuing And for
default of such issue to the Right heirs of me the said William
Item I give unto my wife my second best bed with the furniture
Shackspere for ever ^ Item I give & bequeath to my said Daughter
Judith my broad silver gilt bowl All the Rest of my goods Chattels
Leases plate Jewels & household stuff whatsoever after my debts and
legacies paid & my funeral expenses discharged I give devise
& bequeath to my Son in Law John Hall gent & my daughter
Susanna his wife whom I ordain & make executors of this my
                                    the said
Last will & testament And I do entreat & Appoint ^ Thomas
Russell Esquire& ffrauncis Collins gent to be overseers hereof And
do Revoke All former wills & publish this to be my last
will & testament In witness whereof I have hereunto put my
 hand
~~Seal~~ the day & Year first above Written

By me William Shakspeare

Witness to the publishing
Hereof   Fra: collyns
Julius Shawe
John Robinson
Hamnet Sadler
Robert Whattcott

Appendix B

Books Displayed in the Appleby Triptych

The Center Panel

In Countess Margaret's hand:

1. *The Book of the Psalms of David*

On the shelf, top to bottom:

2. *Manuscript of Alchemical Extractions*

3 All Seneca's *Works*, translated into English.

4. *The Holy Bible*

The Left Wing

Upper shelf, above:

5. *The Manuel of Epictetus*

6. Boethius, *Book of Philosophical Comfort*

7. S. Daniel, All the Works in Verse

Upper shelf, standing:

8. *The Holy Bible*

9. St. Augustine, *The City of God* (tr. Healy)

10. Eusebius, *The History of the Church*

11. All the works of Dr. Joseph Hall

Upper shelf, left.

12. Sir Philip Sydney, *Arcadia*

13. All Edmond Spencer's Works

14. Ovid's *Metamorphoses* (tr. Golding)

Upper shelf, right:

15. John Dowman, *The Christian Warfare*

16. Du Bartas, *Divine Weeks and Works* (tr. Sylvester)

17. Chaucer, *Works*

Lower shelf:

18. De La Primaudaye, *The French Academy* (3 vols.)

19. Castiglione, *The Courtier*

Lower shelf, lying:

20. Tasso, *Godfrey of Boloigne*

21. Le Roy, *The Variety of Things*

22. S. Daniel, *The Chronicles of England*

23. Montaigne, *Essays* (tr. Florio)

24. John Gerard, *Herbal*

On the floor:

25. Camden, *Britannia*

26. Ortelius, *Theater of the Whole World* (tr. Coignet)

27. Agrippa, *Vanity of the Sciences* (tr. Sandford)

28. Cervantes, *Don Quixote* (tr. Shelton)

The Right Wing

Upper Shelf, fallen:

29. Sandys, *Paraphrase of the Psalms of David*

30. Commines, *History* (tr. into English)

31. John Moore, *A Mappe of Man's Mortality*

32. Ben Jonson, *Works*

33. John Donne, *Poems*

Upper Shelf, standing

34. Henry Cuffe, *The Ages of Man's Life*

35. George Herbert, *Poems*

36. John Barclay, *Argenis* (tr.)

37. Antoninus, *Meditations* (tr. Casaubon)

38. John King, Bishop of London, *Sermons*

Upper shelf, lying:

39. William Austin, *Meditations and Devotions*

40. John Donne, *Sermons*

41. Marcellinus, *Roman History* (tr. P. Holland)

By the hand:

42. *The Holy Bible*

43. Charron, *Book of Wisdom* (tr. into English)

Lower Shelf

44. George Strode, *Anatomy of Mortality*

45. Plutarch, *Lives*, in French

46. Guicciardini, *History*, in French

47. Plutarch, *Morals*, in French

48. Sir Foulke Greville, *Lord Brooke, His Works*

49.   Hackwell, *Apologie for the Power of God*

50.   Wotton, *The Elements of Architecture*

Notes on the Triptych

The biography *Lady Anne Clifford* by Richard T. Spence is the source for the titles of the books as they appear in the pictorial representation on the triptych (190-191). The inscriptions on the triptych are transcribed in the Appendix of the book *Lady Anne Clifford*, by Dr. George Williamson (498-500).

In the inscriptions on the triptych, Primaudaye's *French Academy* is listed three times. It is unclear if these are separate volumes that appear as separate books in the triptych. Two books appear on the triptych shelves but are not listed in the inscription: Du Bartus' *Divine Weeks and Works* (Sylvester translation) and Marcellinus' *Roman History* (translated by Philemon Holland). It would seem that these two books were added to the visuals after the inscription was written.

In addition to the discussion of the triptych books in the biographies, an informative essay by Graham Parry, "The Great Picture of Lady Anne Clifford" is in *Art and Patronage in the Caroline Courts, Essays in honour of Sir Oliver Millar*, edited by David Howarth.

Bibliography

Acheson, Katherine O. *The Diary of Anne Clifford 1616-1619, A Critical Edition*. Garland Publishing. 1995.

Ackroyd, Peter. *Shakespeare: The Biography.* Doubleday, 2005.

Adams, Simon. *Leicester and the Court: Essays on Elizabethan Politics*. Manchester University Press, 2002.

Aikin, Lucy. *Memoirs of the Court of King James the First*. London: Longman, Hurst, Rees Orme, Brown, 1822.

Akrigg, G. P. V. *Jacobean Pageant*. Harvard University Press, 1963.

Akrigg, G. P. V. *Shakespeare & the Earl of Southampton*. Hamish Hamilton, 1968.

Alsop, J. D. "Religious Preambles in Early Modern English Wills as Fomulae." *Journal of Ecclesiastical History*, Vol. 40, No. 1, 1989.

Anderson, Mark. *Shakespeare By Another Name*. Gotham Books, 2005.

Arber, Edward, ed., *A Transcript of the Registers of the Company of Stationers of London 1554-1640, vol. iii*. London: Privately printed, 1876; reprint, Mass: Peter Smith, 1967.

Arkell, Tom. "Interpreting Probate Inventories." *When Death do Us Part*. Leopard's Head Press, 2004.

Arkell, Tom, Nesta Evans, Nigel Goose, eds. *When Death Do Us Part*. Leopard's Head Press, 2004.

Barnard, Toby and Jane Clark, eds. *Lord Burlington: Architecture, Art and Life*. Hambledon Press, 1995.

Barnes, Susan J., Nora De Poorter, Oliver Millar and Horst Vey, eds. *Van Dyck, A Complete Catalogue of the Paintings*. Yale University Press, 2004.

Barnett, Richard C. *Place, Profit and Power: A Study of the Servants of William Cecil, Elizabethan Statesman*. University of North Carolina

Press, 1969.

Beauclerk, Charles. *Shakespeare's Lost Kingdom*. Grove Press, 2010.

Bell, H.E. *An Introduction to the History and Records of the Court of Wards & Liveries*. Cambridge University Press, 1953.

Bernard, G.W. "The Downfall of Sir Thomas Seymour." *The Tudor Nobility*, G. W. Bernard, ed. Manchester University Press, 1992.

Berry, Reginald. *A Pope Chronology*. G. K. Hall & Co, 1988.

Bevington, David. *Tudor Drama and Politics: A Critical Approach to Topical Meaning*. Harvard University Press, 1968.

Black, J. B. *The Reign of Elizabeth 1558-1603*. Clarendon Press, 1959.

Brittan, John. *Beauties of Wiltshire, Vol I*. London: J. D. Dewick, 1801.

Brown, Ivor and George Fearon. *Amazing Monument: A Short History of the Shakespeare Industry*. New York: Kennikat Press, 1970. Originally published, 1939.

Brown, R. Allen. *Origins of English Feudalism*. Harper & Row, 1973.

Bullough, Geoffrey. *Narrative and Dramatic Sources of Shakespeare*. London: Routledge and Keegan Paul, 1966. In eight volumes.

Carleton, Dudley. *Dudley Carleton to John Chamberlain 1603-1624 Jacobean Letters*, Maurice Lee, Jr., ed. Rutgers University Press, 1972.

Cecil, David. *The Cecils of Hatfield House: An English Ruling Family*. Houghton Mifflin Company, 1973.

Chamberlain, John. *The Letters of John Chamberlain*, Norman Egbert McClure, ed. Philadelphia: American Philosophical Society, 1939, reprint 1962.

Chamberlin, Frederick. *The Private Character of Queen Elizabeth*. Dodd, Mead & Co., 1922.

Chambers, E. K. *William Shakespeare: A Study of Facts and Problems*,

Clarendon Press, 1930.

Clare, Janet. *'Art made tongue-tied by authority': Elizabeth and Jacobean Dramatic Censorship.* Manchester University Press, 1999.

Cohen, Bernice and Alan. "The Riddle of the Countess of Pembroke." *De Vere Society Newsletter*, June 2009.

Collins, Arthur. *The Life of That Great Statesman William Cecil, Lord Burghley.* London: Robert Gosling and Thomas Wotten, 1732. Reprint Kessinger Publishing.

Conrad, Peter. "Contested Will: Who Wrote Shakespeare? By James Shapiro." The Guardian, April 3, 2010.

Correspondence of the Reverend Joseph Greene: Parson, Schoolmaster and Antiquary, Levi Fox, ed. London: Her Majesty's Stationery Office, 1965.

Cowdry, Richard. *A Description of the Pictures, Statues, Busto's, Basso-Relievos, and other curiosities at the Earl of Pembroke's House at Wilton.* London: J. Robinson, 1751.

Cox, Jane. "Section on the Will and Signatures." *Shakespeare in the Public Records*, David Thomas, ed. London: Her Majesty's Stationery Office, 1985.

Cox, Jeff and Nancy Cox. "Probate 1500-1800: A System in Transition." *When Death Do Us Part.* Leopard's Head Press Limited, 2004.

Creighton, Mandell. *Queen Elizabeth.* New York: Thomas Y Crowell Company, 1899.

Croft, Pauline, ed. *Patronage, Culture and Power: The Early Cecils.* Yale University Press, 2002.

Crowson, P. S. *Tudor Foreign Policy.* Adam & Charles Black, 1973.

Cust, Lionel. *King Edward VII and his court: some reminiscences by Sir Lionel Cust, K.C.V.G.* New York: E.P.Dutton, 1930.

Bibliography

Cust, Lionel. *Van Dyck.* London: George Bell and Sons, 1900.

Dean, David. "Elizabethan Government and Politics." *A Companion to Tudor Britain.* Wiley-Blackwell, 2009.

De Lisle, Leanda and Peter Stanford. *The Catholics and Their Houses.* HarperCollins, 1995.

Devon, Frederick. *Issues of the Exchequer: Payments Made During the Reign of King James I.* Great Britain: John Murray Publisher, 1837. Reprint. Forgotten Books, 2015.

Dickinson, Janet. *Court Politics and the Earl of Essex 1589-1601.* Pickering & Chatto, 2012.

Dictionary of National Biography, Leslie Stephen and Sidney Lee, eds. Oxford University Press, 1968.

Dietz, Frederick C. *An Economic History of England.* Henry Holt & Co., 1942.

Dietz, Frederick C. "The Exchequer in Elizabeth's Reign." *Smith College Studies in History*, Vol. VIII, No. 2, 1923.

Donaldson, Ian. *Ben Jonson: A Life.* Oxford University Press, 2013.

Duffin, Ross W. *Shakespeare's Songbook.* W. W. Norton & Company, 2004.

Dugdale, William. *Antiquities of Warwickshire.* London: Thomas Warren, 1656.

Du Maurier, Daphne. *The Winding Stair: Sir Francis Bacon, His Rise and Fall.* Doubleday & Company, 1977.

Eccles, Mark. *Shakespeare in Warwickshire.* University of Wisconsin Press, 1961.

Edmondson, Paul, and Stanley Wells, eds. *Shakespeare Beyond Doubt: Evidence, Argument, Controversy,* Cambridge University Press, 2013.

Eliot, T. S. "Hamlet and His Problems." *The Sacred Wood: Essays on Poetry and Criticism.* New York: Alfred A. Knopf, 1921.

Emmison, F. G. *Elizabethan Life: Wills of Essex Gentry & Merchants.* Chelmsford: Essex County Council, 1978.

Emmison, F. G. *Elizabethan Life: Wills of Essex Gentry & Yeoman.* Chelmsford: Essex County Council, 1980.

Erickson, Amy Louise. "Reading Probate Records." *When Death Do Us Part.* Leopard's Head Press, 2004.

Erickson, Amy Louise. *Women and Property in Early Modern England.* Routledge, 2005.

Erickson, Carolly, *Bloody Mary.* St Martin's Press, 1978.

Erickson, Carolly. *The First Elizabeth.* St Martin's Press, 1983.

Erskine-Hill, Howard. "Avowed Friend and Patron: The Third Earl of Burlington and Alexander Pope." *Lord Burlington: Architecture, Art and Life,* Toby Barnard and Jane Clark, eds. Hambledon Press, 1995.

Foister, Susan. "Foreigners at Court: Holbein, Van Dyck and the Painter-Stainers Company." *Art and Patronage in the Caroline Court, Essays in honour of Sir Oliver Millar.* Cambridge University Press, 1993.

Fowler, William Plumer. *Shakespeare Revealed in Oxford's Letters.* New Hampshire: Peter E. Randall, 1986.

Fox, Levi. "An Early Copy of Shakespeare's Will." *Shakepseare Survey 4,* Allardyce Nicoll, ed. Cambridge University Press, 1951.

Fox, Robin. *Shakespeare's Education: Schools, Lawsuits, Theater and the Tudor Miracle.* Germany: Laugwitz Verlag, 2012.

Foyster, Elizabeth. *Manhood in Early Modern England.* Longman, 1999.

Fraser, Antonia. *The Six Wives of Henry VIII.* Alfred A. Knopf, 1993.

Freeman, Arthur and Janet Ing Freeman, *John Payne Collier: Scholarship and Forgery in the Nineteenth Century.* Yale University Press, 2004.

Bibliography

Fripp, Edgar. *Shakespeare's Haunts*. Oxford University Press, 1929.

Fullom, S. W. *History of William Shakespeare Player and Poet: With New Facts and Traditions*. London: Saunders, Otley, and Co, 1862.

Gambarini of Lucca. *A Description of the Earl of Pembroke's Pictures*. Westminster: A. Campbell, 1731.

Gilvary, Kevin, ed. *Dating Shakespeare's Plays: A Critical Review of the Evidence*. UK: Parapress, 2010.

Gohn, Jack Benoit. "*Richard II*: Shakespeare's Legal Brief on the Royal Prerogative and the Succession to the Throne." *The Georgetown Law Journal*, Vol. 70, No. 3. 1982.

Golding, Louis Thorn. *An Elizabethan Puritan*. New York: Richard R. Smith, 1937.

Goose, Nigel and Nesta Evans. "Wills as an Historical Source." *When Death Do Us Part*. Leopard's Head Press Limited, 2004.

Gordenker, Emilie. *Anthony Van Dyck and the Representations of Dress in Seventeenth-Century Portraiture*. Turnhout: Brepols Publishers, 2002.

Green, Martin. *Wriothesley's Roses: In Shakespeare's Sonnets, Poems and Plays*. Baltimore, Maryland: Clevedon Books, 1993.

Green, Nina. "The Fall of the House of Oxford." *Brief Chronicles, Vol 1*. The Shakespeare Oxford Fellowship, 2009.

Greenblatt, Stephen. *Will in the World: How Shakespeare Became Shakespeare*. W. W. Norton & Company, 2004.

Greer, Germaine. *Shakespeare's Wife*. HarperCollins Publishers, 2007.

Grosart, Alexander B. *Miscellanies of the Fuller Worthies Library*, Vol 4. Printed for private circulation, 1872.

Halliwell, James O. (later Halliwell-Phillips). *Shakespeare's Will Copied from the Original in the Prerogative Court*. London: John Russell

Smith, 1851. Reprinted from an original in the Folger Shake-speare Library, AMS Press, 1974.

Halliwell-Phillipps, J. O. *Outlines of the Life of Shakespeare*. London: Longmans, Green, and Co., 1882.

Hammer, Paul E.J. *Elizabeth's Wars: War, Government and Society in Tudor England, 1544-1604*. Palgrave, 2003.

Hammer, Paul E.J. "Shakespeare's *Richard II*, the Play of 7 February 1601, and the Essex Rising." *The Shakespeare Quarterly* 50.1. Folger Shakespeare Library, 2008.

Handover, P.M. *The Second Cecil: The Rise to Power 1563-1604*. Eyre & Spottiswoode, 1959.

Hannay, Margaret P. *Phillip's Phoenix: Mary Sidney, Countess of Pembroke*. Oxford University Press, 1990.

Haynes, Samuel, ed. *The State Papers of William Cecil, Lord Burghley*. London: William Boyer, 1740.

Hazard, Mary. *Elizabethan Silent Language*. University of Nebraska Press, 2000.

Hazlitt, William. *Picture Galleries of England*. London: C. Templeman, 1836.

Hearn, Karen. *Dynasties: Painting in Tudor and Jacobean England, 1530-1630*. New York: Rizzoli International Publications, 1996.

Helmholz, Richard H. "Married Women's Wills in Later Medieval England." *Wife and Widow in Medieval England*. University of Michigan Press, 1993.

Herbert, Sidney. *A Catalogue of the Paintings and Drawings at Wilton House*. London: Phaidon Press, 1968.

Hibbard, G. R. *Thomas Nashe*. Harvard University Press, 1962.

Hicks, Michael. *Bastard Feudalism*. Longman, 1995.

Hodges, Mary. "Widows of the 'Middling Sort' and their Assets in Two Seventeenth-Century Towns." *When Death do Us Part.* Leopard's Head Press Limited, 2004.

Holden, Anthony. *William Shakespeare: His Life and Work.* London: Little, Brown and Company, 1999.

Holmes, Martin. *Proud Northern Lady.* London: Phillimore & Co., 1975.

Honan, Park. *Shakespeare: A Life.* Oxford University Press, 1999.

Honigmann, E. A. J. *Shakespeare: the 'lost years.'* Manchester University Press, 1998.

Honigmann, E. A. J. "Shakespeare's Will and the Testamentary Tradition." *Shakespeare and Cultural Traditions: Selected Proceedings of the International Shakespeare Association World Congress, Tokyo, 1991,* Tetsuo Kishi, Roger Pringle and Stanley Wells, eds. University of Delaware, 1994.

Honigmann, E.A.J. and Susan Brock, eds. *Playhouse Wills 1558-1642 An edition of wills by Shakespeare and his contemporaries in the London theater.* Manchester University Press, 1993.

Houlbrooke, Ralph. *Church Courts and the People During the English Reformation 1520-1570.* Oxford University Press, 1979.

Houlbrooke, Ralph. *Death, Religion & the Family in England 1480-1750.* Clarendon Press, 1998.

Howarth, David, ed. *Art and Patronage in the Caroline Courts, Essays in honour of Sir Oliver Millar.* Cambridge University Press, 1993.

Howarth, David. *Images of Rule: Art and Politics in the English Renaissance, 1485-1649.* University of California Press, 1997.

Hurstfield, Joel. *The Queen's Wards: Wardship and Marriage Under Elizabeth.* Great Britain: Green and Co, 1958.

Hutchinson, Robert. *The Last Days of Henry VIII.* Weidenfield & Nicolson, 2005.

Bibliography

Ingram, Martin. *Church Courts, Sex and Marriage in England, 1570-1640.* Cambridge University Press, 1987.

Ives, Eric. *Lady Jane Grey: A Tudor Mystery.* Wiley-Blackwell, 2009.

James, Susan E. *Kateryn Parr: The Making of a Queen.* Ashgate, 1999.

Jameson, Anna. *Handbook to the Public Galleries of Art in and near London.* London: John Murray, 1842. Reprint Kessinger Publishing, 2004.

Jones, Roger. "Richard Mead, Thomas Guy, the South Sea Bubble, and the Founding of Guy's Hospital." *The Journal of the Royal Society of Medicine*, 2010.

Jordan, W. K. *Philanthropy in England, 1480-1640.* New York: Russell Sage Foundation, 1959.

Kay, Dennis. *Shakespeare: His Life, Work and Era.* Sidgwick & Jackson, 1992.

Kennedy, James. *A New Description of Pictures.* London: Benjamin Collins, 1758.

Klein, Arthur J. *Intolerance in the Reign of Elizabeth the Queen.* NY: Kennikat Press, 1968. Originally published 1917.

Lacey, Robert. *Robert, Earl of Essex: An Elizabethan Icarus.* Phoenix Press, 1971.

Lees-Milne, James. *Earls of Creation: Five Great Patrons of Eighteenth-Century Art.* London House & Maxwell, 1963.

Lever, Tresham. *The Herberts of Wilton.* John Murray, 1967.

Lewis, B. Roland. *The Shakespeare Documents.* Stanford University Press, 1940.

Lightbrown, Ronald W. "Issac Besnier, Sculptor to Charles I, and His Work for Court Patrons." *Art and Patronage in the Caroline Court.* Cambridge University Press, 1993.

Lindley, David. *The Trials of Frances Howard.* Routledge, 1996.

Bibliography

Llewellyn, Nigel. *Funeral Monuments in Post-Reformation England.* Cambridge University Press, 2001.

Loades, David. *The Cecils: Privilege and Power Behind the Throne.* Bloomsbury Publishing, 2013.

Looney, John Thomas. *Shakespeare Identified.* London: Cecil Palmer, 1920.

Lord Longford. *A History of the House of Lords.* Sutton Publishing Limited, 1999.

Lovell, Mary S. *Bess of Hardwick: Empire Builder.* W.W. Norton, 2006.

Maclean, John. *The Life of Sir Thomas Seymour, Knight.* London: John Camden Hotten, 1869.

Mantel, Hilary. "Contested Will: Who Wrote Shakespeare? By James Shapiro." *The Guardian*, March 19, 2010.

Marcus, Leah S., Janel Mueller, Mary Beth Rose, eds. *Elizabeth I Collected Works.* University of Chicago Press, 2002.

Mead, Richard H. *In the Sunshine of Life: A Biography of Dr. Richard Mead 1673-1754.* Philadelphia: Dorrance & Company, 1974.

Miles, Rosalind. *Ben Jonson: His Life and Work.* Routledge & Kegan Paul, 1986.

Millar, Oliver. *The Age of Charles I.* Tate Gallery Publications, 1972.

Miller, Laura. "Contested Will: Who Wrote Shakespeare?" *Salon*, March 28, 2010

Miller, Ruth L. *Shakespeare Identified: Oxfordian Vistas, Vol II.* New York: Kennikat Press, 1975.

Moir, Anthony. *Anthony Van Dyck.* Harry N. Abrams, Inc, 1994.

Moore, Peter R. "Oxford and the Order of the Garter." *The Lame Storyteller, Poor and Despised.* Germany: Verlag Uwe Laugwitz, 2009.

Mowl, Timothy. *William Kent: Architect, Designer, Opportunist.* Jonathan Cape, 2006.

Mumby, Frank A. *The Girlhood of Elizabeth.* London: Constable & Company, 1909.

Nelson, Alan. *Monstrous Adversary: The Life of Edward de Vere 17th Earl of Oxford.* Liverpool University Press, 2003.

Nicholl, Charles. *A Cup of News: The Life of Thomas Nashe.* Routledge & Kegan Paul, 1984.

Nicholl, Charles. *The Reckoning: The Murder of Christopher Marlowe.* University of Chicago Press, 1992.

Nicolson, Adam. *Earls of Paradise.* Harper Collins Publishers, 2008.

Niederkorn, William S. "A Historic Whodunit: If Shakespeare Didn't, Who Did?" *New York Times*, February 10, 2002.

Niederkorn, William S. "Absolute Will." *The Brooklyn Rail*, April 2, 2010.

Norris, Herbert. *Tudor Costume and Fashion.* Dover Publications, Inc., 1997.

North, Christine. "Merchants and Retailers in Seventeenth Century Cornwall," *When Death Do Us Part.* Leopard's Head Press Limited, 2004.

North Country Wills: Being abstracts of wills relating to the counties of York, Nottingham, Northumberland, Cumberland, and Westmoreland at Somerset House and Lambeth Palace, 1558 to 1604, Vol 2. London: Bernard Quaritch, 1912.

North Country Wills: Publications of the Surtees Society, Vol. II. Durham: Andrews & Co., 1912.

Norton, Elizabeth. *The Temptation of Elizabeth Tudor.* Pegasus Books, 2016.

Norton Facsimile, Charlton Hinman, ed. W.W. Norton & Company,

1968.

O'Donoghue, Freeman. *Catalogue of Engraved British Portraits in the British Museum*, Vol. 5. London: Longmans, 1922.

Ogburn, Charlton, Jr. *The Mysterious William Shakespeare: The Myth and the Reality*. Dodd, Mead & Company, 1984.

Ogburn, Dorothy and Charlton. *This Star of England*. New York: Coward-McCann, 1952.

Ollard, Richard. "Clarendon and the Art of Prose Portraiture in the Age of Charles II." *Art and Patronage in the Caroline Court, Essays in Honour of Sir Oliver Millar*. Cambridge University Press, 1993.

Oxford Dictionary of National Biography, Lawrence Goldman, ed. Oxford University Press, 2004.

Parry, Graham. "The Great Picture of Lady Anne Clifford." *Art and Patronage in the Caroline Courts: Essays in honour of Sir Oliver Millar*. Cambridge University Press, 1993.

Parry, Graham. "Van Dyck and the Caroline Court Poets." *Van Dyck 350*, Susan J. Barnes and Arthur K. Wheelock, Jr., eds. University Press of New England, 1994.

Patterson, Annabel. *Censorship and Interpretation: The Conditions of Writing and Reading in Early Modern England*. University of Wisconsin Press, 1984.

Paul, Christopher. Review of *Edward de Vere: The Crisis and Consequences of Wardship* by Daphne Pearson. *English Historical Review*, Vol. 121/493:1173.

Paul, Christopher. "The 'Prince Tudor' Dilemma: Hip Thesis, Hypothesis, or Old Wives Tale?" *The Oxfordian*, Stephanie Hopkins Hughes, ed., Vol. V, 2002.

Pearson, Daphne. *Edward de Vere: The Crisis and Consequences of Wardship*. Ashgate Publishing, 2005.

Pointon, A. J. *The Man Who Was Never Shakespeare: The Theft of William Shakspere's Identity.* UK: Parapress, 2011.

Porter, Linda. *Katherine the Queen: The Remarkable Life of Katherine Parr, the Last Wife of Henry VIII.* St. Martin's Press, 2010.

Prendergast, Thomas A. *Poetical Dust: Poet's Corner and the Making of Britain.* University of Philadelphia Press, 2015.

Price, Diana. *Shakespeare's Unorthodox Biography*: *New Evidence of an Authorship Problem.* Greenwood Press, 2001.

Prosser, Eleanor. *Shakespeare's Anonymous Editors*: *Scribe and Compositor in the Folio Text of "2 Henry IV."* Stanford University Press, 1981.

Read, Conyers. *Lord Burghley and Queen Elizabeth.* London: Jonathan Cape, 1965.

Richardson. *Aedes Pembrochianae.* Great Britain: Salisbury Press, 1795. Twelfth Edition accessed through Google Digitized Books.

Riden, Philip, ed. *Probate Records and the Local Community*. Great Britain: Alan Sutton, 1985.

Riggs, David. *Ben Jonson: A Life.* Harvard University Press, 1989.

Riggs, David. *The World of Christopher Marlowe.* Henry Holt and Company, 2005.

Riverside Shakespeare, G. Blakemore Evans, ed. Houghton Mifflin Company, 1974.

Roe, Richard Paul. *Shakespeare's Guide to Italy.* Harper Perennial, 2011.

Rogers, Joyce. *The Second Best Bed: Shakespeare's Will in a New Light.* Connecticut: Greenwood Press, 1993.

Rogers, Malcolm. "'Golden Houses for Shadows': Some Portraits of Thomas Killigrew and His Family." *Art and Patronage in the Caroline Court.* Cambridge University Press, 1993.

Bibliography

Roscoe, Ingrid. "The Monument to the Memory of Shakespeare." *The Journal of Church Monuments Society*, IX, 1994.

Rose, Lloyd. "Who Wrote Shakespeare? Author James Shapiro offers an answer." *The Washington Post*, June 6, 2010.

Rosenbaum, Ron. *The Shakespeare Wars.* Random House, 2008.

Rosenberg, Saul. "About an Author, Much Ado." *The Wall Street Journal*, April 16, 2010.

Rowse, A. L. *Shakespeare the Man.* Macmillan, 1973.

Russell, John W. Review of *The Queen's Wards* in *Shakespeare Authorship Society Review #3.*

Salgado, Gamini. *The Elizabethan Underworld.* Wrens Park Publishing, 1992.

Schoenbaum, Samuel. *Shakespeare's Lives.* Clarendon Press, 1991.

Schoenbaum, Samuel. *William Shakespeare: A Documentary Life.* Oxford University Press, 1975.

Shahan, John M., and Alexander Waugh, eds. *Shakespeare Beyond Doubt? Exposing an Industry in Denial.* USA: Llumina Press, 2013.

Shapiro, James. *Contested Will: Who Wrote Shakespeare?* Simon & Schuster, 2010.

Sharpe, Kevin. *Sir Robert Cotton 1586-1631.* Oxford University Press, 1979. Reprinted in 2002.

Simpson, Frank. "New Place: the only representation of Shakespeare's house from an unpublished manuscript." *Shakespeare Survey 5*, Allardyce Nicoll, ed. Cambridge University Press, 1952.

Smith, Alan Gordon. *William Cecil: The Power Behind Elizabeth.* London: Kegan Paul & Co, 1934.

Smith, Sir Thomas. *De Republica Anglorum*, 1583. Reprint Menston: Scolar Press Limited, 1970.

Snook, Edith. *Women, Reading and the Cultural Politics of Early Modern England.* Ashgate Publishing Limited, 2005.

Spence, Richard T. *Lady Anne Clifford, Countess of Pembroke, Dorset and Montgomery (1590-1676).* Sutton Publishing Limited, 1997.

Spring, Eileen. *Law, Land, & Family: Aristocratic Inheritance in England, 1300 to 1800.* University of North Caroline Press, 1993.

Spufford, Margaret. *Contrasting Communities: English Villagers in the Sixteenth and Seventeenth Centuries.* Cambridge University Press, 1974.

Starkey, David. *Elizabeth: Apprenticeship.* Vintage, 2001.

Starkey, David. *Elizabeth: The Struggle for the Throne.* HarperCollins, 2001.

Starkey, David. *Six Wives: The Queens of Henry VIII.* HarperCollins, 2003.

Stevens, John Paul. "The Shakespeare Canon of Statutory Construction," *University of Pennsylvania Law Review,* Vol.140, No.4, 1992.

Stone, Lawrence. *Crisis of the Aristocracy,* Clarendon Press, 1965.

Stone, Lawrence. *Crisis of the Aristocracy,* abridged edition. Oxford University Press, 1967.

Stopes, Charlotte Carmichael. *The Life of Henry, Third Earl of Southampton, Shakespeare's Patron.* New York: AMS Press, 1922.

Stretton, Tim. *Women Waging Law in Elizabethan England.* Cambridge University Press, 1998.

Strickland, Agnes. *The Life of Queen Elizabeth.* London: Hutchinson & Co, 1904.

Stritmatter, Roger. *"Is This the Bard We See Before Us? Or Someone Else?" The Washington Post,* March 18, 2007.

Stritmatter, Roger A. and Lynne Kositsky. *On the Date, Sources and*

Bibliography

Design of Shakespeare's The Tempest. McFarland & Co., 2013.

Stritmatter, Roger A. *The Marginalia of Edward de Vere's Geneva Bible: Providential Discovery, Literary Reasoning and Historical Consequence.* University of Massachusetts at Amherst, 2001.

Strong, Roy. *The Cult of Elizabeth: Elizabethan Portraiture and Pageantry.* Great Britain: Thames and Hudson, 1977.

Strong, Roy. *The English Icon: Elizabethan & Jacobean Portraiture.* London: Routledge & Kegan Paul, 1969.

Strong, Roy. *Tudor and Jacobean Portraits in the National Portrait Gallery.* London: HM Stationary Office, 1969. In two volumes.

Sumner, Ann and Polly Amos. "Kenelm Digby and Venetia Stanley: The Love Story of the Seventeenth Century." *Death, Passion, and Politics Van Dyck's Portraits of Venetia Stanley and George Digby.* Dulwich Picture Gallery, 1996.

Swinburne, Henry. *A brief treatise of Testaments and last Wills, Part VII.* London: John Windet, 1590.

Tannenbaum, Samuel A. *Problems in Shakespere's Penmanship including a Study of The Poet's Will.* New York: The Century Company, 1927. New York: Kraus Reprint Corporation, 1966.

The Theatrical City: Culture, Theater and Politics in London 1576-1649, C. Smith, David L. Smith, Richard Strier and David Bevington, eds. Cambridge University Press, 1995.

Tittler, Robert and Norman Jones, eds. *A Companion to Tudor Britain.* Wiley-Blackwell, 2009.

Tonkin, Boyd. "Contested Will: Who Wrote Shakespeare? By James Shapiro." *Independent,* March 26, 2010.

Toynbee, Margaret R. "A Charles I Conversation Piece." *The Burlington Magazine,* Volume lxxxix, 1947.

Vaisey, D. G. "Probate Inventories and Provincial Retailers." *Probate Records and the Local Community,* Philip Riden, ed. Alan Sutton,

1985.

Waagen, Gustav. *Treasures of Art in Great Britain, Vol. iii.* London: John Murray, 1838. Reprint Elbiron Classics.

Walker, Sue Sheridan, ed. *Wife and Widow in Medieval England.* University of Michigan Press, 1993.

Walker, Sue Sheridan. "Litigation as a Personal Quest: Suing for dower in the Royal Courts, circa 1272-1350." *Wife and Widow in Medieval England*, University of Michigan Press, 1993.

Walpole, Horace. *Anecdotes of Painting in England, Vol. ii.* London: J. Dodsley, 1786.

Ward, B. M. *The Seventeenth Earl of Oxford.* London: John Murray, 1928.

Weir, Alison. *Henry VIII: The King and His Court.* Ballantine Books, 2001.

Weir, Alison. *The Life of Elizabeth I.* Ballantine Books, 1999.

Whalen, Richard. "The 'Prince Tudor' Hypothesis: A Brief Survey of the Pros and Cons." *Shakespeare Oxford Society Newsletter,* Spring, 2006.

Whalen, Richard. "The Stratford Bust: A Monumental Fraud," *Report Me and My Cause Aright: The Shakespeare Oxford Society Fiftieth Anniversary Anthology*, 2007.

Whalen, Richard F. *Shakespeare – Who Was He?* Praeger Publishers, 1994.

Whittemore, Hank. *100 Reasons Shake-speare was the Earl of Oxford.* Massachusetts: Forever Press, 2016.

Whittemore, Hank. *The Monument.* Meadow Geese Press, 2005.

Wilkinson, Nevile R. *Wilton House Pictures.* London: Cheswick Press, 1907.

Williamson, George C. *Lady Anne Clifford Countess of Dorset, Pembroke*

Bibliography

& Montgomery 1590-1676: Her Life, Letters and Work. Kendall: Titus Wilson and Son, 1922. Reprint Forgotten Books, 2017.

Wills and Inventories from the Registers of the Commissary of Bury St. Edmund's and the Archdeacon of Sudbury, Samuel Tymms, ed. Camden Society, 1850.

Wills and Inventories from the Registry at Durham, Part IV. London: Wm. Dawson & Sons. Reprinted 1968 with the permission of The Surtees Society.

Wills and Inventories of the Archdeaconry of Richmond, James Raine, editor for the Surtees Society. Durham: George Andrews, 1853.

Wood, Michael. *Shakespeare.* New York: Basic Books, 2000.

Wrigley, E.A. and R. S. Schofield. *The Population History of England 1541-1871.* Cambridge University Press, 1981. Republished in 1989.

Index

Made in the USA
San Bernardino, CA
01 December 2019